RELIGION
A PREFACE

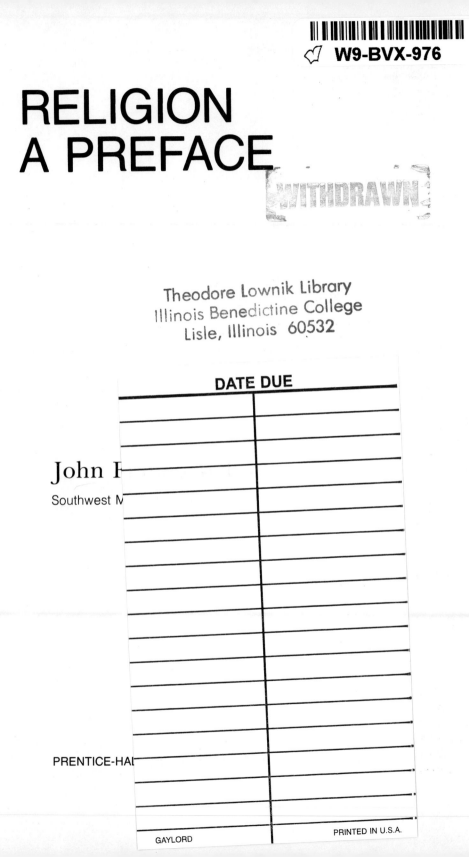

DATE DUE

John F

Southwest M

PRENTICE-HAI

Library of Congress Cataloging in Publication Data

WILSON, JOHN FRANCIS.
 Religion: a preface.

 Includes bibliographical references and index.
 1. Religion. 2. Religions. I. Title.
BL48.W494 200 81-15316
ISBN 0-13-773192-2 AACR2

200
W749r

ISBN 0-13-773192-2

Editorial/production supervision by Daniel Mausner
Cover design by Ray Lungren (Tony Ferrara Studio)
Manufacturing buyer: Harry P. Baisley

Printed in the United States of America

10 9 8 7 6 5 4 3 2 1

PRENTICE-HALL INTERNATIONAL, INC., *London*
PRENTICE-HALL OF AUSTRALIA PTY. LIMITED, *Sydney*
PRENTICE-HALL OF CANADA, LTD., *Toronto*
PRENTICE-HALL OF INDIA PRIVATE LIMITED, *New Delhi*
PRENTICE-HALL OF JAPAN, INC., *Tokyo*
PRENTICE-HALL OF SOUTHEAST ASIA PTE. LTD., *Singapore*
WHITEHALL BOOKS LIMITED, *Wellington, New Zealand*

TO MY PARENTS

Who were my own Preface to Religion

CONTENTS

PREFACE

The ancient Hebrew Scriptures tell the story of Uzzah, who reached out and touched the sacred ark containing stone tablets inscribed with the Ten Commandments. Uzzah dropped dead. Not for any wickedness, mind you, but simply because he got too close to the Divine. Perhaps in the attempt to avoid repeating Uzzah's unfortunate mistake, some people have tended to cut a wide and respectful swath around religion. Others have felt that venturing too close to the sacred is folly, not because some mysterious wrath may consume them, but because up close the mystery would disappear like a highway mirage and leave them faithless and alone on the earth. Better, they opine, to remain in ignorance than to risk an unveiling of the Other and discover only emptiness.

This book is written for the rest of us—we who cannot help ourselves and despite the danger are drawn to the subject of religion like moths to streetlights, fluttering eagerly among the mysteries with an insatiable combination of expectation, fascination, and dread.

The book has modest goals. It is, after all, only a *preface* to the study of religion. It does not presume to provide more than a place to begin. If it is used as a text, it is an unpresumptuous one that must be supplemented with much additional reading, especially of primary religious documents, and with skilled lectures and discussion. If it is read by those who have set off on an individual search—intellectual or spiritual—or those who merely wish to see how religion fits into their own world of art or science or philosophy or auto mechanics, then such people can expect only a quick trip designed to help them get the lay of the territory—like a ten-minute helicopter ride over Disneyland.

Some will no doubt complain that the trip was unsatisfying or even unpleasant, that we were wanting in intellectual depth or even that we lacked proper piety. Others will find offense when they detect the author's bias peeking up here and there—as though anyone ever said much about religion and at the same time remained objective with any degree of purity. Sometimes complicated things will be made to seem too simple when the author's desire to communicate ran away with him.

Despite all this we have plunged ahead, guided by the principle and the hope that this book will help those who are merely beginning their journey and who should not be told more than they want to know. The direction this book takes was forged on the anvil of day-to-day classroom contact and private discussions with young adults. It is not the result of erudite discussions with fellow scholars—who will undoubtedly learn nothing by reading it.

The motif that ties the diverse subjects in the book together is religion and human culture. Or, to transpose the same thing into a question, "What has the human race *done* with religion?" Most of the classic academic categories are here somewhere (the philosophy of religion, the psychology of religion, comparative religion, Biblical studies, the sociology of religion, etc.). But because most beginners care little for the pigeonholes scholars use to organize themselves, not a great deal will be made of them.

The reader will probably be a product of Western culture, and the book's plan has such a reader in mind. It will alternately try to help that reader dig deeper into what is very close and familiar to him or her and then carry him or her as far afield as possible. Perhaps the reader will develop a taste for depth and breadth and want to go much farther than this book will take him or her. I certainly hope so.

Thanks are due to Dr. Gerrit tenZythoff for his consistent encouragement; JoAnne Brown, Kristin Engdahl, and Kristine Spurgeon for technical assistance; Dr. John B. Magee, for *Religion and Modern Man*, a book that blazes a trail and sets the standards for introductions to the study of religion and that provides much of the foundation for Chapters Two, Three, Nine, and Eleven of the present work; my friends and colleagues in the university and my family for providing the milieu in which books can grow; and the thousands of students at Southwest Missouri State University whose facial expressions have said to me either "Please explain that one more time" or "Oh, now I see!"

JOHN FRANCIS WILSON
Springfield, Missouri

CHAPTER ONE
RELIGION AND EDUCATION

THE PLACE OF RELIGIOUS STUDIES

The universities have come to accept religious studies. More than 60 percent of the "secular" universities in the United States offer courses dealing with specifically religious questions. One might ask, "How can this be?" Is that not the responsibility of the churches rather than institutions of higher learning? What has religion to do with getting an education? Has not the Supreme Court banned religion in the schools?

The last question is the easiest of all to answer. No, it is not illegal for religious studies to be taught in college. The Supreme Court of the United States, in its famous decision on prayer in the public schools, indicated that the *practice* of religious rituals in public schools, rituals that are required and are carried on at public expense, is unconstitutional. But it clearly stated that studying *about* religion is not only legal, but necessary in any really serious attempt to educate.[1]

---

[1] In its 1963 decision in *Abington* v. *Schempp,* the U.S. Supreme Court declared devotional scripture reading and prayer in the public school classroom unconstitutional. However, it added that "it might well be said that one's education is not complete without a study of comparative religion or the history of religion and its relationship to the advancement of civilization. It certainly may be said that the Bible is worthy of study for its literary and historic qualities. Nothing we have said here indicates that such study of the Bible or religion, when presented objectively as part of a secular program of education, may not be effected consistent with the First Amendment."

For a thorough investigation of the various facets of this question, see David E. Engel, ed., *Religion in Public Education: Readings in Religion and the Public School* (New York: Paulist Press, 1974).

Why is religious studies such an important part of an education today?[2] A number of reasons can be given.

Recent Revival of Religious Interest

Religion has acted in history much like a camp fire. At times it recedes and seems to have grown cold and dead. Then it suddenly flashes into flame again, fed by a live coal here or there, hidden among the ashes. Then, after burning brightly a while, the flame is smothered in smoke and disappears once again.

This phenomenon can be seen in the history of the United States, which seems to experience sweeping revivals of religious interest every second or third generation, followed by a return to a more materialistic and secular way of thinking.

At this time we seem to be in a "hot" period. Religion and religious movements are very much a part of the current scene. They are very visible. They include old forms revitalized and new forms flaming for the first time.

The United States is not the only place where this is true. Postwar Japan, for example, has seen a host of aggressive "new" religions (many having roots in older religious forms) arise. One of the most striking examples is Soka Gakkai, which has made millions of converts, including many Americans, and which, through its political activities, has become a significant force in Japanese life.[3]

In the United States, interest in the occult is another kind of flaming of fire in the ashes. The success of the movie *The Exorcist* and the preoccupation with demon possession, witchcraft, fortune-telling, and astrology all testify to a renewal of interest in the "other" world. Books about reincarnation, spirits, and the possibility of reaching beyond death, or of reaching people in the other world, sell by the millions. Astrology is a multimillion-dollar business. It dates its origin to thousands of years before the rise of science. Its world view is nonscientific, even antiscientific, yet millions of people are guided in their daily lives by their horoscope "readings."

This interest extends, particularly among the young, to the religious ideas and forms of the East. On the streets of Dallas, Texas, one hears the tinkling of bells and the chant,

Hare Krsna, Hare Krsna, Krsna Krsna, Hare, Hare
Hare Rama, Hare Rama, Rama Rama, Hare, Hare.

---

[2]In this section, as elsewhere throughout this book, the work of John B. Magee, *Religion and Modern Man: A Study of the Religious Meaning of Being Human* (New York: Harper & Row, 1967), has been enormously helpful.

[3]See H. Byron Earhart, *Japanese Religion: Unity and Diversity,* 2nd ed. (Encino, Calif.: Dickenson, 1974), Part III, for a survey of the Japanese new religions.

There they stand, earnest, robe clad, their pale white shaved heads with a single tassel of hair remaining, their wives with children-on-hips, calling to passersby to accept the peace of Krishna. Dallas, Texas!

The Astrodome in Houston appeared to be an immense oriental temple when the teenaged Guru Maharaj Ji introduced his Divine Light Mission to thousands of young WASPS, crying out

Boyle Shri, Sat Gurudev, Maharaj KI JAI!
Boyle Shri, Sat Gurudev, Maharaj KI JAI!

At Madison Square Garden the Korean messiah figure Sun Moon has brought to the multitudes the new age and a new faith.

On Johnny Carson's *Tonight* show, the serene face of the Mahareshi Mahesh Yogi flickers on the screen, expounding the virtues of transcendental meditation.

Obviously, there are religious questions in the air today. And to become educated is to look for the "why's" and the "how's" connected with those questions.

Even the overtly nonreligious and antireligious movements of our day have had to make some compromises to the flames from the ashes. The Chinese communist system, for example, calls for the abolition of religion through education of children in atheism from the nursery to adulthood. But many beliefs and activities we normally connect with religion have reappeared in Chinese life, though called by other names.

Mao Tse-Tung, during his long dominion over his country, attained virtually divine status, his icons everywhere, his words collected into Bibles. His sayings were scripture by which one guided one's life and learned the truth.[4] Great ceremonies feature both praise and prayer, though called by other names. No medieval monk ever showed greater or more total religious devotion than Wang Tao-ming, the young Chinese communist whom we shall discuss in the next chapter.

Will not an educated person want to study this phenomenon and try to understand it?

A Good Time for Religious Studies

This is a good time to study religion, because we have much more information available than we formerly had. There are several reasons for this. One is that we know much more about the original languages of the scriptures of various religions. This is important because often real under-

---

[4]The "Little Red Book" served for a time as the equivalent of sacred scripture for 20 percent of the world's people. See Stuart R. Schram, ed., *Quotations from Chairman Mao Tse-Tung* (New York: Praeger, 1968), for a good annotated English version.

standing of a religion depends on reading its teachings in their original form. Today, many people in the West can study the Hindu scriptures in the Sanskrit language. Many others can read the Koran, the holy book of Islam, in Arabic, the Hebrew Scriptures in Hebrew, and the New Testament in Greek. These languages are taught in our universities; they are no longer exotic mysteries. So language study has been the prelude to better understanding.

There is a second reason why this is a good time to study religion: it is much easier to get objective information now. For most of history, the only reason anyone ever studied anyone else's religion was to prove that it was *wrong*. That was the purpose the "student" had in mind before he or she started. Small wonder that such a student ends up defining the other religion as being a series of superstitions, flaws in thinking, and corruptions of real truth! (In other words, one tends to find what one is looking for.)

Of course, the time comes when one must make up one's own mind—and that will mean choosing *for* some ideas and *against* others. But before deciding for or against, say, Buddhism, one's responsibility is first to look at Buddhism for what it *is*. In other words, one must gather as much objective information as possible.

It is much easier today to find such information. And the university is becoming a better and better place in which to find it.

Decoding Ancient Religious Texts. This stone tablet, found in 1881, provides a text to explain the religious ceremony depicted. The tablet was placed in an earthenware box by the Babylonian King Nabopolassar, evidently so that if the idol and temple depicted were destroyed, future generations would know how to reconstruct them. Modern decoding of such ancient documents has led to an explosion in knowledge of ancient religious beliefs. (British Museum)

Also, travel is relatively easy now. Travel means the mixing of ideas. It gives one a chance to observe and critique what one has read by means of firsthand experience. For many centuries the only way in which anyone could possibly learn anything about the Shinto religion in Japan was to read a book by some very daring soul who had gotten on a ship and sailed to Japan. There he or she had had many adventures and had observed many strange customs and had written them down for our entertainment and amazement. We read them as exotic things, far beyond the scope of our own lives.

But today multitudes of people visit Japan. For many people in our century the Far East became a practical reality when they were pressed into military service and sent off to war there. It no longer takes great wealth to walk among the ancient temples of India, to stand inside the fabled mosques of Arabia, to observe the tribal ceremonies of Africa. All it takes is a little determination and ingenuity.

If those who set out in this way are sensitive enough, and inquisitive enough, and open enough, they can come home with a great deal of information. The present wealth of information makes this a good time to study religion.

Religious Studies as a Search for Clarity

Religious studies are popular now because interest in religion is on the upswing and because more objective information is available than ever before. A third reason grows out of the fact that college is, at least theoretically, the place where people clarify their thinking. Probably no other word is used so nebulously as the word "religion." It covers many different ideas; already, in the opening pages of this book, we have used the word in several different ways, to refer to several different things.

This situation makes it difficult to communicate. The word "religion" is perceived in dozens of ways, depending on the vantage point of the various hearers, their experiences, their feelings, the books they have read, the people they have met, and so on. So one of the things this book attempts to do is *clarify*. The word "religion" is much too complex for any one definition. We must begin to develop a thoughtful way in which to handle these definitions, however, and that is one of the main tasks of education.

Education and Freedom

Studying religion in college is an important part of the process of emancipation. People seek education for various reasons. A major goal for most is vocational training, learning so as to get a job. Many professors, particularly those in technical fields, tend to think that this is almost the exclusive purpose of education. Everything else must be sacrificed, if need be, to "make our graduates competitive in the job market." And an even higher percentage of students concurs. Their thinking runs something like this:

"I will study certain subjects to gain certain skills needed to get a certain job and make a certain amount of money. There is a nice straight, logical line between each of these items, connecting them tightly together. That connection is why I'm here. Courses that don't fit into this line are only endured. They are dirty tricks played on us by egg heads, obstacle courses designed by starry-eyed idealists who won't give us our license to go out and make money until we play their Mickey Mouse game."

Administratively, any course that cannot be shown to apply directly to getting a job is always in jeopardy. In times of financial crisis, it is likely to be the first to go. "We don't have time or money for that kind of peripheral material," the university seems to be saying. "We have to get these students trained so they can get the good jobs and make the good money."

Undeniably, education has some vocational goals. But an education with only vocational goals is a deficient and dangerous education. One of the reasons for studying religion, and other "impractical" subjects, is that true education involves not only training, but also *emancipation*.

The mastery of technological skills enables us to build remarkable machines. Our technological machine runs on the strength of our technological skills. But technology has not been able to replace the need for values. People who are oriented solely toward technical information and technical skill tend to suffer from a "value deficiency." Sadly, some people,

(Marc Anderson)

very highly educated in highly technical ways, discover at a certain age that all that they really know is one very narrow field. They are unable to even carry on a reasonable conversation about anything else. They feel trapped. Listen to one medical specialist:

"If you want me to talk about the inner ear I'll do it. I'll tell you anything you want to know. But if you want me to make an informed, intelligent comment about politics, or art, or heaven forbid, religion, well, forget it. I'm just lost. I don't know where to start."

This comes from a person who sometimes has to make what are basically moral decisions, decisions that have to do with values. A physician may decide, for example, whether you will live or die. You do not want an intellectually narrow person there; you want someone who can move in many directions, one who is free and open and comfortable in the world. You want an emancipated human being.

Human values are caught, struggle, and die in the web of ignorance. Certain primitive tribes think that twins are dangerous. So they take them, newborn, and leave them in the forest to die of exposure or be carried away by animals. To learn that this is not necessary is to be emancipated. To respect the life in those twins is *freedom*—for them, for their mother, for the tribe.

In the eighteenth century, a really sick person was taken to a barber, who would slit the person's wrists and let him or her bleed a while. This, supposedly, got all the "poisons" out. At least one account of the death of George Washington says that he was bled to death by someone trying to cure him. When people learned more facts, they were freed from this deadly misunderstanding. They were emancipated.

And what is true of these is also true of human relationships, and true of ultimate questions, and true of "religious" questions—the more you know, the freer you become. Jesus put it succinctly:[5]

You will know the truth, and the truth will make you free.

So there is a connection between truth and freedom. And education can be not simply training, but a way to get oneself free, to open up one's life to all kinds of new possibilities, to become a person.

A college degree is no longer a ticket to financial success anyway. There are much quicker and less expensive ways to get a job—often one with more prestige and money than those available to a "merely" emancipated person.

Many college graduates do janitorial work and drive taxis and operate service stations and sell insurance. There is certainly no tragedy in that—no tragedy, that is, if these persons have been emancipated. Not a

---

[5]John 8:32. All Biblical quotations are from the *Revised Standard Version* unless otherwise noted.

dollar or a day of it was wasted. They got exactly what they paid for—a kind of handle on life, a kind of freedom. It would be a tragedy only if they had spent all that time and money solely to train as a left-handed computer technician, and then could not find an opening for a left-handed computer technician, and then had to take a job as a cabbie. *That* would be a failure and a waste.

In modern times vocation has tended to become an eight-hour-a-day affair. The key questions are, "What about the other sixteen hours?" "How will I approach life?" "How will I approach other people?" "How will I read, and what will I read?" "How will I watch television, and what will I watch?" "How will I react to what is going on in my world?"

Religious studies is one very important area in which these questions are faced head on. It is part of the concept of education as emancipation.

Seeking Our Roots

A fifth reason for studying religion is to gain a better understanding of our culture. Our culture has numerous and pervasive religious presuppositions. They may be well hidden, but they are there. They can be detected even in families in which no one member has darkened a church door in seventy-five years. These presuppositions still operate in the way in which these families make decisions, in the things the parents tell the children, in the manner in which they live from day to day. There are some religious roots.

What is true of families is also true of society as a whole: religious presuppositions operate in the way in which we as a people make decisions, make laws, treat certain issues or certain people. Western Europe and America, it is said, are "bound up with Judeo-Christian thought forms."[6]

In some ways the university has always recognized this. Various disciplines there have been forced to deal with religious issues, because religious issues have so often exerted an influence on human behavior. Political science must deal with religious issues, for example, and education must, and business must.

In religious studies we meet the issues directly. We say, "If religion has always been so much a part of our culture, should we not study it? Perhaps in doing that we will come to understand our culture better." And so we do.

Religious studies, undertaken in the Western world, will try to understand the religious presuppositions of the West. But religious studies, undertaken anywhere, must deal with the subject of humanity—the universal human being. In religion people search for themselves and try to find out what they *mean*, not as Americans, or Englishmen, or Danes, or Italians, but as human beings.

[6]Magee, *Religion*, p. 7.

One might even argue that religion is the primary discipline in the study of humanity. Biology, anthropology, sociology, and history all deal with important aspects of humanity's nature and activities. Religion asks the questions about *meaning* and *value*. What kind of judgment can be made on things-as-they-are? On human beings as they are? What do *I* mean? Do I mean *anything*? Am I going anywhere? If so, where? Do I have any present meaning, or any future purpose? Who *am* I, anyway?

These are the distinctly "religious" questions we must ask about humanity. We can, of course, search for answers among the test tubes and computers. But the problem is that the answers seem to come up in a totally unsatisfying way: What am I? "Well, you are a blob of protoplasm, . . . here by chance . . . and going nowhere." Not a very satisfying answer.

But maybe the answer gets no farther than that because we are asking it in the wrong place. On a once popular television space fantasy, a very friendly computer, when asked questions such as these, would always reply, "It does not compute." If the machine's answer is inadequate, it may not mean that no adequate answer exists. It may mean that the machine has none.

Religious studies is a search for the answers elsewhere.

Religion and Personal Values

A seventh reason for religious studies is the need to develop an intelligent way in which to judge whether a given religious concept is right or wrong. Not all ideas are true. That is a basic axiom, as true in religious studies as in any other academic discipline. Somehow the idea exists that to believe that someone else's religious ideas are untrue is to be intolerant and bigoted and narrow minded. But we do not think similarly of other disciplines. When we hear the claim that one must bleed a patient to heal that person, we do not hesitate to say, "That is wrong!" When someone says that the Declaration of Independence was signed in 1492 we immediately reply, "That is incorrect!"

But when religious concepts are at issue, we become very hesitant. We may claim that this hesitancy is born of tolerance, but more likely it betrays our insecurity. When insecure persons are questioned about their convictions, they will probably respond by becoming angry. They regard the question to be a personal threat. That is why so many religious discussions turn into arguments—all heat and no light, all superficial prejudices and very few intelligent opinions.

Others, claiming tolerance, decline to discuss religion or make religious judgments, due to apathy. It is not really that they are so tolerant. They simply do not want to bother. So comes the rationalization: "Oh, I don't think I want to comment on that. I think everyone has a right to his or her own belief. I never discuss religion or politics. Who am I to say what's right and wrong?" After all, it is much easier to plead ignorance than face the issues.

But the fact is that such people are making judgments; they cannot avoid it. They are simply choosing to make them without any intelligent investigation.

Such judgments usually crumble quickly under fire. Uninformed people tend either to get dogmatic and make fools of themselves or to sway in the wind like palm trees in a hurricane. When confronted with a new idea, especially if it sounds profound, they fall for it immediately. And then they fall for the next one, too. And the next one.

Religious studies will help us decide—perhaps *for*, perhaps *against*, but at least much more intelligently.

An eighth reason for the study of religion has to do with human developmental needs. Psychologists point out that at certain stages in a person's life each of us has certain specific developmental tasks. At one stage it may be "learning how to get our eyes focused." At another "getting our thumb and fingers to work together." Or "learning to share with others." The motor needs and psychological needs come, step by step, in the road to maturity.

One of the most pressing developmental needs of the college years is the need to acquire a *personal value system*. It is a time when one decides whether to keep what he or she has been taught or abandon it. It is a time when one draws one's own conclusions about what is real and what is fake, what is basic and what is secondary. Of course many students do this without consciously realizing that they are doing it. They do not reflect on the process; they just "let it happen." Others feel such a significant task is worth at least a few hours of sober thought.

Quite often this second group turns to religious studies for some help.

SOME PRACTICAL SUGGESTIONS
ABOUT STUDYING RELIGION

How does one proceed in attempting a mature, intelligent study of religion? Here are some basic suggestions:

Begin Where You Are

The French philosopher René Descartes claimed that to find truth one had to clear one's mind of all preconceptions. One had to start with a clean slate, at absolute ground zero, and build up from there. Unfortunately, there are several reasons why this approach does not work very well in the study of religion. There is a *philosophical* reason, for example. Our minds have already developed certain categories and certain approaches toward data. It is too late to simply wipe everything out of our minds and pretend to know nothing at all. We do know some things. We know a certain language, for example. We think in forms compatible with that language. In this way objectivity is compromised at the very beginning of the thought process. We have to begin where we are.

Another reason this is true is a *psychological* one. It is psychologically damaging to say, "All the things I've always believed or been told are false. I will discard them all. I'm going to start all over again with nothing at all, and move up from there." Unfortunately, one of the worst places of all to be, psychologically, is nowhere at all.

Often people falling into severe psychosis are overwhelmed by a sense of not knowing anything, of not being sure of anything. Everything shifts like loose sand. There is nothing to hang on to anywhere.

So, begin where you are.

Here are three slightly different ways of saying the same thing:

Do Not Jump Without Your Parachute

Think of what you believe now—the way in which you hold your life together, the way in which you keep things going—think of that as being a *parachute*. A parachute lets you down easily. When you are up in the rarified atmosphere of new ideas, bombarded on every side, it is not wise to jump without your parachute. Instead, hang on to those things that have always held you together and allow them to let you down gently.

Of course by the time you reach the ground you may have changed in all sorts of important ways. You may even decide to use a different parachute from now on. But in the meantime do not discard the one you have—not until you have the new one road tested. In other words, do not despise what you have received.

Sometimes people read a few books and take a few courses and decide that "Everything anybody ever told me before now is wrong. Now I know where the truth is. It resides with my fraternity brothers, and with one or two of my profs. Everything I ever heard before now is out."

There comes a kind of sinking feeling, or perhaps with others a kind of rebellious feeling, that says, "Some things I have always believed are obviously wrong. Therefore *everything* I have always believed is obviously wrong." Of course that kind of thinking is not very rational, but it happens nevertheless.

You see, some of the things that people have told you in the past may be true. Some may be false, of course, but some may be true. So do not count out the old family traditions all together. New ideas are not always better than old ones.

One other way to say it is, Do not consider the exotic to be preferable. Of course it may or may not be preferable, but it is never preferable simply because it is exotic. Sometimes people begin to learn something about a religious system practiced far away in some storybook place. They see how people there deal with religious questions. It all sounds plausible, and it seems to have some strengths, and some answers they have never heard. So they quickly conclude, *they* are right and *we* are wrong!

Perhaps. But that conclusion may not have come from a sober reflection on the facts. It may have come from an approach that says, "Anything that is different must be right. Anything that sounds like what I have always heard must be wrong."

The exotic may turn out to be preferable. But the fact that something is exotic, and that you have never heard it before, does not automatically make it true. So, begin where you are.

Creative Listening and Learning

Another basic suggestion is to: *listen and then talk.* Be sure that you understand the new idea before you either accept it or try to refute it. It is amazing how superficial discussions about religion can be sometimes. Often that is because no one is paying attention to anyone else. Everyone is talking and no one is listening. All the other person wants to do is to make a point, and all you want to do is to make your point, and no one is learning anything. Neither of you is studying religion—you are just arguing. The first step toward real learning is to listen, and to listen very carefully. Ask questions. Be sure that you understand what the other person is saying or what his or her new idea really is.

And try to look at what is best in the other point of view. If you want to know how a religious system different from your own deals with things, do not start with a book written to refute that system. Read one written by someone who believes it. Allow the other person the benefit of the doubt. Let the other person explain things to you at their best.

Then you are in a better position to say, "Now I've heard it at its best. I know the facts. And I've come to the conclusion that it is true here, and here, and here. But not here, and here, and here." But that kind of talk can come only after you have done a lot of hard listening.

There is another kind of nonlistener—the gullible one. This person does not really want an explanation. He or she is looking for a guru, to believe what the guru says to believe. This is a kind of emotional and intellectual escape method that says, "I'll accept that because I like you" or "because you are my teacher." That is really no better than saying, "I'm not going to believe you because I do not like you." Either way, you are not really listening. That means that no communication is taking place, and it probably also means that you are developing some distorted ideas about what the other person believes.

Sometimes statements are made about the tenets of a certain religion that are completely distorted and untrue. But the statements stay alive because no one bothers to ask the people involved whether they are true or not.

It is very important to listen. It minimizes sloppy thinking, sloppy statements, gross generalizations, and distortions of the other person's point of view. It results in clarification and real communication and learning.

You do not have to agree with someone to be able to listen to him or her. After all, it is really no threat to your personhood to listen to an idea different from your own. You do not have to get upset about it. You do not have to rant and rave and scream. Often it is not necessary to refute or agree with what you are hearing.

Of course there are times when a good, spirited discussion of differences is enjoyable and profitable—especially if all people involved are sure enough of themselves emotionally and can handle it. Nothing is quite as stimulating as a really good discussion about religious questions, about the basic questions of meaning. It can be a growing experience.

Some people say that it is never appropriate to discuss religious differences. On the contrary, religious differences are among the most important things to discuss. Of course if "discussion" means simply shouting the other person down without listening to that person, then the process is a waste of time. But if one is trying to understand, and not simply to refute, then it is an excellent activity.

The same principle applies to reading. Freud said that religion is a childhood neurosis. Marx said it is an opium people take to escape the real world. Both leveled their major attack upon Christianity. Now a Christian reader might become very angry about this and throw the book down. Or he or she might look around a bit and discover that, sure enough, some people do use Christianity like opium, and some do retain childhood neuroses. People with serious mental difficulties are often religious, and their religion often reflects their neurotic approach to life. People in positions of power and wealth have often used religious teachings to hold the lower classes in poverty, telling them to look for their "pie in the sky by and by." So you see, Marx and Freud are not entirely wrong after all, are they?

When someone criticizes your religion, it is always a good idea to see whether the criticism is not directed toward a *misuse* of that religion. It may not be a valid attack upon the *essence* of what you believe at all. But you would not have noticed that if you had not taken time to listen.

Our next suggestion for studying religion is to *keep on learning*. Someone once described another person as "knowing too much for his own good." Such a thing is probably impossible. One might know too many wrong things for one's own good; but one will never have too many facts, or too much truth. More information is always helpful. Some people have very strong religious opinions that are precisely the same as those same people held fifty years ago. There has been absolutely no growth, no developing insight, no deepening understanding.

These people make frustrating conversationalists. They seem to have a bumper sticker taped to their forehead that says, "My Mind Is Already Made Up; Don't Try to Confuse Me with Facts." They seem to be saying, "I don't want to hear anymore. I went through that whole thing a long time ago and I've made up my mind. I want no new evidence, pro or con. I just do not want to talk about it anymore."

People who do not keep learning about religion tend to resort to gross oversimplifications; they sound very narrow minded and bigoted, and they tend to make unintelligent comments. Sometimes they are very sophisticated in other areas, but when it comes to religion these usually suave and fluent types can say absolutely crazy things. They usually say them very confidently and have no idea how absurd they sound to anyone with a smattering of facts at his or her disposal.

Religious studies must not be thought of as the accumulation of a few convictions, followed by a lifetime of stubborn loyalty to those same convictions. Rather, it is a process that must keep happening to be of any use.

The Objective Study of Religion

Our next suggestion: *look at religion objectively.* There are some things about religion that can and should be looked at without any presuppositions, special pleading, or desire to make or prove a point. The accumulating of raw data, of uninterpreted facts, is an important step in religious understanding. (It is not the *only* step, of course.)

Three major areas for the objective study of religion are:

1. The history of religion
2. The sociology of religion
3. The psychology of religion

The first area, the *history of religion,* is itself divided into several categories: *anthropology,* for example, deals with the nature of religion in preliterate cultures. Even though these cultures leave no written documents, they often possess highly developed religious concepts. The anthropologists study these cultures and thereby learn some important things about religion.

A special area within anthropology is *archaeology.* Archaeologists can be very helpful in religious studies because they can tell us about religious concepts and practices in cultures now gone. Since we can no longer talk to these people, we must learn about them through the artifacts they left behind. Archaeology often deals with religion because people tend to leave behind artifacts having to do with the things they considered most important—"religious" things. For example, the most permanent, massive, and impressive buildings in most ancient societies had religious purposes—altars, temples, and tombs. Tombs are especially revealing, because death is a kind of direct contact with the "other" world, and burial customs often reflect the deepest thinking of a people about ultimate questions.

Documentary criticism is the historical, objective study of written materials. The documentary critic takes the literature of the past (most of which is religious) and "decodes" it. He or she studies the languages of these documents (most of them in dead languages), dates them, and interprets them as much as possible in their original cultural and historical context.

Comparative religions is a study that takes certain categories (e.g., the concept of sin) and traces and compares those categories in various religions. By observing the similarities and differences from one religion to another, it adds to our fund of objective facts.

A second area for the objective study of religion is the *sociology of religion*. Here scholars observe the effect of culture on religion and religion on culture. This should not be an attempt to prove any religion right or wrong. Rather, it should be an objective attempt to see how humanity's religious beliefs have influenced the way in which human beings have developed social structures or the way in which social structures have created or changed religious ideas.

The *psychology of religion* is a third area for objective study. Psychologists and theologians often deal with the same or similar matters. One can sometimes learn a great deal about religion from psychological research. For example, "conversion," or radical personal change, has both psychological and theological dimensions. So do "guilt" and "anxiety" and "meaning."

The study of the mental processes of abnormal individuals is also of interest to students of religion. While we might reject the notion that *all* religion grows out of neurosis, it is certainly true that neurotic people are often religious. And they tend to be religious in neurotic ways. It is important to take some note of this.

Several years ago a student, an excellent athlete, came to see me. He had been under tremendous psychological pressures. He said he wanted to relate to me a "religious experience" that had happened to him.

"I was running around the indoor track today," he said, "when I realized that if Jesus would help me I could run faster than any human being ever had. I was thinking about that when suddenly I *saw him,* suspended in air in front of me, on his cross. He kept saying, 'Come on! Come on!' So I ran faster and faster, trying to catch up with him. But he kept moving just beyond my reach. So I ran even faster. I broke all the world indoor track records."

Shortly after our discussion the young man went berserk and tried to run down several people in his sports car and had to be hospitalized.

Here was a person whose mind was unraveling, and part of his reaction to this was "religious." So you can see how religion and abnormal psychology sometimes share concerns. It would be unfortunate, of course, if a psychologist were to claim that *all* religious expressions are psychologically abnormal. This kind of attitude is more often a prejudice than a scientific opinion.

The Subjective Study of Religion

Another suggestion: *do not neglect the subjective.* A purely scientific or objective study of religion is not sufficient to really understand it. In fact, the greatest strength of the scientific method becomes something of a limitation in studying religion, because simply analyzing religious ideas produces no evaluation of them. Analysis tells us what something is, that is, what *parts* make it up; but analysis cannot determine whether the thing is good or bad or mediocre. One is left without any sense of the *wholeness* of the thing investigated.

An example might help to illustrate this problem. Every student in a university class was given a goldfish in a little glass bowl. The assignment was to take the goldfish home and in three weeks bring to class an essay entitled "What Is a Goldfish?"

People have different kinds of minds, and so the students went at this project in different kinds of ways. People who chose the scientific route immediately began with analysis, as you would expect. Pity the poor goldfish that belonged to these people! Its fate was set; it was headed for dissection, right? That, after all, is what one does to find out what a goldfish *is*. So they took their goldfish apart, categorized, weighed, and counted the parts. They came back to class with some highly technical analytical statistical studies on the goldfish. But they had hardly said everything that can be said about a goldfish!

Other students approached the problem from the viewpoint of wholeness, or evaluation. Many of their essays resorted to poetry because to them the goldfish was "the glint of gold when the sun shines through the delicate veins of the flowing fins." Or "quiet movement, serenity, untroubled gentleness." They were seeing the goldfish in a very different way—subjectively. They were reacting to a goldfish, to what it meant to them, to its *value*. Some students even gave their goldfish a name and came to love it.

The things this latter group said were true. They were part of the reality of a goldfish. In some ways, they were the most important realities. For the subjective qualities of something may be more important "truths" than its objective qualities. For instance, think of your friends. They are so tall, so old, so this or that, statistically, analytically. But you will never know the truth about a friend when you insist on knowing him or her only in that way.

Of course subjective study can get a little frightening. It is very demanding. It is much easier to take a fact, lay it out, and count and measure it than it is to begin to ask, "Is this fact *important*? Is it important *to me*?"

Subjective study of religion can make one uncomfortable at times, but it is nevertheless very important.

Syncretism

Sometimes students accumulate information faster than they can assimilate it. The mass of data does not immediately fall into consistent order in their minds. They may, in fact, start jamming conflicting ideas into their "system" and end up with a hodgepodge. They pick up a book on Hinduism, grab an attractive idea or two, and glue them onto their system of thinking. Then they do the same with Islam, Zen, and so on.

The word we will use for the hodgepodge approach is *syncretism*. The student's mind is not moving fast enough to realize that it is picking up and accepting ideas that are mutually exclusive.

"But isn't it a good idea just to take the best from all religions, rather than settling on just one of them?"

This sounds good, but there are some serious problems in such an approach. It implies that the great world faiths have so little internal integrity that one can simply yank off a little here and pinch off a little there. On the contrary, these systems are usually made up of complex interwoven concepts. They are like a spider's web in which each strand depends on the tension of the other strands to hold itself together. One cannot simply detach and isolate an idea, because that idea may well have little meaning standing by itself; it becomes merely an isolated piece of data, supported by nothing.

The great religions have been considered "great" because there is a profound inner web of integrity in them. To study them properly, one must always watch for and appreciate that web.

CHAPTER TWO
DEFINING "RELIGION"

A WORD WITH NUMEROUS DEFINITIONS

"Religion" is one of those very common words that are often the hardest of all to define. Everyone uses it, but few people have a very well developed idea of what they *mean* when they use it.

Often, one's definition of "religion" reveals much more about the point of view or prejudices of the definer than it does about religion itself. If the word evokes positive emotions the definition is positive; if it evokes negative emotions the definition is negative.

Some of religion's nineteenth-century critics furnish good examples of this fact. *Sigmund Freud* (1865–1939) said that religion was an illusion, a neurosis, "born of the need to make tolerable the helplessness of man, and built out of the material offered by memories of the helplessness of his own childhood and the childhood of the human race."[1] What we learn here is not so much what religion is, as what the *Freudian concept* of religion is.

The same could be said about *Karl Marx*'s (1818–1883) definition: "Religion is the sigh of the oppressed creature, the sentiment of the

---

[1]Sigmund Freud, *The Future of an Illusion*, trans. W. D. Robson-Scott (New York: Liveright, 1955), pp. 52–58.

heartless world, the soul of soulless conditions. It is the opium of the people."[2]

Emile Durkheim (1858–1917), a famous sociologist and a founder of sociology, predictably defined religion in terms of its relationship to sociology. He said that "the idea of society is the soul of religion." That is, it is "collective sentiments . . . fixing themselves upon external objects." In other words, groups of people have certain things in which they believe as a group—collectively. They project these ideas somewhere external to themselves into an "upper world" and make that projection their "religion." The showing of a motion picture furnishes an analogy. The things depicted on the screen are not really happening. All that is really happening is that light is falling on a screen in various patterns. Durkheim thought that to be the case with religion, that it is the reflection of people's collective thoughts. These thoughts are projected upward on a screen we call "heaven" or "the other world." But they have no actual existence. The "sacred" is no more than a projection of the ideas of a society in the secular world, thrown up onto a heavenly screen.[3]

Ludwig Feuerbach (1804–1872), a famous critic of religious ideas, did, however, attempt a positive definition of "religion" from his own point of view. He said, "Man is the beginning of religion, the center of religion, the end of religion."[4] Religion "is the dream of the human spirit."[5] There could be no clearer statement of the view of the scientific humanist. Religion, he says, originates with the human being. It is a collection of people's highest dreams for themselves and their world.

One of the most negative definitions from the nineteenth century is that of *Salomon Reinach* (1858–1932). Religion, he said, is "a sum of scruples which impedes the free exercise of our faculties."[6] There is something in this definition that gives us an incisive insight into the mind of Reinach. For him, religion is whatever keeps one from really being free. Of course pro-religious definitions show the same pattern. They often say more about the person offering the definition than they do about religion.

We need to develop some categories to help us make judgments about such definitions. Religion has more than one face. And each face has its

[2]Karl Marx, *Early Writings,* trans. and ed. T. B. Bottomore (New York: McGraw-Hill, 1963), pp. 43–44.

[3]Emile Durkheim, *The Elementary Forms of Religious Life,* trans. Joseph Ward Swaim (London: Allen & Unwin, 1968), pp. 418–419.

[4]Ludwig Feurerbach, *Das Wesen des Christentums* (Leipzig: Druck und Verlag von Philipp Redanjun., 1841, 1904), Kap. 19. Quoted in E. S. Brightman, *A Philosophy of Religion* (Englewood Cliffs, N.J.: Prentice-Hall, 1940), p. 16.

[5]Dagobert D. Runes, *Dictionary of Philosophy* (Totowa, N.J.: Littlefield, Adams, 1955), p. 108.

[6]Salomon Reinach, *Orpheus, A History of Religions,* trans. Florence Simmonds (New York: Liveright, 1935), p. 3.

own kinds of definitions. One might define religion in several different ways if one is defining several different faces of religion. Differing definitions do not necessarily conflict. One may define one face, whereas another defines a different face. Sometimes people argue needlessly about definitions because one has one face in mind and the other has some other face in mind. The first step in such discussion is to be sure that everyone is attempting to deal with the same face.

We will assign names to four major faces or aspects of religion to help us in discussing it. There are four types of definitions:[7]

Descriptive
Normative
Essential
Functional

A *descriptive* definition is simply whatever a given person or group chooses to *call* religion.

"What is your religion?"
"I'm a Baptist."
"I'm a Buddhist."
"I'm a Druid."
"I'm a Sun Worshipper."

Whatever you call your religion is, descriptively, your religion. Whenever I describe you as an adherent of that religion ("You are a Unitarian"), I am giving a descriptive definition. I am making no judgments; I am simply stating the case descriptively.

A *normative* definition has an "ought to" or a "should" in it. It occurs whenever someone defines religion according to what he or she feels it should be. This definition introduces the concept of judgment. It implies rightness or wrongness. It implies that certain systems that call themselves religions are not. For example,

Religion should meet man's emotional needs.
Religion should deal with living a better life.

An *essential* definition tries to be comprehensive. It tries to define religion in such a way that all religious expressions fit the definition. It seeks the essence that is the root of all religion. For example,

Religion is man's way of relating to the transcendent.
Religion is a state of being grasped by an ultimate concern.

---

[7]The categories are from John B. Magee, *Religion and Modern Man: A Study of the Religious Meaning of Being Human* (New York: Harper & Row, 1967), p. 20.

As you can see, these are very broad definitions that try to deal with every instance of religion.

Often beginning students, asked to define religion essentially, say that "Religion is the means by which man relates to God." But there are religions that make no reference to "God." Some forms of Buddhism, for example, are basically atheistic, or at least divine beings play no part in the practice of these faiths. So an essential definition would have to be broader than that.

A *functional* definition describes religion in terms of what it does or what its effect is. Marx's definition ("Religion is the opium of the people") falls into this category. He defines religion as he sees it working. He sees it as a stultifying phenomenon. It so distracts people that they do not worry about their real problems. That is a functional definition. Here is another example of a functional definition: "Religion is the power that frees man from his sins." This example sees religion working in a very different way, but it is the same kind of definition—a functional one.

For us to talk to each other intelligently, we need to come to some agreement on which face of religion we want to discuss. If I insist on talking about what religion *should* be, but you will only talk about what it *is*, we can argue at length and never communicate with each other. I say, "Religion should make people love one another." You reply, "Religion has resulted in many people having been burned at the stake." We are not communicating because we are trying to compare apples with oranges. You are talking about religion descriptively, and I am talking about it normatively. We will have to agree on which face of religion we wish to discuss before there will be any progress.

RELIGION AS ULTIMATE CONCERN

The essential definition or religion that we will use as a "working definition" is short and concise: *religion is ultimate concern.* This may or may not be the best essential definition. It is certainly not the only one. But it will at least help to clarify our thinking. We borrow the phrase "ultimate concern" from the philosopher-theologian *Paul Tillich* (1886–1965). Religion, he notes, is "the state of being grasped by something unconditional, holy, absolute."[8] If this definition is accepted, then a person is acting "religiously," even if one does not recognize it or admit it, when one

1. Struggles with the ultimate and final *meaning* of life.
2. Feels an ultimate *obligation*, something that must be done, no matter what.

[8]Paul Tillich, *The Protestant Era* (Chicago: University of Chicago Press, 1948), p. 59.

3.   Relates oneself, by action or devotion, to what one believes is ultimately *real*.

Ultimate concern is, then, something that would cause one to sacrifice everything else. It is the ruler by which one measures everything. It is that which is ultimate—really real. There is not the slightest touch of illusion in it. It is at the root of everything, and everything grows out of and depends on it.

When we think about what is really *real*, what one must really *do*, and what existence really *means*, then we are doing *religion*, regardless of our denominational commitment or theological commitment or lack of it. These questions belong to everybody. We either deal with them ("do religion") or we do not. And the way in which we deal with them is, essentially, our religion.[9]

Here are some examples of essentially religious questions: "Is there anything so dear to me that I would allow myself to be put against the wall and shot, rather than compromise?" "Are there things that I would do, even if I knew I would be shot for doing them?" "Are there things that I would refuse to do, even if refusal meant certain death?" "What is the last thing among my possessions (material and nonmaterial) that I would be willing to give up?"

Ultimate Concern and Atheism

From the perspective of this definition, no one is really a pure atheist. Atheism is not the lack of religion, defined as ultimate concern. It is the disbelief in some particular god. There are, therefore, various varieties of atheists. There are some who do not believe in the Judeo-Christian god. There are some who do not believe in the Hindu god or gods. There are some who do not believe in the African gods or the "gods" of scientific humanism. Atheism, in this context, implies a negative judgment toward what may be considered ultimate to someone else. It is not an alternative religion.

The atheist does have a religion, that is, an ultimate concern or concerns. He is atheistic only with reference to certain gods, say, Yahweh, or Krishna, or Marduke. And, of course, all of us are atheists with reference to some gods. No one believes in all of them: the very act of believing in one god usually necessitates disbelief in many others.

Everyone has some "god"—if we use the word to mean some "ultimate concern or concerns," something that is of ultimate meaning in his or her life, something that means more than anything else. When one com-

---

[9]Here we stray from Tillich's own use of the phrase "ultimate concern" since, for him, if the concern were not *really* ultimate, the activity would not strictly speaking be "religious." See Paul Tillich, *The Dynamics of Faith*, (New York: Harper & Row, 1957).

mits oneself to something in this ultimate way, then o
becomes an atheist with reference to other gods or

So, when religion is defined in this way, every/
atheist and in some sense a believer.

Crypto and Pseudo and False Religions

The term *crypto* means "hidden." Cryptoreligion is the word we will
use to describe an ultimate concern that wears a secular mask. It does not
think of itself as a religion. It avoids using religious terms such as "god" or
"holy spirit" or "church." But it is an ultimate concern; it matters more than
anything else to the person who possesses it.

Patriotism is the cryptoreligion of some people. Their love for and
commitment to their country is absolutely the most ultimate of their concerns. They will willingly die to protect it or serve it. They sense an
immense, all-comprising obligation toward it. They may say, "I'm not a
religious person; I'm a patriot." But according to our working definition
they *are* religious. Patriotism is their cryptoreligion.

In the last part of this chapter we will look at Wang Tao-ming, a young
Chinese communist, whose commitment to a certain political ideology is
one of the clearest possible examples of religion wearing a secular mask.

The term *pseudo* means "false." A pseudoreligion is one that claims to
be, or outwardly appears to be, dealing with ultimate concerns, but actually
is not. Its adherents claim that it guides all their thinking and actions, and
they claim to base their lives upon its teachings, but actually they do not.

On any given Sunday in the United States, hundreds of people sit
through various rituals that purport to deal with ultimate concerns. They
say words and sing hymns that speak of ultimate commitments. They hear
sermons saying, "What's really real is this. What one must die for is *this*."
The people listen, and appear to agree, but they would not really die for
those things at all. They do not believe those are the "realest" things at all.

They adhere to the rituals and use the vocabulary of ultimate concern, but the result is a pseudoreligion. Their real commitments are hidden behind the façade. Sometimes they cannot even admit to themselves
what they really believe, what is really basic to them, what really guides
their actions and decisions. In other words, their real religion is hidden
behind the pseudo one. So what one says, or even superficially believes is
ultimate for him or her, may not really be ultimate at all.

Even though our working definition makes everyone "religious" in
the essential sense, it does not follow that all religions are equally true.
People can truly, sincerely, and totally commit themselves to something as
ultimate when it is not ultimate. They may believe with all their hearts that
it is true and real and basic, when actually it is none of those things.

When Mount Vesuvius began to pour ashes and lava over the ancient
Roman city of Pompeii (A.D. 79), there was time to escape. But in the face of

tense danger, some people lingered long enough to run back into their ouses to rescue what was ultimately important to them. As they rushed back into the streets the ash poured down upon them and covered them, snuffing out their lives. Their bodies disintegrated, but left a perfect mold or impression in the hardening volcanic ash.

Centuries later the archaeologists began to excavate the city. Whenever they discovered one of the human molds, they would make a small hole and fill the cavity full of a liquid substance that would then harden. Next they carefully removed the ash, leaving a perfect model of the ancient citizen of Pompeii just as he or she looked at the moment of death.

Do you know what those people had run back to get, causing them to lose their lives? The ancient hands still clutched them:

Bags of gold!

Here were people who had taken an ultimate stand; they had risked everything for what they thought most important. From our perspective, two thousand years later, it seems pathetic and tragic to trade life for a bag of gold, especially since, being dead, one could hardly use it. These people had paid the ultimate price for something that was unworthy of it. They had worshipped a false god.

And, indeed, when anyone exhalts the nonultimate to the place of the ultimate, one worships a false god and follows a false religion. Of course we might disagree about what *is* ultimate—people always have. Still, sad as it may be, the fact remains that in these disagreements some people may turn out to be wrong.

Death and the Ultimate

The people of Pompeii died in their struggle to grasp the ultimate. Death has always been intimately associated with the ultimate, because it raises the question of meaning and the question of reality more directly than does any other human experience. Why? Because it is final and it is certain. One can avoid almost anything—love, sensitivity, responsibility, relationships—but one cannot avoid dying.

Of course people can employ a kind of mental maneuver that avoids the *issue* of dying (but not the reality of it). I call it the *invincibility syndrome*. I experienced it myself, in my closest brush with death.

It happened not six blocks from my home. I was driving along rather absentmindedly, engaged in some obscure errand. Suddenly I was conscious of a white flash to the right rear of my car. I had been hit broadside by a big stationwagon. My car went out of control and took off, sailing through the air. When I looked out the front window I found myself confronted with two choices: hit a telephone pole or hit the back end of a paint truck.

Actually, I had no choice at all, since my car was careening out of control. Rather, I had the role of a very interested observer, wondering which object I was going to slam into.

Well, there I was, sailing toward an inevitable head-on collision. But do you think I was scared? Not a bit. Now I have been frightened half to death a time or two when I almost hit a dog running in front of my car. That really made my heart pump. But this time—no fear at all. I felt completely invincible. I *knew* this kind of thing could not happen to me.

But of course it did. As it happened I hit the paint truck instead of the telephone pole. I remember seeing the equipment in the back of the truck explode into the air. The front end of the station wagon was resting partially in my lap, headlight and all, and the front end of my car had simply disintegrated. Pieces of vehicles were lying everywhere.

My first thought was, "Oh, no. My eyes! I can't see anything." Then I realized that my glasses had been knocked off. I was conscious of having little bits of glass in my hair. But I just sat there calmly, still feeling invincible.

A police officer came up, looked in the window and asked, "Are you all right?"

"Well, I don't feel anything. Maybe I'm paralyzed from the neck down. Or maybe I'm dead—never having been dead I don't know what *that* feels like."

The look on the patrolman's face said, "Boy, have I ever gotten hold of a live one here!"

The whole adventure was very instructive to me—because I will never forget that sense of invincibility. You would think at least at a time like that you would admit that you are mortal—that it is possible for you to be killed. But, no, I still felt that that happens only to other people.

Nevertheless, the statistics are overwhelmingly against living forever. Still many people have treated death more like an obscenity than a reality. Someone has said that all the obscenities in the last generation were sexual but that all the obscenities of this generation deal with death. We can accept it in movies. We have a morbid curiosity to see blood spurting on the screen. But we do not want to deal with death as a real, personal kind of issue.

We seem unwilling to look at it calmly and say, "In view of the fact that I am not immortal, what does today mean? What does tomorrow mean? What does existence mean?"

Once I was conducting a class discussion on death and various theories were being bandied about. In that class, one student, fifth row back, fourth person over, was four hours from his death. He did not know it, of course. No one did. He had a number of things to say on the subject. He left school that afternoon, and drove toward his home a few miles away. As he crossed a railroad track a fast-moving train struck his car broadside and killed him.

I have often thought about the difference between our theorizing that afternoon and the *reality* of the thing. I have wondered how he would have treated that discussion if he had known that before the next day dawned he would be dead.

Fyodor Dostoyevsky, in his novel *The Idiot*, describes a man who had this opportunity. He was condemned for a political offense to be shot by firing squad. Soon he found himself with only five more minutes.[10]

> He told me that those five minutes seemed to him an infinite time, a vast wealth; he felt that he had so many lives left in those five minutes that there was no need yet to think of the last moment, so much so that he divided his time up. He set aside time to take leave of his comrades, two minutes for that; then he kept another two minutes to think for the last time; and then a minute to look about him for the last time. He remembered very well having divided his time like that. He was dying at twenty-seven, strong and healthy. As he took leave of his comrades, he remembered asking one of them a somewhat irrelevant question and being particularly interested in the answer. Then when he said good-bye, the two minutes came that he had set apart for *thinking* to himself. He knew beforehand what he would think about. He wanted to realize as quickly and clearly as possible how it could be that now he existed and was living and in three minutes he would be *something*—someone or something. But what? Where? He meant to decide all that in those two minutes!

The sentence was changed at the last moment, so the man lived to share his "final" thoughts. But the questions he grappled with are real questions for every human being—and should be dealt with openly and calmly—not as whispered obscenities.

To deal with such ultimate questions is one of the important parts of "doing religion."

RELIGION AND HUMAN EXISTENTIAL NEED

Now we turn to defining religion *functionally*, that is, defining it in terms of what it *does*. What purpose does it have? How does it function? What are its

---

[10]Fyodor Dostoevsky, *The Idiot*, trans. Constance Garnett (New York: Macmillan, 1913), p. 57. Emphasis added.

results? The working functional definition for religion that we will propose is this:

Religion is the means by which a person fulfills existential needs.

The word "existential" is a rather complicated one, but we are using the word in a simple way: an *existential need* is a need that an individual has because he or she is a human being. It is a need that comes out of one's existence as a human being. It is called existential to distinguish it from needs caused by particular society (sociological needs) or time frame (historical needs). A "human existential need" is the need of a human being. It exists whenever human beings exist and in whatever culture they live. In other words, it is a need that all people, everywhere, have always had.

Technology does not function well to fulfill this kind of need. If anything, human existential needs have a way of becoming even more pressing in technosocieties because physical needs are not so much of a problem in such societies. People in technosocieties are fairly safe from invasion, starvation, and diseases. There are more opportunities to get inside oneself. The needs that grow out of *existence* begin to surface. Ironically, the more progress people have made toward meeting external needs, the more conscious they often become of unmet internal needs.

Many examples of this phenomenon can be seen in the children of upper-middle-class families. Their parents worked very hard. They had struggled through the Great Depression. They had somehow overcome, gotten themselves a good bank account, a couple of nice cars, a vacation home, maybe even a boat. The children always had the confidence that funds were available for whatever they wanted to do. If they wanted to take ballet lessons they could do so. If they wanted to go to Europe they could do that too.

But in numerous cases the reaction of the children has been rebellion—a total rejection of the life-style that brought them such comfort. Sometimes they have become leaders of the "prophetic minority"—the counterculture critics of their parents' life-style. Like the poor young man in the movie *The Graduate*, they find the world of their parents abhorrent—even shocking. By the thousands, they turn their backs on such a world and drop out.

In other words, the very people who have had their physical and financial needs most consistently and completely met have often become the most unhappy with life itself and have gone off on a desperate search for something with more and deeper meaning.

"Religion" is whatever these or any other human beings have used to meet these existential needs. And while many different religions have functioned in this way, they have all functioned to meet the *same* needs.

We will look at some of the most significant of these needs and some of the religious responses to them.

Precariousness

The first human existential need (the following are not listed in order of importance, necessarily), is

The need to overcome the sense of precariousness.

People of ancient and modern times share the sense of shakiness, the feeling that nothing is solid, that things are unstable, that there is no really unmovable place to stand. You have undoubtedly felt it yourself. There seems to be nothing to hang onto very well. Everything seems to be flowing, shifting like desert sand. You feel that you are about to plunge into some great emotional or psychological chasm. You dream of falling through space, grabbing for trees along the side of the cliff, feeling them slip out of your hands. You just keep falling and falling.

Religion has responded by attempting to provide some sense of personal stability, some sense of cosmological stability, some sense of wholeness. It has tried to supply the conviction that there are some solid places, some solid foundations, unmoved and unmovable. It expresses itself in such statements as this one, from Max Ehrmann's poem "Desiderata":

You are a child of the Universe;
You have a right to be here.

Or in dozens of hymns that speak of solid rocks and safe harbors:

On Christ the solid rock I stand,
All other ground is sinking sand.

Loneliness

A second universal human existential need is to *escape from loneliness*. This is not the loneliness that results from not having friends or from being physically alone. It is an existential loneliness. "Alienation" and "separation" are synonyms. It is much deeper than physical loneliness. It can occur in the middle of 50,000 people at a football game. It can happen to you when you are looking into the eyes of the person you love most, somebody you know would gladly die for you.

It is a kind of ache that says, "When all is said and done, the truth is that I am alone."

In college I used to feel it most right after supper. It is beginning to get dark. You have been to supper and return to your room. It is dark there, too, and you do not know if you even want to turn the light on. You feel very alone. It is not homesickness—you were home last weekend. It is not a lack of friends—you have plenty.

No, it has something to do with your whole existence, with the act of being. You begin to think, "Here is this infinite universe—billions of stars and millions of light-years. And here am I—tiny speck of existence and all alone."

There it is: existential loneliness.

This experience can take various forms. Sometimes it is a sense of alienation from the whole universe. You ask "What's going on here? Who am I? Where is this place? Where am I? Where else could I go?" You feel trapped. You feel alone. You feel separated from what is ultimately real. You wonder where the real center of things may be, where the real action is taking place. Am I at the center, you ask, or am I out on the edge somewhere?

Or it may take the form of alienation from other people. The question keeps pursuing you: "Who *are* all these people?" It can happen as well at the family dinner table as in a crowd of strangers. You can be married twenty years and this loneliness can hit you and you can look across the table at the person you have eaten with, lived with, slept with, shared tragedy and joy with—you can look him or her right in the eyes and think, "I have no idea who you are."

Or it can come to you as self-alienation. You can look in the mirror and say, "I have no idea who I am. I cannot get hold of what this is—what this body is, what this mind is. I am looking at a stranger."

Religion tries to respond to existential loneliness. But not all religions attempt to deal with it in the same way. They share a common question, but they provide differing answers. In the case of loneliness, they define the problem differently.

Western religions (primarily Judaism, Islam, and Christianity) maintain that the reason for alienation is *sin*. In fact, sin *is* alienation. It is turning one's back on what is real. It is isolating oneself. It is something that you have done. You have pulled back. You have refused to accept the open-armed plea of God to gather you into union with Him, and thus into union with what is real. There can be no peace with the world, self, or others until this union is consummated. Augustine, the great Christian theologian, said it this way: "Our hearts are restless till they rest in Thee."

It is like having a serious argument with a dear friend. Although you are on the same campus, you try to avoid each other. Every moment is eaten up, stolen, by the attempt to maintain the separation.

So it is with humanity and God. Though God reaches out, humanity seeks to avoid a meeting, seeks to avoid coming face to face with what is real. And so humans suffer loneliness.

Eastern religions, for example, Hinduism and Buddhism, approach the problem differently. They see humanity's basic problem, and the source of its loneliness, in its *ignorance*. Human beings do not know the real situation. If they understood, if they could perceive reality; if they could think clearly, then they would not feel alienated and would be at peace with themselves again.

And so the Eastern holy man sits down and pulls himself together, especially through meditation, to the point where he is at one with the universe, and the universe is friendly toward him, and he can feel at home. He reaches inward toward enlightenment—toward a proper understanding. Ignorance is washed away by true perception, and the loneliness is gone.

In both East and West, once the broken cord is mended between human persons and the ultimate, then alienation from self and others also disappears.

Meaning

A third universal human need is the need to *find meaning*. From the most ancient songs, poems, and books, to the most modern, these themes appear over and over again: What does suffering mean? Why do I suffer? Why do you suffer? What do joy and beauty mean? Where do they come from, and why?

Human beings have found as much mystery in joy as in suffering, although the latter gets most of the attention. How could I deserve this? Why do I feel so good? Why are things so nice? And, what does death mean? And, in view of death, what does life mean?

Religion attempts to deal with the question of meaning by suggesting the reordering of perception. It says, in one way or another, that reality is not what it appears to be on the surface. Reality lies deep; it lies behind what a human being superficially experiences. Religion calls, in one way or another, for *faith in the unseen*. It maintains, in fact, that the unseen is more real than the outward and obvious. One must cut through the obvious; one must dig deeper, below the surface, to reach reality and meaning.

Religions may disagree as to what this reality and meaning are, but they agree that they are not what the superficial and casual observer believes them to be. Religion would argue that there is some kind of meaning in suffering, joy, and death. This meaning might be hidden; one might never really get hold of it. But one has the assurance that somehow, behind all seeming chaos and lack of meaning there is order, that the universe is not an accident, that things fit together, even though they do not fit together in our perception. To return to the words in "Desiderata,"

> And whether or not it is clear to you, no doubt the universe is unfolding as it should.

Our perception sees these mysteries as parallel lines, permanently

separated from each other. But a master physicist, using the most highly
sophisticated equipment, may find that seemingly parallel lines lack one
billionth of a degree of being truly parallel and are moving imperceptibly
toward each other. He may then confidently predict that somewhere out in
space, millions of light-years away, those lines will come together at a point
of perfect harmony.

In the same way, the religious masters have seen imperceptible
movements among the seemingly incongruous and contradictory events of
life. They have therefore predicted confidently that out there, far beyond
human capacity to perceive, the mysteries are resolved into perfect harmony. Truth, then, is not what may first *appear* to be true.

The way in which one searches for and finds truth differs from one
religious system to another. Again, we can generally distinguish East from
West.

The Eastern religions reach for truth through inner meditation.
They do this because they hold that the ultimate realities are hidden deep
within the human being, so one must reach down into oneself to grasp
them. One does this through the process of meditation.

The other approach, more common in Western religions, understands the ultimate to be outside and above the human being. This ultimate
reaches down to humankind from the outside. The process is called
revelation. When one accepts this revelation as truth, one is able to perceive
things as they really are.

In either case, West or East, when one finds out the truth, one finds
that it is not what it had first seemed to be. One finds that one has
reordered one's perception.

Holiness and Joy

A fourth universal human need is to find a way to deal with the
"holy." The word "holy" is used here in a specialized way. We are not using
the word as in the sentence, "I can't stand Harvey; he has such a holier-
than-thou attitude." We are using the word in the special way Rudolf Otto
used it in his famous book *The Idea of the Holy.*[11] All humans share, he says,
the experience of the "numinous." They sense themselves to be, at least on
some occasions, in the presence of an otherness.

This experience is expressed in various ways. Primitive peoples speak
of taboos:

"Don't go under that tree!"
"Why not?"
"Because it is a holy place."

[11]Rudolf Otto, *The Idea of the Holy,* trans. John W. Harvey (Baltimore, Md.: Penguin
Books, 1959).

When Moses saw a burning bush in the desert of Sinai he heard a voice commanding him,[12]

"Take off your shoes!"
"Why?"
"You are standing on holy ground."

Humans have always experienced this brush with "the other" and have always tried to deal with it. And religion has always offered some way for people to cope with the Holy. One of the functions of religion, then, is to provide people a way in which to relate to the otherness that they sense in their world.

Religion has approached the Holy in two ways. The first approach we will call *ritual*. It provides special actions that one performs to show his or her reverence for the Other, or at least to keep from angering It. Elaborate systems of sacred places, sacred objects, sacred names, sacred actions, sacred persons, and sacred writings have been developed. Through these, people try to become safely involved with the Other—to be able to live with it without being constantly in terror.

The second approach is by way of *morality*. Most of the so-called "higher religions" (the more developed ones, by modern standards) give an ethical content to the Holy. They would claim that the sense of Other-

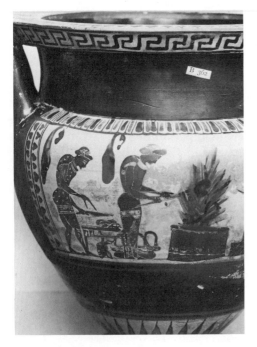

Religious Ritual. One way human beings have attempted to relate to the "other world" is through ritual ceremonies such as sacrifice. In this scene on an ancient Greek vase, two youths offer a goat as a burnt offering to the god Hermes. One youth roasts part of the goat on a spit. Other parts of the corpse lie on the table and floor and are suspended from the ceiling. By offering the life of the animal, they hope either to placate the god's anger or to gain his favor. (British Museum)

[12]Exodus 3:1–6.

ness triggered by ghost stories is not real contact with the Other. But the fascination and sense of Otherness one feels *is* real, they would say. And it is an indication of a real Otherness—one that has real existence.

But, this viewpoint would argue, what this Otherness wants is, primarily, for one to live with a certain life-style that is pleasing to or conforms to It. And if one will live in this way, one will have peace with the Other. So, in these religious systems, there is more emphasis on the kind of person one is than upon the kind of rituals he or she performs. That does not mean there are no rituals, of course, but it does mean that the emphasis is on ethics or life-style.

A fifth universal existential human need is for *joy*. People need a sense of well-being, of things going well. Sometimes the need gets even more intense and demands ecstasy. So it can vary from seeking a simple, calm feeling of peace, to a search for an overflowing, screaming, riproaring happiness.

Even the most ancient religious literature speaks of joy and how to achieve it. Religion has always responded to this need by seeking to provide people with a means of joy, to intellectual and emotional peace, to deep ecstasy. Again, not all religions stress this equally, or in the same way. Some seek for exuberance and are very expressive; others concentrate on the securing of inner peace. But almost all of them deal often and profoundly with joy.

The British author and literary critic C. S. Lewis called his spiritual autobiography, which traced his journey to religious faith, *Surprised by Joy*.[13] That phrase expresses well the theme of countless religious writers throughout the centuries.

A functional definition of religion, then, is "the means by which men fulfill their universal human existential needs." We can see this definition working in a classic example of cryptoreligion.

Wang Tao-ming was a member of the Red Chinese People's Liberation Army, serving as a deputy political instructor. His commitment to the revolution and to Chairman Mao functioned precisely the way more overt religious beliefs and practices do. His writing, in fact, is profoundly religious.

He mentions, for example, a revolutionary hero named Lei Feng who "by studying and applying Chairman Mao's work in a vital way . . . understood the significance of life."[14] He himself came to see that "I must study Chairman Mao's works earnestly and give myself a correct answer to the question of what I live for and whom should I serve." He committed himself to spending every waking moment in the search for true happiness. And when he asked himself "What is happiness?" the reply was

---

[13]C. S. Lewis, *Surprised by Joy* (New York: Harcourt Brace, 1956).

[14]Quotations are from *Mao Tse-Tung's Thought Is the Invincible Weapon* (Peking: Foreign University Press, 1968).

clear: "The proletarian concept of happiness is struggle, revolution, work and serving the people."

No Christian ever spoke of Jesus or the Bible with more intensity than Wang Tao-ming spoke of Mao and his teachings: "Just like the tender seedlings which cannot grow without sunshine, I cannot make an iota of progress without learning from Mao Tse-tung's thought. . . . Mao Tse-tung's thought is the unsetting red sun in my heart and I will forever consider myself a seedling which cannot do without the sunshine even for a single moment."

In summary, then, the search for joy, for meaning, for an escape from alienation and loneliness, for a relationship with the "other" is a *religious* search.

Traditionally attired Chinese walk through a Peking park during a celebration of the twenty fifth anniversary of the People's Republic of China, October 1, 1974. Thousands of residents of the Chinese capital flocked to six major parks to participate. (UPI)

CHAPTER THREE
THE MANY FORMS OF RELIGION

RELIGION: A DESCRIPTIVE DEFINITION

Religion's fourth face is its *descriptive* one. If you were to ask, "What is the major religion in India?" and I answered, "Hinduism," we would both be talking about religion descriptively. When one observes and records what people call "religion" and then states his or her findings objectively, that person is dealing with religion descriptively. Religion is, in this sense, whatever an individual or a group calls religion.

Religion, defined descriptively, has appeared in thousands of forms. To study it in this way is like walking through a huge art gallery observing paintings in the style of hundreds of great artists. Because there is so much, and because the forms seem so diverse, it is easy to become confused. We will try to simplify the process a bit by putting the religions of the world into three major categories:

> Primitive religions
> Cultural religions
> Supracultural religions

No evolutionary order is implied here. Primitive religion does not necessarily evolve into cultural religion and then into supracultural religion. Actually, religions seem to slide both up and down the scale, landing in first one category and then another. And at any moment in history it is possible to find all three types of religion existing side by side.

PRIMITIVE RELIGION

Use of the word "primitive" may be misleading. Primitive religions are not necessarily crude, nor are those who belong to such religions necessarily ignorant and simple minded. As scholars learn more about primitive religions, they find them to be dealing in sensitive and often complicated ways with the human existential needs we have discussed.[1]

Unfortunately, Western colonialists often entered a primitive or underdeveloped country, made some superficial observations, and pronounced what they saw to be simple minded. The people were thought of as savages, hardly superior to the "other animals" of the jungle.

Fortunately, more careful study has now been done. The result is a more sympathetic verdict upon these systems. Rather than regarding primitive religions as a sort of primeval form out of which other religions have evolved, we now may appreciate these forms in their own right. They are remarkably stable religious systems, often changing little over thousands of years.

They only thrive in isolation, however. While the primitive community is bound together tightly and shielded from outside ideas, the primitive religion is strong. But when it is forced to cope with new cultures and new ideas, the primitive religion begins to crumble.

It does *not* evolve into a "higher" form. At least, it is difficult to find examples of such an evolution in historic times. Rather, changes have more often come dramatically, and usually through the influence of the tremendous religious genius of one person or group of persons. The history of religion is in large part a story of great religious geniuses, gurus, saints, and prophets. What these people have said and done has always been tied to the past, of course, but it has had something unique, ingenious, and new in it.

Furthermore, the followers of these geniuses seldom reach the spiritual heights of their teachers. The normal movement in religion is as likely to be degeneration as upward evolution. Compare, for example, the richness of the *Tao Te Ching*, the sacred book of Taoism, with the set of superstitions and rituals that later carried the same name. Or compare the richness of the teachings of Jesus and Paul with many of the ideas called Christian during the Dark Ages.

Religions most often start at their apex. What comes afterward is a constant struggle to prevent degeneration and the loss of the spark of

---

[1]Among the many excellent sources for further information on primitive religions, see W. Richard Comstock, *The Study of Religion and Primitive Religions* (New York: Harper & Row, 1972), and John B. Noss, *Man's Religions*, 4th ed. (New York: Macmillan, 1969), pp. 1–34.

genius that created them. Primitive religion, then, is not necessarily the original form of religion.

Primitive religion is not dead. It is still a thriving force in the twentieth century. In fact, some 10 percent of all living persons practice some form of primitive religion. Most of these are in Africa, with Asia coming next. In South America there are one million such worshippers, and in the United States they number in the tens of thousands.

Perhaps this last fact is surprising. But consider the "native religion" of America—that of the Indians. It is primitive religion in its classic form. And, far from dying, it is now experiencing a kind of revival. This is especially true among some of the youngest and best educated Indians, who see the old faith as an alternative to the one they feel has been forced upon their fathers and grandfathers by white oppressors.

And then, of course, there are various forms of primitive religion among the aboriginal populations of Australia.

The following are some of the characteristics usually common to the many types of primitive religions.

Primitive Religion's Omissions

Primitive religions are characterized by the lack of certain things. They lack, first, an *organized system of thought*. They consist of many more or less disconnected ideas with no particular attempt to fit these ideas into a "theology." There is no attempt to create a rational progression of thought or overarching set of concepts.

Scene from a festival in Mauritius, the Indian Ocean nation. (Christian Zuber, Rapho/Photo Researchers, Inc.)

Second, they lack *theological development*. In a religion such as Christianity, we find the development of various dogmas or concepts that were only in germ form in the New Testament. An example is the doctrine of the Trinity, which spelled out the relationship between the Father, Son, and Holy Spirit. For hundreds of years Christian theologians struggled to develop a way of stating this relationship that would integrate all the various data in the New Testament. Eventually they came up with various creedal statements that were not found in the New Testament but, rather, it was maintained, developed the ideas found there.

In primitive religions such theological development is lacking. Belief and practice remain constant; primitive "theologians" seldom convene conferences to work out new responses to new situations.

Third, primitive religions lack *sacred writings*. There is nothing in them comparable to the Bible or the Koran. Most primitive religions exist in preliterate or nonliterate cultures—among people who have no written language. Thus the past must be retained in other ways. Usually the traditions are kept and guarded by an old holy man who knows and remembers everything. They have been passed to him by another man older than he, and he is training someone to pass them along after his own death.[2] In addition to this oral tradition there is the use of artistic symbols. In the caves of France, for example, are found hundreds of ancient pictures painted on the walls. While their mysteries are not solved entirely, they seem to have served in religious ceremonies thousands of years ago. And as the generations passed, they provided guidance and help in retaining the beliefs of the people and in passing them along.

Fourth, primitive religions lack *literature*. Because they have no written history, the remembrances of the past eventually take on the qualities of myth. Primitive people realize that they are, and must be, tied to their forebearers. But they do not remember them by name, or date, as we think of remembering history. Rather, they remember them through symbols and myths. Great persons of the past may become animals; they may be thought of as living in a misty netherworld, where they slay monsters that threaten their descendants. In these myths lie the essence of the past, and its *real* truth, as far as primitive peoples are concerned.

The High God and the World of Spirits

Even the simplest and most remote jungle tribes seem to believe in the existence of a "high god." He is the father of everything; often he is identified as the creator of everything. He is the generative force from which everything has come.

---

[2]An interesting modern example of this is found in the relationship between Carlos Castaneda and the Yaqui Indian holy man Don Juan. See *The Teaching of Don Juan: A Yaqui Way of Knowledge* (Berkeley: University of California Press, 1968).

He usually is thought to have little to do with people's everyday life, however. He is far away; although he is responsible for everything and has authority over everything, he chooses to stay out of the picture.

When he is discussed male pronouns may be used, but he is really asexual. The picture that emerges of him is not very clear.

Normally, no images are made of the high god, nor are temples erected to him. Thus, when early explorers entered primitive villages, they found many idols, but no evidence of this high deity. Only after a long and intimate study could belief in such a being be uncovered, because the people had no images, no ritual, or no altars to him and seldom mentioned him at all. Yet patient study has eventually shown that this belief in a high god is characteristic of most, if not all, primitive religions.

Another characteristic of primitive religion is the belief in *spirits*. A significant mistake was made in early studies. Scholars observed and recorded the long lists of divine beings and the many rituals and sacrifices connected with them and concluded that the primitive religions had many, many gods. That is, they were thought to be extremely *polytheistic*. Now we know that it is more accurate to speak of the one great father-god and of many, many spirits. There is, in fact, a whole world inhabited by spirits, each with its own name and characteristics. Early scholars erroneously referred to these as "gods."

Primitive religions recognize, and relate themselves to, two categories of spirits. There are, first, the spirits of the dead. This includes the spirits of ancestors, and particularly recent ancestors—fathers, grandfathers, and so on. These are thought of as lingering on earth after their bodies have died. They will, in fact, continue to remain in the area so long as anyone is alive who can remember their names and continue to keep in contact with them through prayer.

It is very important to have children who can remember and reverence one after his or her death. It is also very important to retain these ceremonies and prayers because if they are neglected the ancestors fade away.

This concept is one of the hardest for primitive people to relinquish, even when they are converted to other religious forms. They become very concerned that if the ceremonies end their forefathers will lose their identities—that they will have "killed" them.

The spirit of a recently dead person is believed to be very close to the corpse, especially for the first few hours after death. It is very important to convince the deceased that the survivors are stricken with grief, lest he become angry and cause them trouble. So some tribes have the custom, for example, of requiring young girls, sisters of a dead older brother, to hack off two or three fingers at the first joint. Other types of disfigurement are also practiced. These are to convince the deceased that life is not just going on as usual, but that he is highly respected and sorely missed.

A friend of mine who lived for years in a primitive village tells an interesting story that illustrates how vividly and concretely the spirit world is believed to interact with the physical world. The village in which my friend lived had not had rain for several months and the situation was getting desperate. So the village council met and decided to ask for help from the previous chief, who had been dead several years. They wanted to urge him to make some contacts for them in the spirit world to see if the rain could be started again.

The contact began with two old women who had known the chief personally. They went to his grave, which was unmarked but carefully remembered, and danced on it. Since my friend was trusted and respected, he was allowed to watch and even take photographs.

The women danced and called out the chief's name. They sang songs about the good old days. "Do you remember the time we had a great feast and how we all drank beer until sunrise?" they asked in song.

Then the old man's son went to the grave. He carried with him a pot of beer (a favorite drink of the old chief), which he poured onto the grave. Then he turned the pot over and sat down on it. He leaned forward with his ear close to the ground and said, "Now, Father, first I want to explain this white man with the little black box. Don't worry about it. He has had it all along and it doesn't seem to hurt anybody. He has lived here a long time and is our friend, so he can hear what we talk about."

Then the son and the women carried on a long conversation with the grave about the rain situation. My friend said that it was perfectly obvious to everyone there that a real conversation was occurring.

I do not know whether it rained, but obviously there was a vivid sense of communication with the spirit world.

The second kind of spirits are not of people, but *are spirits of mountains, rivers, animals, and other natural elements.* Every stream, every tree, every valley has a certain spiritual power that controls it. If one wants to cross the stream or climb the tree or hunt in the valley, one must make peace with the controlling spirit. The old fairy tale about Billygoat Gruff, who guarded the bridge, may well be a dim memory of some ancient European form of primitive religion.

In primitive religion, there is a strong sense of being one with nature. Nature has a mind of its own, and one must learn to deal with it. Humans are only one part of nature and must be very careful how they deal with the other parts. If a tree is cut down, certain things must be said and done to convince the spirit of the tree that there is no intention to harm him or usurp his powers. An American Navaho Indian pointed out that his people have a respect for the world in which they live far greater than does the white man. The white man is an exploiter of nature, whereas the Navaho is a partner to nature. This is because the Navaho does not see the world as simply matter, a mere combination of molecules; he sees the world as being animated, alive, having will, having mind, having soul. This statement introduces the next characteristic of primitive religion: *animism.*

An animist believes that material objects and nonhuman creatures have mind, will, passion, feeling, and so on. They have *mana.* Mana is the soul or life that inhabits and animates such things. Some objects have a special power and are called fetishes, amulets, or talismans. These might be feathers from an eagle, the tooth of some ferocious animal, or the scalp of an enemy. They may be kept in a special pouch and brought out on special occasions when their owners need some contact with the spiritual world.

Power in Primitive Religion

Another aspect of primitive religion is the use of *magic.* In magic an attempt is made to use the forces of the invisible world through various occult rituals. The magician knows secret words and ceremonies. He must be very careful to get all the words right; he must stand in precisely the right spot; he must proceed correctly at every point to get in touch with this other world.

In one of Carlos Castaneda's books, an old Yaqui Indian introduces Castaneda into this world of animism and magic. He explains the rules—where one must sit, what time of day it must be, the direction one must face, and so on. The old Indian says that each person has a "place" and that one cannot hope to get in touch unless he or she is sitting in his or her place. So he makes Castaneda crawl around for hours, searching for his place.

"How will I know when I have found it?"

"You will know."

The old man tells him it is on his front porch someplace. Castaneda spends additional hours crawling over every inch of the porch. The old man says that this is very important, because he will not be able to understand or work *anything* until Castaneda finds his place.[3]

There are two kinds of magic: natural and supernatural. For *natural magic* one uses charms, omens, and divinations. For example, one might look at the entrails of a chicken or throw an object into the air and watch the direction in which it falls. The result will give a clue as to how to solve a problem at hand.

Supernatural magic, however, is a much more sober matter. It is often used for evil purposes by witches or sorcerers. You probably remember the witch doctors in the Tarzan movies who were always putting a hex on someone. But actually a witch doctor is just what the name implies. He is the one who can combat what an evil witch has done. A witch doctor is not a witch. Such a person is sometimes called a medicine man or, more pre-

[3]Castaneda, *The Teachings of Don Juan: A Yaqui Way of Knowledge,* pp. 14–19.

cisely, a *shaman*. He knows how to reverse the spells cast by evil witches. He is able to contact and at times even control the powers of the other world.

Because the primitive religionist senses such an intimacy with the other world, he tends to conclude that almost everything that happens is influenced from over on the other side. If a family's house burns down, for example, its members immediately begin to search for an evil witch—because there must have been a witch somewhere using supernatural powers to make such a thing happen.

A friend of mine, living in a village in Zambia, had a rather frightening experience of this kind. He and his family had lived in the village for several years. One day he was cooking over an open fire. Somehow the fire got out of control and caught his hut on fire. Soon the fire spread and the whole village was in flames. He was very concerned, not only because of the loss, but because he knew that the people would begin to look for a witch who had caused such a terrible thing to happen. And, of course, *he* was a likely candidate!

Fortunately, he did not come under suspicion. There was, however, a great deal of discussion about who the witch might be and why he would do such a thing.

Even more ominous is the use of the death hex by a witch. Often persons who are hexed actually die (the power of suggestion?).

We can see that the other world, the Holy as we called it earlier, is very real in the primitive religions. Coping with this other world takes a great deal of time. The material world is constantly being influenced by what is happening in the other world, by powers in the *other* reality. Of course, the scientific humanist would deny that such a world exists. He or she would maintain that only this world is real, that the other one is imagination. Primitive religion would reply that not only is the other world real, but it is the place where the most important events transpire. And if human beings are going to survive in this world, they must always keep good contact and good relations with the other world.

While the primitive world view is usually associated with tribal societies, it can sometimes be found directly in the middle of the most modern technological societies too. I was once invited to attend the spring rites of a rather large group of people who described themselves as "followers of the old religion," "neopagans," or simply "witches" (but not evildoers, as with the "witches" mentioned). The gathering took place in Kansas City, Missouri, almost within sight of a huge modern medical complex. Participants were from all age groups and educational levels. The ceremonies were dedicated to "the Goddess" who, said the worshippers, has been variously called Diana, Venus, Ishtar, Anath, Isis, and so on throughout history. The names of the goddess derive from the great ancient culture religions (discussed in the next section), but the world view of the group corresponds closely to that of the primitive nature worship that predates the ancient empires.

Indeed, said the worshippers, this is the "natural" religion of the human race, followed everywhere by those who have not been "corrupted." They have been worshipping as I saw them, they claim, throughout the ages—a faithful few who have retained the "old ways."

Prayers are offered to the four winds as a sacred circle is drawn within the modern apartment living room. Participants are crowded together in the room. The air is heavy with incense (and marijuana). The atmosphere is reverent. The liturgy proceeds as a black woman and a Hawaiian man in white robes chant praises to the Goddess. A priestess with long golden hair moves through the crowd dispensing blessings and serving the ceremonial wine. Four priests recite the long ceremony. Cries of joy go up as another priestess, representing the Goddess, sweeps into the room, her hair adorned with spring flowers and her sheer blue gown and veils flowing. The worshippers shout in joy at the arrival of the fertile powers of the earth and the meeting dissolves into wild dancing, drinking, and unrestrained celebration.

Kansas City, Missouri!

CULTURAL RELIGION

A second group of religions in our gallery is the cultural religions. They are tied closely to the concept of civilization; each one has an intimate relationship to a particular civilization—rising when it rises, falling when it falls. By definition, then, a cultural religion is one that lasts only until the culture or civilization that practices it passes away.

There are many ancient examples of this. The first great cultural religions date from the rise of civilization—somewhere between 4,000 B.C. and 3,000 B.C. When Egypt was a great power, gods such as Amon and Ra and goddesses such as Isis were widely known and worshipped—but no more. They died when the culture that supported them died. The same can be said for the great god Marduke and the great goddess Ishtar, who fell with the powerful cultures of ancient Mesopotamia. And the gods of ancient Greece, the gods of the poems of Homer, disappeared with that civilization, except, of course, for those that were adopted by the Romans. While Rome ruled the world the cultural religion of Rome flourished. When Rome disintegrated, so did her gods.[4]

The explanation for this phenomenon can be found in the two major characteristics of the cultural religions: their relationship with *tradition* and their relationship with the *power structure*.

Cultural religion has a vital connection with tradition. It serves as the *conveyor* of tradition, being the vehicle by which tradition passes from one

---

[4]A classic work on the Graeco-Roman kind of culture religion is H. J. Rose, *Religion in Greece and Rome* (New York: Harper & Row, 1959). See also Marvin P. Nilsson, *Greek Folk Religion* (New York: Harper & Row, 1940).

Cultural Religion and Polytheism. Cultural religions, unlike supracultural ones, usually pay homage to many gods. The seal from which this impression was made belonged to an Akkadian scribe named Adda about 2300 B.C. Depicted is the sun god rising from between two mountains, holding aloft his emblem, the saw. To his right stands the god of the deep with fish-laden waters flowing behind him and a bird in his hand. His attendant, Janus-headed Usmu, stands behind him. Istar, the winged goddess of war, rises from the mountain on the left, quivers of arrows on her back, while another god, perhaps Ninurta, advances with his bow. (British Museum)

generation to another. It goes further: it also serves as the *sanctifier* of tradition. It pronounces this benediction:

The Blessings of God, may they rest on the way *we* do things.

Priests of the cultural religion appear at every important cultural event, pronouncing it holy and good, tying it to the will of the deity.

Not only does cultural religion convey and sanctify tradition, it also seeks to *protect* tradition. It responds intensely, sometimes even violently, when tradition seems threatened.

Cultural religion always has a vital connection with the power structure. This, no doubt, is the reason why it resists all kinds of innovation. It enjoys a good relationship with those who hold power. And it is always to the advantage of those in power to maintain the status quo. Change may well result in a shift in power, and this becomes disastrous for both the power structure and the religion it supports.

In fact, one of the surest tests in classifying religions is to observe what happens when a given culture is threatened with a new cultural idea. The priests of the cultural religion will be the first to object. This will be true whether the new idea is overtly "religious" or not. One would expect such a reaction to a new religious idea. But the cultural religion will also feel threatened if it is an idea about wearing clothes differently, or wearing hair in a different style, or living in a different kind of housing, or rearranging the family structure in some way, or getting paid in a different manner, or changing the ownership of businesses and factories.

The cultural religion's representatives will immediately perceive some connection between the proposed change and the will and the *law of God*. They will begin to crusade against the change in the *name of God*.

The story has been repeated thousands of times in history. It is a perfectly predictable form of behavior. Once the bond between theology and culture is fixed, everything else follows.

Modern examples might include such religious forms as the pre-revolutionary Russian Orthodox Church or, even more recently, the Church of Ethiopia. These very ancient forms of Christianity had so completely tied themselves to the status quo that each came to depend almost entirely on the emperor and the power structure he represented. In each case, when the emperor was overthrown, the church found itself in great trouble. It had fought every change, but change had won in spite of its opposition. Now, without the emperor to protect it, its future became very dim.

The modern totalitarian states, right wing and left wing, have had their cultural religions, though they have often been cryptoreligions. In Nazi Germany, as in other fascist states, there has been the worship of "the people," of "the spirit of the Fatherland," and so on. In communist states, as we have seen already, the same process exists, although overtly religious language is seldom used to describe it.

Some have detected the same process at work in the custom of some American Protestant churches of placing side by side, at the front of the house of worship, two flags, one bearing the cross and the other the Stars and Stripes.

SUPRACULTURAL RELIGION

The third major section in our gallery of religious types consists of the supracultural faiths. A supracultural religion may be defined as one that can and does *escape cultural bounds*. It is "over" or "above" culture, thus, supra. It is able to move from one culture into another one. It is able to survive the death of its host culture (the one in which it first appeared). The religion of Ishtar and Marduke died with the Babylonian empire—no Babylon, no Marduke. A supracultural religion would have been able to survive in such a case.

Certain characteristics help us to identify supracultural religions. First, they serve a *prophetic* role as well as a *priestly* one. These two words are used in special ways: a priest sanctifies, a prophet judges. A priest says, "God bless what we are doing"; a prophet says, "God is appalled by what we are doing." A priest speaks the blessings of deity on the way in which a culture is presently conducting itself, whereas a prophet speaks to evaluate culture in the name of a higher law.

Supracultural religions are not entirely prophetic. All religions serve a priestly function to some extent. But the prophetic element is present and active to a greater extent in supracultural religions.

Since they criticize, and do not simply sanctify, supracultural religions are often at odds with the power structure. A cultural religion gets into trouble when its host culture collapses. But a supracultural religion tends to be in trouble all the time. The power structure sees it as a threat and often opposes it—sometimes even physically.

This aspect of supracultural religion is called "prophetic" because it is illustrated by the "prophets" of the Hebrew Scriptures. These men fearlessly approached the kings of their day, saying, "If you do not change your policies, then, in the name of God, you will be punished for your deeds!"

Of course, that sort of talk does not make one very popular at the palace. Prophets are seldom invited to gala evenings there. Kings much prefer to be surrounded by priests rather than by prophets. On one occasion the eighth-century B.C. prophet Amos went up to speak out against the false altar at Bethel. On the way he was met by a representative of the king who said, "Why don't you go back down South where you came from and prophesy there? We have all the prophets we need up here!"[5] That is the way supracultural religion is often treated.

A second characteristic of supracultural religion is its *interest in human existential needs*. It is more concerned to serve these needs (which were discussed at length in Chapter Two) than in cultural preservation. People need a sense of joy, they need to find meaning in the things that happen to them, and they need freedom from the feelings of alienation and precariousness that plague them. Supracultural religions focus on these questions rather than bemoan changes in society or in "our way of life."

This helps us to see why such religions can survive the death of the culture that hosts them. They are not overly concerned about such things. They are much more interested in the needs of *human beings* than of any particular *group* of human beings. They can therefore jump from one culture to another, because human needs are the same everywhere and at all times. It is the human predicament, and not a given political or cultural predicament, that occupies their energies.

A third characteristic of supracultural religions is their emphasis on the *internal* aspects of religion. There is a movement, for example, from

Magic ⟶ to ⟶ Ethics

Other religious types, at various levels of sophistication, attempt to control the powers of the other world with secret or sacred words and rituals. The supracultural religion, on the other hand, is more apt to emphasize the *kind*

[5]Amos 7:10–13.

of person one is and the kind of *personal decisions* he or she makes (the person's "ethics") than the ceremonies or sorceries he or she may know.

Put another way, there is a movement from

Ritual ⟶ to ⟶ Inner attitude

Other religious forms place great importance on using the correct forms and ceremonies. Every step, every word, must be precisely executed. Of course supracultural religions have ceremonies, too. But the difference is in emphasis. In them, the emphasis lies on what a person is, in his or her heart, more than on what he or she is doing outwardly.

The ancient prophet Amos, whom we have mentioned, furnishes a classic example of this "ethicising." Speaking for God, he says,[6]

I hate, I spurn your pilgrim-feasts;
I will not delight in your sacred ceremonies.
When you present your sacrifices and offerings
I will not accept them,
nor look on the buffaloes of your shared-offerings.
Spare me the sound of your songs;
I cannot endure the music of your lutes.
Let Justice roll on like a river
and righteousness like an ever-flowing stream.

The whole concept of sacrifice is transformed in the supracultural religion from

Propitiatory sacrifice ⟶ to ⟶ Self-sacrifice

Propitiatory sacrifice emphasizes the offering of something external to oneself, such as the killing of the best of one's animals or the burning of the finest grain of the harvest. Self-sacrifice involves giving one's own life in service to ultimate causes. "Present your bodies as a living sacrifice," says the Christian Apostle Paul, "for this is your proper ritual."[7]

A fourth characteristic of supracultural religions is their conception of ultimate reality as being either *monotheistic* or *monistic* rather than polytheistic. Culture religions are characterized by many gods. The adherents are pulled in many ways. They owe their allegiance to many things. Their loyalties are divided. They are polytheistic.

In the supracultural religions, reality is thought of as *one* thing. Thus, the adherent is committed to and subservient to only one thing. Supracultural religions differ in that some of them are monotheistic and some are monistic. *Monotheism* is the belief that there is one God, one ultimate reality. But it also carries with it the idea that human beings are separate from that one God and must relate themselves to Him. God creates the world, places it external to Himself, and then places human beings in that external world. *Monism*, on the other hand, is the belief that everything is God. The

[6]Amos 5:21–24 (*New English Bible*).
[7]Romans 12:1–2.

world is God, nature is God, the universe is God, and I too am God, to the extent that I am a part of this universe. Communion with God, then, is a form of self-communion with the great Oneness or with the great All.

To generalize, we can say that monism is more characteristic of Eastern religious forms and monotheism of Western ones.

The Sources of Supracultural Religion

The term "supracultural" should not be taken to imply that such religions are completely detached from culture, of course. Historically, the supracultural religions were born within culture. They borrowed profusely from the thought forms and vocabularies of the culture religions around them. But they also showed the ability to vastly expand these concepts and words and to universalize them—making them apply to people of very different cultures and vocabularies. For the most part, supracultural religions were rocked in the cradle of some cultural religion.

Usually, the spark that ignited the supracultural explosion of a new religious form can be traced to one person or one small group of persons. Supracultural religions are not the work of committees or the result of general trends in culture. Rather, they owe their existence to the religious genius who appears, seemingly out of nowhere, using the language and ideas of his or her culture and his or her people, but developing them in ingeniously broad and universal ways. Sometimes a few others share in this process with the genius, but more often he or she works alone. A supracultural religion is born!

The result is the initiation of a struggle between the new religion and its host culture. The two exist together in a state of constant tension. The culture tries very hard to "recapture" the supracultural religion and pull it back, to smother it within its cultural origins. Often a religion slips back and forth between the cultural and supracultural as it alternately loses and wins in this struggle.

Christianity serves as an example. The history of Christianity is, in one sense, the history of a supracultural religion trying to escape from the various cultures in which it has existed. Each of these cultures has tried to maintain that "Christianity belongs to *us*. It is part and parcel of *our way of doing things*. We are a *Christian* culture. To be Christian is to be culturally like *us*."

Thus, early Christian missionaries who went from England and the United States into Africa often made no noticeable distinction between Western culture and the Christian religion. They insisted not only that the people in that different culture accept the universal concepts of Christianity about universal human needs, but also that they take baths more regularly and dress more "modestly"—practices having little or no connection with the universal insights of Jesus.

When the "Christians" of medieval Western Europe went off on the Crusades, they came in contact with the "Christians" of Byzantium, who had a very different culture and language. After a period of puzzlement, the Westerners began slaughtering the Easterners right along with the "unbelievers." Evidently they were not able to conceive of Christians who were not culturally like themselves. Their actions proved that their type of Christianity was indistinguishable in their minds from Western European culture. Of course, the same sort of thing has happened to other supracultural religions like Buddhism, for example.

So you can see that a religion may exist in two forms at the same time. In some places, and by some people, it may be practiced as a supracultural religion; in other places it may function as a classic cultural religion.

Examples of Supracultural Religions

We will divide the major religious systems that have proved their ability to cross cultural lines into three groups. The first group appeared during the centuries between 1,000 B.C. and 500 B.C. It is one of the amazing facts of history that the most persistent religious ideas of humanity, including those most prevalent today, appeared during these centuries. It was in many ways the most creative period for religious ideas in the history of humankind. Not all these ideas were developed fully during this period, but they were present at least in germ form. With few exceptions, the major religions of the world today find their origins during this time. The following are some specific examples.

Greece entered the period with a classic polytheistic cultural religion. Then there arose people who struggled intensely with the ultimate questions about existence—people like Socrates, Plato, and Aristotle. In their quest for reality they developed a truly supracultural way of looking at things. Within the philosophies of these men, and others like them, can be found almost every possible direction of rationalistic philosophical thinking about the meaning of human existence. The philosophical alternatives they proposed have influenced and guided men and women in numerous succeeding cultures.

Meanwhile, during the same period, something dramatic was happening in the tiny country of Israel, a relatively short distance to the southeast of Greece. The religion of Israel had, prior to this time, followed rather classic culture-religion lines. It was a religion of the children of Israel, wandering in the desert, on their way to the promised land. It was a religion for them and for them alone. It contained a strong emphasis on propitiatory sacrifice and ritual and priestly ties to the power structure. Then during the years from 1,000 B.C. to 500 B.C. a group of prophets arose, one at a time, here and there (this was no committee!), with an amazingly similar message.

The God of Israel is the God of the Nations, they began to say. He desires mercy and not sacrifice. It is His will to pull the human race together. He operates among and above the empires of humanity, bringing about His purposes in history. He seeks people who will make a covenant with Him in their hearts. Speaking as the mouthpieces of Yahweh, the God of Israel, men such as Amos and Jeremiah and Isaiah proclaimed a supracultural God.

And in Iran (ancient Persia) a remarkable religious genius named Zoroaster was bringing about a similar change in the old Aryan culture religion. The remarkable coincidences continued in India, where Gautama, the founder of Buddhism, was developing insights that allowed a new faith to emerge from the old Hindu culture religion—a faith that eventually spread far from its Indian homeland to become a world religion. Within Hinduism itself there were genuinely creative stirrings at the same time. During these centuries were produced the two most profound documents of Hinduism, documents that reflect many of the most basic supracultural characteristics. These include a collection known as the Upanishads and then, somewhat later, the classic Bhagavad Gita or Song of God.

The first century A.D. is a pivotal one in the history of supracultural religion. Three of the major religions of the world arose around this same hundred years. None were entirely new; all were built on earlier foundations.

This was, of course, the founding century of Christianity. Christianity had two host cultures—a sort of grandmother and grandfather, you might say. The first was Israel, particularly the Israel of the great prophets just mentioned. The second was the Graeco-Roman world into which Christianity came. When the early Christians spoke of their faith they used not only the language of the sacred books of Israel, but also the Greek language, the language that had formed the thinking of the Roman Empire.

Judaism also underwent another major change during this century. The Jewish state had been severely damaged by the Romans around A.D. 70. At the close of the century, a group of rabbis met at the city of Jamnia. Their deliberations were a kind of climax to a process of development that had started many years before and resulted in the religion called Judaism. The old forms—blood sacrifices, the priesthood, the divinely anointed kingship—all disappeared entirely. While Judaism is perhaps still tied to a given culture more than the other religions we are discussing in this section, it is also very resilient and has been able to survive in diverse cultural situations for many centuries. Thus it is included here.

The third of the first-century developments took place within Buddhism and resulted in what is called Mahayana Buddhism, a religion that has spread into many parts of the earth and has become a truly world religion. A further discussion of this religion will come in Chapter 4.

There are a number of significant supracultural movements of a later date, also. In the heart of the culture religion of Arabia there arose, in the seventh century A.D., another remarkable religious thinker—Muhammad. Out of the raw materials of his culture, he expounded universal concepts about the nature of God, the nature of reality, and the meaning of existence. The new faith, Islam, eventually conquered the far-flung cultures of North Africa, Central Africa, the Middle East, Iran, and Turkey.

Of all the major religions, Hinduism has found it most difficult to escape from its host culture. Between the ninth and twelfth centuries A.D., however, a form of Hinduism appeared that has "exported" very well. Vedantic Hinduism is the form most frequently accepted by non-Indians, since it moves most easily into other cultures.

The twelfth century also saw the development of Zen Buddhism. Zen has demonstrated its ability to cross cultural lines. There are, for example, thousands of Zen Buddhists in California who are Caucasians, not Orientals.

Several of the religions mentioned in this chapter will be investigated in detail in the following chapters. For now, it is important to remember that in the gallery of religious forms there are three major sections: primitive religions, cultural religions, and supracultural religions. In each section there are hundreds of individual pictures of faith, ready for viewing by the student of religion.

CHAPTER FOUR
THE SPIRITUAL WORLD
OF EASTERN RELIGION

THE EASTERN WORLD VIEW

Scientific humanism is a Western phenomenon, which, as we shall see, grew out of the secularization of the Medieval Man. But most of the world is *not* Western. Most of the world's population resides on the side of the world we call "the East," in nations such as China, India, Japan, and Indochina.

The scientific humanist, whose viewpoint will be discussed at length in Chapter 10, says that reality could be found only in the material world. But in the East, while people might not believe in the existence of a personal God (and thus be atheists from a Western point of view), neither do they believe that only matter is real. In other words, they might be atheistic, but never materialistic.

The real world is not the material world at all, they would say. The real world is not obvious like the material world. It is rather, a spiritual world that lies behind and beyond the world of the eyes and ears of human beings. This means that the physical world around us and the events that occur in that world (historical events) are no more than what the Hindus call Maya, or "illusion," and *Lila*, or "the play of the gods."

The Westerner tries to become rich, to become famous, to gain physical comfort. Ambition drives him or her toward the "top"— materially. Once on top, the Westerner is pronounced a "success." Desire and ambition are the stuff of life. Without them people are doomed to mediocrity and failure.

According to many of the holy men of the East, however, desire and ambition create nothing but problems. In fact, our troubles are caused by our desires. So to feed one's ambition is sure to bring nothing but more misery. It will only result in pain.

Furthermore, says the way of the East, you move closer to truth and reality not by striving and great effort, but by being very quiet—by not doing anything. Taoism, for example, one of the ancient religions of China, speaks of the great Tao as the spiritual eternal reality, the thing behind and beyond everything else. But the Tao can never be found with test tubes and laboratory experiments. Rather, says the Taoist, you find it by doing nothing at all, by allowing yourself to flow with the true spiritual nature of things. It is a process called Wu-Wei. By doing this (or, rather, by not doing it!) one quietly gets oneself on the track of the Tao or the "way," thereby gaining access to things as they really are.

Of course, this is a completely different way to search for truth than that of the Western scientific humanist, who studies hard, works hard, experiments, struggles, and strives.

The Taoist, instead, may retreat to the countryside and seek a sense of oneness with all things. He or she seeks an end to striving. Unless one calms oneself, says the Taoist, one will never know the truth.

Another Eastern religion, Hinduism, offers the practice of yoga. Here the approach to truth lies in self-denial, in pulling in one's senses like a tortoise pulls its legs and head into its shell. By closing out the outside world of illusion and looking deep into oneself, one moves toward truth. The yogi, sitting in the lotus position, eyes closed, cuts off all stimulation from outside. The physical world disappears. The *truth* appears. The yogi would have little use for a laboratory filled with electronic devices, as they would show only more and more sophisticated views of illusion.

Even one's own body partakes of illusion. The Hindu holy man says that the real *you* is not your physical body at all. It is rather the *Atman* or the "soul." There is something in you which is the infinite, ultimate reality. And by reaching inward, by shaking off everything not connected with the Atman, one is lost in the wonder of the absolute—in the true.

So, if you want to find truth, you search, not out there somewhere, in the physical world, but within. Only by excluding what is outside can you attain the depths of what is inside.

THE INTERACTION OF EASTERN AND WESTERN IDEAS

Modern China is a striking battleground between the Eastern and Western ways to search for truth. This huge country, home of one third of humankind, has operated historically on the basis of the Eastern view of truth. The major religions of China—Taoism, Buddhism, Confucianism—all shared some of the ideas we have been discussing.

But then, suddenly, revolution came to China in the 1940s and 1950s. It was a communist revolution. No one adheres more completely to the Western technophilosophy of materialism than does the communist. He represents the pinnacle in the evolution of Autonomous Man, a way of being human discussed in Chapter Nine.

And so a group of Chinese began restructuring Chinese society on the basis of ideas learned from Westerners such as Karl Marx. These ideas were almost completely opposite to all the ancient ideas of Chinese society. The basic concept behind the new ideas was "dialectic materialism." It held that nothing exists but matter—matter clashing with matter and creating new forms of matter. Taoism had found reality in the Tao, or the way, which, it said, was more basic than matter. But Maoism (the Chinese form of communism), said that only matter was real. Confucianism had said that ethics grow out of the "will of Heaven." Confucius did not exactly mean "God" in the Western sense, but he did mean that there was some kind of higher plan that people were supposed to follow on earth. It was a spiritual kind of ethic. But Maoism looked to this earth alone for rules of behavior.

China, then, became a battleground between two very different ideas: the ancient idea that only the spiritual world is ultimately real and the communist idea that only the material world is ultimately real. No wonder that the friction that resulted caused the death of millions of people.

Some people believe that the old ideas in China will eventually smother the new ones, since the latter are, after all, imported into China from a foreign and hostile world.

In an earlier chapter we quoted from Wang Tao-ming, the young Chinese communist. It is striking to see how he deprecated himself, striving to rid himself of all personal desires. By letting go of himself, he says, he will find the true meaning of life. He seems to be a sort of Taoist who does not believe in Taoism. His "letting go" is not a giving of himself to the Tao, but to Mao, who is a physical, political reality.

There are few Buddhists in India, not because Hinduism fought Buddhism but because it "hugged it to death." It simply accepted and incorporated the Buddhist ideas into itself and went on its way, depriving Buddhism of any reason to continue as a separate faith. Will the old ideas in China do the same thing to communism? The communist leaders recognized the danger. That is why they have developed elaborate systems to separate children from their natural families, putting them in places where they will hear only the new ideas, hoping to raise them as new people without any sense of the reality of the spiritual world.

In the meantime, the Chinese leaders have to carry on a continuous "revolution." Periodically it is necessary to stir up the young against the old.

Thus, during the famous Red Guard period, students were encouraged to kidnap their professors in the universities, put dunce caps on them, and march them around in humiliation. This was punishment meted out because the professors were not yet free of the old ideas.

From time to time great campaigns are mounted in China against Confucius. Although dead for hundreds of years, he is attacked in the press as though he were about to take over the country! This can only mean that the old ideas are still around and are strong enough to be considered a threat to the materialists. Post-Mao China continues to struggle to find its place between the two worlds of spiritualism and materialism. Mao himself is treated less and less like a divine being, but the tension he introduced into Chinese culture is sure to have its effect for generations to come.

In the West, the clash of ideas seems to be moving in exactly the opposite direction. Is it not curious that, while China took over scientific humanism and is trying to build a society on it, many elements in the West have decided that scientific humanism will not work and are beginning to look with favor toward the old Eastern religions! The interest in transcendental meditation, the Hare Krishna sect, the popularity of Zen Buddhism, the practice of drug-induced meditative techniques—all these represent a "looking Eastward" by the children of Western technology.

HUMAN EXISTENTIAL NEEDS: A REVIEW

Earlier we saw that the supracultural religions, the "higher religions," existed to try to meet human existential needs—the needs that all people everywhere have always had. In beginning to study the writings of Eastern holy men, this fact should constantly be kept in mind. One should keep asking the question, "How does this particular religious concept seek to answer the basic problems of human existence?"

A review of some of these basic problems might help.

1. *The sense of precariousness*—religion tries to provide a sense of wholeness and stability.
2. *The experience of alienation, separation, and loneliness*—religion tries to provide a sense of kinship with the ultimate. As we have seen, the Eastern religions often speak of looking into one's own soul to discover in it the great oneness and to commune with that oneness.
3. *The demand for meaning*—religion seeks to fulfill this need by reordering perception, helping one to see that things are not what they seem to be. The Eastern religions teach that through meditation one learns what is illusion and what is real.
4. *The right relationship with the "holy"*—in the supracultural religions, this need is fulfilled through ethics, or rules of behavior, as well as through ceremonies and rites.

5. *The need for joy*—religion seeks to supply emotional and intellectual peace. As you read the Eastern holy writings, you can see many suggestions and guidelines, often calling for the use of exercises and meditative techniques, to attain this goal.

There are many excellent books on each of the Eastern religions. It is not necessary to repeat what has been done so well elsewhere.[1] We will limit ourselves to a brief survey about two major religions of the East—Hinduism and Buddhism—to gain some additional "feel" for the Eastern way.

THE HINDU ANSWER

Here is a basic list of Hindu words:

Bhagavad Gita
Krishna
Arjuna
Caste
Dharma
Atman
Brahman
Karma
Moksha
Maya
Lila

The Bhagavad Gita is one of the most famous Hindu holy writings. In it, the god Krishna appears to the warrior Arjuna. In Krishna's conversation with Arjuna we have one of the clearest and most concise explanations of the Hindu world view. Arjuna is upset by the prospect of killing people in war. Krishna explains to him that people are divided into *castes*. Certain people are born warriors, certain others merchants, certain others priests, and so on. The castes are firmly set; there is no movement from one to the other. One does not simply decide what to major in, go off to school and then get a job. One must fulfill the duties of the caste in which he or she was born. Those duties are called one's *dharma*.

If, then, one is in the warrior caste, one's dharma is to fight and kill. If one is in the merchant class, one's dharma is to sell; if a priest, to pray and meditate, for example.

The *atman* or the "self" is the indestructable reality that is the real person. It is never dying and travels through several bodies, not just the one in which it dwells now. Finally, after a long, long struggle and pilgrim-

---

[1]See Lewis M. Hoppe, *Religions of the World* (Beverly Hills, Calif.: Glencoe, 1976), and Houston Smith, *The Religions of Man* (New York: Harper & Row, 1958).

Arjuna and Krishna on a chariot. South Indian painting, c 1800 A.D. (British Museum)

age, it manages to reunite itself with *brahman*, or the "ultimate." Brahman is the eternal oneness in its purity. Brahman is God—but we must not think of the Western meaning of "God."

The self, or the atman, goes through body after body, both animal and human, in a continual search. Finally, it is fused with brahman entirely, so that it no longer exists as a separate entity in any way.

The principle of *karma* is, as someone has said, the belief that "the universe keeps books." That is, when you do good things, you generate good karma and move forward in your search for brahman. When you do bad things, you generate bad karma and slip backward. "Moving forward" means progressing through a series of reincarnations, with each body being a bit higher up the scale than the last. By doing well in a given reincarnation, that is, by performing its dharma well, one accumulates good karma. And good karma sends one higher up the ladder in his or her next reincarnation.

So, if a man like Arjuna does well as a warrior, he may progress upward, finally becoming a brahman (the highest caste). There, as a priest, he will enable himself to spend all his time in spiritual exercises. This will increase his chances of going into the final stage where he is not reincarnated at all, but becomes fully one with the ultimate.

This last state is *moksha*. It is being beyond existence, being released from one's individuality, being fused with the oneness. The holy men say that it is like a drop of rain water falling into the sea. It no longer has any of experiences peculiarly connected with being a drop of water, because it has become one with the infinite ocean. So humanity hopes to free itself from the wheel of existence, from being reincarnated over and over again. Human beings hope to cease to exist—not in the sense that they become *nothing* but in the sense that they become *everything*.

One of the ways in which one achieves this state is by coming to know what it means to say "I am brahman." To say this with true enlightenment is to say that what is real in me is the ultimate realness, the ultimate oneness. And so the holy man may sit motionless for days saying, over and over, "I am brahman." He will say this thousands of times, until he gradually begins to catch hold of what that means. In this way, he frees himself from ignorance.

In Hindu thinking ignorance is anything that keeps one from true self-awareness, anything that keeps one from seeing what he or she really is. And in particular, one of the worst forms of ignorance is the "illusion of multiplicity"—the idea that there are lots of things. One who has really been enlightened will know that there are *not* lots of things—there is only *one* thing. Everything is illusion except that one thing, and one must come into complete union with that one thing to be free from all ignorance.

Maya is illusion. It is seeing things wrongly, perceiving incorrectly. Maya is the curtain that hides the truth from us. When this curtain is pulled back we meet the truth face to face. And when this is done, we see and know that the world and history are nothing but *lila*—the play of brahman.

The truly holy Hindu will observe what is going on around him like a spectator at a play. He will never get involved in what happens on the stage, beyond simply watching it in a detached way. He may be slightly interested in the plot, but he realizes that what he sees is not really happening.

Twice in my life I have seen someone lose his sense of perspective at a dramatic production. The first was a college play. One of the actors, whom I knew, was an unstable and very disturbed person. By some fluke, he was given a part in the play that almost exactly paralleled his own life. According to the plot, this character gradually falls deeper and deeper into despair and at the end of the play he is left prostate on the stage, hopelessly lost.

The curtain closed and the audience began to applaud. Suddenly this fellow appeared at one of the wings and rushed to center stage. The audience thought the play had simply been provided with a brief epilogue and became quiet to hear the final lines.

But as the actor began to talk the mood changed to shock. "You just do not understand," he said. "I've got to have help. HELP ME!"

We gradually came to the terrible realization that these were not lines in the play. The actor had lost his identity in that of the character he had played. He was that person. The plot had been real. The real world had slipped away, and the stage had taken its place. The poor fellow had to be carried away, sobbing and calling for help.

The second incident occurred in a movie theater where the film *Easy Rider* was being shown. This film builds up in the last few moments, carefully manipulating the audience into a frenzy of hate. When the climax occurred a young man behind me jumped to his feet and began to curse and flail his arms at the screen. He had forgotten that he was only watching a movie.

The Hindu holy man would say that the young man's mistake is the one made by all unenlightened people, who do not realize that all the events around them are but charades being acted out by the gods, mere images flickering on silver screens. People are foolish when they treat the things around them as though they are real. People are wise when they learn to be witnesses and not players, spectators and not actors.

Hinduism's attitude of tolerance is well known. There are, say the holy men, many ways to salvation. Any of them will eventually work, although some will take much longer than others. This is why most religions that have tried to enter India have eventually been "hugged to death." Instead of being resisted, they are simply accepted as also valid, though perhaps inferior ways to reach out for brahman.

The three classical paths of Hinduism are *karma marga* (the path of works) in which the believer wins moksha by performing the caste duties well; *bahkti marga* (the path of devotion), in which the believer devotes all of life to brahman, or perhaps to one of brahman's incarnations such as Krishna; and *jnana marga* (the path of knowledge), in which the believer meditates until enlightenment comes.

There are, of course, thousands of other paths, but the Hindus believe these three to be particularly successful. And whatever path one chooses, a person will find the practice of yoga very helpful in traveling along it.

Yoga is a highly developed series of physical and psychological exercises designed to help one shut out the unreal outer world and get into oneself. It is truly amazing what the master yogi can do with his body and mind. He can control muscles that we ordinarily think of as involuntary.

He may gain so much control over his stomach muscles, for example, that he may form a perfect letter "J" by simply tensing certain muscles and relaxing others. He can cause them to move up and down, back and forth, even round and round. There are also the psychological exercises, which develop the ability to control the mind's activities.

Most of us have very little mental control. This fact can be illustrated by the following little test: For the next thirty seconds, do *not* think of a *white bear.*

Were you able to do it? I doubt it. Even though you had not thought of one in ages, just being told not to think of one makes it very hard to keep a white bear from popping into the mind, no matter how hard we try.

The yogi, on the other hand, can cast all thoughts from his mind, bringing it to perfect rest. There is spiritual value in this, say the holy men, for it enables one to avoid the illusions that fill the mind and frees the soul to commune with the real.

Before we move on to look at Buddhism, remember that, just as there are over four hundred kinds of Christianity, there are also hundreds of kinds of Hinduism. We have generalized, and any serious student of this religion, or any other, must dig much deeper to really understand.

THE BUDDHIST ANSWER

Buddhism begins with the story of its founder, Siddhartha Gautama. Siddhartha was born about 563 B.C. in India. He began life with every material advantage. Born into a very wealthy family of royal blood, he married a beautiful girl, they had a beautiful child, and, according to legends, lived in three beautiful palaces.

Siddhartha was purposely shielded from anything unpleasant or evil. He never saw anyone sick, anyone suffering, anyone old, anyone poor, anyone dead. One day, however, he ventured out into the streets. There he saw a very old man, then someone suffering, and then a corpse.

He was stunned. For days he struggled with this revelation of evil. Finally he decided that he must go out in search of answers. He took a final look at his beautiful wife and family, lying asleep, left them a note and slipped away to seek for what is real and true.

Siddhartha tried several things, including a stint with a group of ascetics so extreme in their self-mortification that their fasting and discipline almost killed him. Finally, down to skin and bones, he decided that, while such men knew a great deal about bringing their bodies into subjection, they really knew no more about the truth than anyone else.

For many years he wandered from guru to guru, always searching, but never finding an answer. Finally one day he sat down beneath the bo tree. There his own inner struggle took place. Before he arose again he had received the Enlightenment. He understood now the nature of the world and the answer to the question of how to live.

Buddhism is the religion that developed from Siddhartha Gautama's teachings following his Enlightenment. It arose in India and flourished there for a thousand years. In many ways the Hindu roots of Buddhism are obvious. Eventually Indian Buddhism disappeared as a separate religion, but by that time the faith had spread widely into other countries and cultures. Today the major concentration of Buddhism is Southeast Asia (Cambodia, Vietnam, Thailand), Japan, and China.

Buddhism exists in two major branches (compare Western Christianity's Protestantism and Catholicism): Theravada Buddhism, more prevalent in the southern countries, and Mahayana Buddhism, more prevalent in the northern countries. To taste the flavor of Buddhism we will look at one of the sacred books of Theravada Buddhism called the Dhammapada.[2]

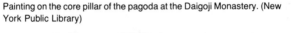

Painting on the core pillar of the pagoda at the Daigoji Monastery. (New York Public Library)

[2]Quotations from *The Dhammapada*, trans. P. Lal (New York: Farrar, Straus & Giroux, 1967).

Siddhartha Gautama the Buddha was not interested in metaphysical speculation. He was interested in life and in getting some hold on it. So he says to a disciple,[3]

Therefore, consider carefully, Malunkyaputta, the things that I have taught and the things that I have not taught. What are things I have not taught?

I have not taught that the world is eternal. I have not taught that the world is not eternal. I have not taught that the world is finite. I have not taught that the world is infinite. I have not taught that the soul and the body are the same. I have not taught that the soul and the body are different. I have not taught that the liberated person exists after death. I have not taught that he does not exist after death. I have not taught that he both exists and does not exist after death; that he neither exists nor does not exist after death.

Why, Malunkyaputta, have I not taught all this? Because all this is useless, it has nothing to do with real Dhamma, it does not lead to cessation of passion, to peace, to supreme wisdom, and the holy life, to Nirvana. That is why I have not taught all this.

And what have I taught, Malunkyaputta? I have taught that suffering exists, that suffering has an origin, that suffering can be ended, that there is a way to end suffering.

Why, Malunkyaputta, have I taught this? Because this is useful, it has to do with real Dhamma, it leads to the cessation of passion, it brings peace, supreme wisdom, the holy life, and Nirvana. That is why I have taught all this.

Therefore, Malunkyaputta, consider carefully what I have taught and what I have not taught.

To make the same point, the Buddha tells a story. People who always want to deal with philosophical questions are like the man who was shot with a poison arrow. When people came to aid him he would not let them touch his wound. Instead, he wanted them to explain to him what kind of arrow it was, where it came from, what kind of poison was on it, the motivation of the person who shot him, and dozens of other similar questions.

None of those questions is important, says the Buddha. The important question is, how can I remove the arrow and stop the suffering it causes? Those who seek the Enlightenment will deal only with that question.

The right path, he says, is the middle one between sensuality, the indulgence of the body, and extreme asceticism, the torture of the body. To his followers he says,[4]

Avoid these two extremes, monks. Which two? On the one hand, low, vulgar, ignoble, and useless indulgence in passion and luxury; on the other, painful,

[3]Quotations from *The Dhammapada*, p. 20.
[4]Ibid., p. 22.

ignoble, and useless practice of self-torture and mortification. Take the
Middle Path advised by the Buddha, for it leads to insight and peace, wisdom
and enlightenment, and to Nirvana.

Nirvana is the goal of the Buddhist. The Theravada Buddhist describes it as a state in which all the flame of desire has been blown out. The
Mahayana Buddhist calls it a state of being so full of the infinite that the
loss of the finite is of no consequence. Nirvana lies beyond all concrete state
of existence.[5]

> But where is the Buddha? Here or There?
> Neither here nor there, sire.
> What do you mean, respected Nagasena?
> Supposing, sire, the flames of a great fire are extinguished,
> where do they go? Here or there? Where?
> Neither here or there. They disappear.

> So, when the Buddha achieved Nirvana, sire, he became neither here
> or there. But you may know him by the Dhamma, for he taught the
> Dhamma, and left it behind.

So we see that the Buddha is beyond existence now and has left behind
only his teachings as a guide for others to follow him. The Buddhist holy
man, says the Dhammapada, is[6]

> Like a bird invisibly flying in the sky,
> He lives without possessions
> knowledge his food, freedom his world,
> while others wonder.

> Like a bird flying invisibly in the sky
> while others wonder, he lives, the saint
> Without passions, indifferent to food,
> aware of the meaning of freedom.

In this poem we can see clearly the detachment so common to Eastern
spirituality. The key to the Buddhist life-style is mental self-possession:

> We are what we think
> Having become what we thought . . .[7]

> Clear thinking leads to Nirvana
> . . .

[5] Ibid., p. 34.
[6] Ibid., p. 71.
[7] Ibid., p. 39.

[The Wise Man] meditates, he preserves,
He works hard for the incomparable freedom
and the bliss of Nirvana . . .[8]

A disciplined mind is the road to Nirvana . . .[9]

We can see that the rewards of Buddhism come from what one does for himself. Siddhartha Gautama the Buddha has left good advice and enlightened teaching, but the believer will gain nirvana only through his *own* efforts.

To think wrong thoughts is to remain separated from nirvana. The kinds of thoughts that are wrong are those that agitate the mind, that prevent the mind from being quiet and calm, like a bird flying invisibly in the sky. In particular, there are four kinds of thoughts that must be purged from the mind: *possessiveness*, *anger*, *hatred*, and *lust*.

Right thoughts, those that contribute to gaining nirvana, include *detachment* and *compassion*. It is best to love other people and to never return evil for evil. This ensures mental tranquility.

And as for the world around, one must simply think to oneself,[10]

The world is a bubble,
the world is a shadow . . .

Buddhism seeks to relieve men of suffering. And before this can be done the believer must come to understand the truths that Siddhartha himself received under the bo tree: the four noble truths.

The *first noble truth* concerns suffering:[11]

For there is suffering, and this is the noble truth of suffering—birth is painful, old age is painful, sickness is painful, death is painful; lamentation, dejection, and despair are painful. Contact with the unpleasant is painful, not getting what you want is painful.

One must then, first recognize the condition of human beings, that they are in anguish.

The *second noble truth* concerns the origin of suffering:[12]

Suffering has an origin, and this is the noble truth of the origin of suffering—desire creates sorrow, desire mixed with pleasure and lust, quick pleasure, desire for life, and desire even for non-life.

[8]Quotations from *The Dhammapada*, p. 45.
[9]Ibid., p. 49.
[10]Ibid., p. 97.
[11]Ibid., p. 23.
[12]Ibid.

Why do people suffer? They suffer because they *desire*. It is desire that creates sorrow—even the desire for life, even the desire to not live.

The *third noble truth* concerns the end of suffering:[13]

> Suffering has an end, and this is the noble truth of the end of suffering—nothing remains of desire, Nirvana is attained, all is given up, renounced, detached, and abandoned.

We want something but cannot get it. We are miserable. We blow out the flame of desire. We are no longer miserable.

Suppose that you see a very attractive member of the opposite sex and immediately fall deeply in love. But the love you feel is not returned. You become miserable, caught in the web of an unfulfilled and unfillable desire. Either you must end the desire, and gain peace, or resort to force, and bring even more unhappiness on yourself.

Some years ago a student told me about a bizarre incident in which the second alternative was used. Deciding that her relationship with her boyfriend had no future, she broke up with him. He was grief striken. Determined to have her, he came to her apartment with a pistol and forced her to come with him to an adjoining state. There he kept the gun in her ribs while a judge, unaware of what was happening, married them.

She did not dare let the judge know what was happening, so she said her vows with a forced smile. But as soon as the ceremony was over and the couple got back to the groom's apartment, she forcefully administered a lamp to his head and called the police before he regained consciousness.

Now she is happily married to someone else and, unless her violent suitor has blown out the flame of his desire, he presumably still lives in misery!

But the real misery, says the Buddha, is not that we do not get what we desire; it is the desire *itself* that makes us miserable. The only sure escape comes when all desire is given up, renounced, detached, and abandoned. And when desire is gone, so will suffering disappear.

The *fourth noble truth* provides the practical plan for attaining nirvana:[14]

> And this is the noble truth that leads to Nirvana—it is the Eightfold Way of right views, right intentions, right speech, right action, right profession, right watchfulness, and right concentration.

It all boils down to this: one must free oneself from craving. Only in this way comes peace.[15]

[13]Ibid.
[14]Ibid.
[15]Ibid., p. 157.

Craving is like a creeper,
it strangles the fool.
He bounds like a monkey, from one birth to another,
looking for fruit.

When craving, like poison,
takes hold of a man,
his sorrows increase
like wild grass.

This is my advice:
"Root out craving! Root it out,
like wild grass is rooted out.
Do not let death destroy you
As river waters destroy reeds."

COMPARING AND CONTRASTING
THE RELIGIONS OF EAST AND WEST

Now we are ready to make some general comparisons between the religious ideas of the East and West. The following chart should help focus our thinking.

Contrasting Eastern and Western Religions

The East	*The West*
1. Broad tolerance	1. Exclusivism
2. Reality monistic and imminent	2. Reality dualistic and transcendent
3. World denying	3. God acts in history and nature
4. Passive acceptance of human condition	4. Active attempt to change human condition
5. Highest goal: union with the ultimate	5. Highest goal: true personhood
6. Cyclical view of history	6. Linear view of history

First, the religions of the East are more likely to assimilate new ideas than to fight them. One may easily belong to several religions at the same time. One Japanese woman told me that she would "be married a Shintoist, live as a Confucianist, and be buried as Buddhist." In the West, acceptance of one faith has traditionally meant rejection of all others. The Gospel of John quotes Jesus as saying, "I am the way, the truth, and the life. No man comes to the Father except by me." This exclusivism is a characteristic of the other major Western religions as well.

Second, in the Eastern faiths reality is monistic; that is, everything that is, is one. Multiplicity is an illusion. And this great Oneness is *here*. Everything that is real is a part of it. But the West thinks of reality as *dualistic*; that is, both matter and spirit exist, both God and the world. So the ultimate reality is "there" (transcendent) as well as "here" (imminent).

Third, Eastern religion is basically world denying. We have seen this illustrated in various ways in our earlier discussion. In contrast, the religions of the West understand God to be active in nature and in history. Nature and history have not been abandoned by the Ultimate; nor *are* they Ultimate in some mystical way. Rather, they are the arena in which God acts. He is separate from them, but works within them. So, instead of denying and withdrawing from them, one looks for God within them.

Fourth, the East tends to accept the human condition passively. The Hindu doctrine of karma attempts to explain why humans suffer (as punishment for bad karma in a previous life). The Buddhist holy man detaches himself from his suffering by ridding himself of desire. In both cases suffering is inevitable, and men must simply learn to live with it. In the West, people actively attempt to *change* the human condition. Rather than learn how to accept starvation with calm resignation, they fight for something to eat. They try to alleviate suffering by filling the need rather than by quenching the need. This difference in approach helps to explain why movements for social and economic change have generally begun in the West.

Fifth, the greatest goal of Eastern religion is to be fused with the Ultimate, to *become* the Ultimate, to lose one's individual identity. One no longer exists in any way separate from the Oneness. One is like a drop of rain water that has fallen into the ocean. For the Western faiths, true personhood is the goal, the attaining of one's fullest potential by being oneself in the most complete way possible.

Sixth, for the East, history is cyclical. That is, history spins around and around, like a wheel. But this movement is not like that of a wagon wheel that is going somewhere. Rather, it resembles the movement of a wheel attached to the side of a barn, simply turning around and around, going nowhere in particular. What has happened will happen again. There is no pattern, simply the idle repetition of similar events. Western religions have a linear view of history. That is, they conceive of history as moving forward all the time, as looking more like a straight line than a circle, as moving more like an arrow than like a wheel.

It is time to remind ourselves again about the difference between a normative definition and a descriptive one. The normative definition of a given religion is what that religion *should* be when it follows its own best lights. A descriptive definition deals with the same religion as a historical phenomenon. Usually the practice of a religion is far inferior to the highest ideals of the founders of that religion.

Few Indians, even the most pious of them, reach up to the highest standards of the Hindu view of life. When one sees Buddhist monks in Southeast Asia leading demonstrations and becoming actively involved in political intrigue, one may think, "Is *that* detachment? Shouldn't they be off in a quiet monastery somewhere meditating?" These things should not be surprising. All religions are one thing in the ideal and another when they actually work out in life situations.

That fact is apparent in the history of Christianity. During the middle ages men were burned at the stake in the name of Jesus. But there is nothing in the teachings of Jesus about burning people at the stake. This is an example of how his teachings have not been worked out in Christian societies, just as Hindu teachings have not been worked out in Hindu societies, or Buddhist teachings in Buddhist societies.

But in fairness we should never judge the ideals of a religion purely on the basis of its historical record—the ideals cannot be blamed for the failures of those who carried the name of those ideals.

So, just as we have looked for the best in the religions of the East, we will do the same for the religions of the West.

CHAPTER FIVE
THE RELIGION OF ISRAEL

THE ACTS OF GOD IN HISTORY

The scholar Edmond Jacob summarizes very well the essence of Biblical religion in this brief statement:[1]

> The special characteristic of biblical revelation is that God binds Himself to historical events to make them the vehicle of the manifestation of his purpose.

The Infinite, the Transcendent, the Other, has come down and become involved in the imminent, the now, the historical, the material world.

The Bible begins with a story that maintains that the human race in its present state is fallen.[2] By "fallen" we simply mean that, due to disobedience, self-assertiveness, and unwillingness to live according to the created order of things, people have created an enormous gulf between themselves and the Ultimate Reality—a gulf for which they have only themselves to blame.

[1]Edmond Jacob, *Theology of the Old Testament* (New York: Harper & Row. 1958), p. 188. Another excellent introduction to the thinking of the Hebrew Scriptures is Otto J. Baab, *The Theology of the Old Testament* (New York: Abingdon, 1949).

[2]Read Genesis 1–3. This account underwent considerable interpretation by Christian theologians. Our use of the term "fallen" should not necessarily be identified directly with traditional Christian doctrines of the depravity of the human race.

Because this gulf exists, people are plagued with certain feelings, feelings we described earlier as "human existential needs." They feel guilt. They sense that the universe is not friendly toward them, that they are separated from what is real, that they are not measuring up to standards. They feel alienated. They are somehow alone. They are cut off from their roots. And they sense a lack of meaning: they are here, but they do not know why. They do not know where they came from. They do not know where they are going.

All these problems come, according to the first few chapters of the Bible, from the human race's rejection of the One who made it, from its disobedience to that One, and from its asserton of its own will above the will of that One. The Biblical story has two parts. The first is "prehistoric"; that is, it deals with the beginning of the world and humanity, painted in broad and poetic strokes. The second interprets a period of history heavily documented by archaeology and surviving records.

In the beginning, Adam and Eve passed their time in a beautiful garden, trimming the trees, the Bible says, living in harmony with nature. Although there were almost no rules or restraints, nevertheless Adam and Eve lost their place in Eden.

To vary the analogy somewhat, it is as though the race began its existence on a high mountain, surrounded by steep cliffs. On top of this mountain is a beautiful garden filled with flowers, fruits, and cool streams of clear water. Then humanity is told, "This lovely place is yours; but never go beyond its boundaries."

The people, however, do step outside the limits of the garden. They lose their footing and slip down the steep cliff. They find themselves unable to climb back up again. They are mired down in a horrible swamp. They can look up and catch only fleeting glances of the beautiful place where they used to live. But they cannot return to it, no matter how they struggle.

This is humanity's condition. People can conceive of a place so much more beautiful than where they are now. They sense themselves to be separated from the real life that is potentially theirs. They are frustrated because they cannot climb to the heights of their dreams and expectations. Unable to climb, they can only look up and dream, or hope, or even sometimes *remember* the paradise from which they came. The human race has fallen farther than it can climb; that is the condition of humankind pictured in the early chapters of Genesis.

However, the Bible continues, this God who made the beautiful garden and put people in it pities their plight and stretches out His arm to restore them. The intimate relationship of Eden, where God walked with Adam in the cool of the evening, is gone. But God will now, through the march of historical events, reach out to humanity and offer to heal the wounds of the past.

He will, moreover, do this in such a way that the human race is not robbed of its own free will. This has always been God's most precious gift to humanity. He could have made it in such a way that it *could* not have fallen. Then it would have lived forever in the garden there would be no need for religion at all. But it would not live in the garden as *human.* It would live there like a plant or an animal, acting out of instinct instead of through moral choice.

But humanity is made, so says the book of Genesis, in the image of God. Humanity has been created with its own personhood and its own will. God is not willing to interfere with that. He chooses to open Himself up to humanity in such a way that the human race can respond to Him openly and freely, without any compulsion.

Such a procedure is, of course, very complicated. Thus the method by which God acts is also a bit complicated. According to the Bible, what God does is to select a tiny group of people who live in the Near East and make a special covenant with them. Then He begins to work out a revelation of Himself in their history. They are to become a "light to the nations," He says.

And by involving Himself with them and acting within their history, He will gradually work out His plan to reconcile the human race to Himself and to restore His people to Eden. This little community is called *Israel.*

The history of Israel, says the Bible. is not ordinary history. It is history with the acts of God mixed in—"holy history," as it were. The events of this history are not just normal events, explainable by the normal theories of cause and effect of the objective scientific historian. Rather, they are events into which God has inserted Himself, making them "vehicles for the manifestation of His purpose."

Of course one can study the events recorded in the Bible as an objective historian. The Biblical writers might not object to such a study. But they would be quick to point out that the acts that they recorded have another dimension beyond the mere objective recounting of them. So, one might maintain that the Red Sea had parted on numerous occasions. One might even furnish scientific explanations. But that it parted at one particular time, just at the moment when the children of Israel could cross and escape the Egyptians, and thereby flee the bondage of Egypt and become a people—that was for the Biblical writers a mighty act filled with the presence of God. In acts such as this, they claimed, God was manifesting Himself and working out His purpose.

It is this point of view that explains why so much of the Hebrew Scripture is an account of the history of Israel. In this history the writers perceived God coming to the human race to redeem it.

Here, very briefly, is how the story continues: God selects a motley group of slaves living in Egypt as the people through whom He will work. They will be a light to the nations. He sends them a leader named Moses who leads them out of Egyptian servitude and into the desert of Sinai. There, on Mount Sinai (presumably somewhere in the region we call the

Sinai Peninsula), God presents Moses with a covenant for the people. It contains the Ten Commandments and, by extension, the codes and law by which these slaves will become His people. On His part, God promises to work with and through them and to be their God.

For many years the people of Israel wander in the wilderness, in the land that is today populated by Bedouin tribepeople and oil sheiks. Finally they enter the land of Canaan (modern Israel and Jordan) and, after a number of centuries of struggle, gradually dominate the local population and build a nation.

First they are organized into semi-independent tribes, and then, eventually, into a monarchy ruled over by kings such as David and Solomon. The monarchy and the nation itself split in two, resulting in a northern kingdom (Israel) and a southern kingdom (Judah). Through stormy centuries these little kingdoms gradually become caught in the great power struggles of the day, caught between the mighty empires to the north, south, and west of them. They are battered around constantly until finally, in 722 B.C., the northern kingdom is destroyed by a massive Assyrian invasion. The people are carried away into exile and lose their identity. History knows them as the ten lost tribes. In a few more generations' time the southern kingdom also falls to the Babylonians and the temple of God is destroyed (687 B.C.).

Some of the southerners (who became known as Jews) are taken into Babylonian exile, there to remain for seventy years. While in exile they firmly retain their cultural identity and their worship of the God who had so many centuries ago revealed Himself to them. Their understanding of the nature of this God was immeasurably strengthened during this time; so much so that when they returned from exile they were ready to present to the world the documents that are often called the Old Testament—documents that have formed the basis for all Western religions.

THE HEBREW PROPHETS: THE
RIGHTEOUS REMNANT

Several times the people of Israel almost disrupt the whole plan. Even though God is working in them, they are perfectly capable of rejecting His work or even working at cross-purposes with Him. Sometimes the light almost goes out entirely. But somehow always a few people remain faithful to the covenant. The Biblical writers call them the *remnant*.

In particular there were the group of persons we call the prophets.[3] These were, says the Old Testament, God's special people, His special

---

[3]For further study, see Stephen Winward, *A Guide to the Prophets* (Richmond, Va.: John Knox, 1968), or Emil G. Kroeling, *The Prophets* (Chicago: Rand McNally, 1969).

spokesmen, who observed and recorded and interpreted the acts of God in history, who learned what God was like and what His will was, and who passed this information to those who wrote it down in the holy books.

As time passed it became more and more clear to these prophets that the full purposes of God were never going to be completed in the normal course of history. There would never be a perfect society, or a restoration to the perfect life of Eden, in the regular process of events. The prophets began to talk more and more about the futility of the way secular human beings were trying to build their kingdoms—military might, politics, and social reform. They began to predict more and more insistently that God would eventually act in a most decisive way, that He would intervene as He had never done before, in a crowning act in which He would bear Himself as fully as the human mind and senses can comprehend. In that intervention would come the restoration to Eden.

The flavor of these dreams can be well illustrated from one of the most profound of the books of the prophets, the Book of Isaiah:[4]

It shall come to pass in the latter days
    that the mountain of the house of the LORD
shall be established as the highest of the
        mountains,
        and shall be raised above the hills;
and all the nations shall flow to it
        and many peoples shall come, and say:
"Come, let us go up to the mountain of the LORD,
        to the house of the God of Jacob;
that he may teach us his ways
        and that we may walk in his paths."
For out of Zion shall go forth the law,
        and the word of the LORD from Jerusalem.
He shall judge between the nations,
        and shall decide for many peoples;
and they shall beat their swords into plowshares.
        and their spears into pruning hooks;
nation shall not lift up sword against nation,
        neither shall they learn war any more.

This beautiful quotation is inscribed on the front of the United Nations building in New York (where the extent of its influence seems doubtful).[5]

Behold, the Lord, the LORD of hosts will lop
        the boughs with terrifying power;

[4]Isa. 2:2–4.
[5]Isa. 10:33–11:9.

the great in height will be hewn down,
    and the lofty will be brought low.
He will cut down the thickets of the forest with an axe,
    and Lebanon with its majestic trees will fall.
There shall come forth a shoot from the stump of Jesse,
    and a branch shall grow out of his roots.
And the spirit of the LORD shall rest upon him,
        the spirit of wisdom and understanding,
        the spirit of counsel and might,
        the spirit of knowledge and the fear of the LORD.
And his delight shall be in the fear of the LORD.

He shall not judge by what his eyes see,
    or decide by what his ears hear;
but with righteousness he shall judge the poor,
    and decide with equity for the meek of the earth;
and he shall smite the earth with the rod of his mouth,
    and with the breath of hip lips he shall slay the
        wicked.
Righteousness shall be the girdle of his waist,
    and faithfulness the girdle of his loins.

The wolf shall dwell with the lamb,
    and the leopard shall lie down with the kid,
and the calf and the lion and the fatling together,
    and the little child shall lead them.
The cow and the bear shall feed;
    their young shall lie down together;
    and the lion shall eat straw like the ox.
The sucking child shall play over the hold of the asp,
    and the weaned child shall put his hand on the
        adder's den.
They shall not hurt or destroy in all my holy mountain;
for the earth shall be full of the knowledge of the LORD
    as the waters cover the sea.

The themes of this dramatic poem are striking: God acts in a very decisive way, like a mighty ax laying the forest of human culture and human attainments low. All these were but frustrating failures, unable to bring human beings to Eden. Then, among the ruins, a tiny shoot springs up from an old stump, promising new life. It is the "stump of Jesse" (Jesse was the father of King David). This "anointed one" or Messiah will institute a truly just social order, where even poor and weak are treated fairly. What results is a paradise void of all violence and death, where every person enjoys a perfect relationship with God.

Here was a truly glorious dream, a dream of God's intervening, of God's ruling, of God's Kingdom, of the coming of the Kingdom of God to humanity. This is the dream of the Hebrew Scriptures. It is the dream, as we have said, that becomes the basis for the Western religions, though the precise understanding of the Messianic motif has been differently understood in each of them.

It is an unfinished dream. And out of its unfinishedness has come the religion we call Judaism.[6] Out of the ancient stories and prophecies comes the amazing hope and strength of the Jewish people throughout the ages, feeding on those events and those dreams.

Yet the fond dreams of the prophets have an unfinished character about them. It is as though someone had shot an arrow into the air toward a goal. It is well aimed and well shot. It is sure to land in its intended place. It is moving swiftly and surely toward its goal. But as we see the arrow go by, we cannot predict where it will land. We do not know its target, for it lies beyond our view, over the horizon. Only the One who shot it knows its destination.

In that simple analogy lies the essence of the Biblical view of history. The accompanying chart helps us to visualize this view. God reaches down and touches history at various points, represented in the chart by arrows. History itself is pictured as an arrow, plunging toward its goal: the Day of Yahweh.

TEMPLE AND TORAH

As important as it may have been, the prophetic movement was not the only religious expression among the ancient Jews. Alongside this movement,

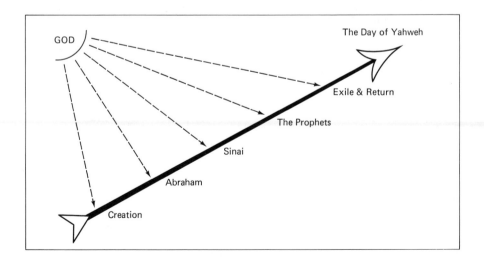

[6]To trace the development of this religion from Biblical times to the present, see Leo Trepp, *Judaism: Development and Life* (Belmont, Calif.: Dickenson, 1966).

existing in dynamic tension with it, was the religion of the temple and the Torah, administered by the priests and the scribes.

The temple in Jerusalem, built originally by King Solomon around 950 B.C. and magnificently rebuilt by King Herod in the first century B.C., was the center of a massive cultus involving thousands of priests. The entire economy of Israel during the second temple period (approximately 400 B.C. to A.D. 70) was dependent on this cultus that attempted to carry out the elaborate sacrificial system outlined in the Torah (the first five books in the Hebrew Scriptures).[7]

With the fall of the Jewish state and the destruction of Jerusalem and the temple by the Romans in A.D. 70, however, the sacrifices were abruptly halted, since the Torah allowed them to be performed nowhere else. For several previous centuries, Jews had settled in many lands throughout the eastern Mediterrean, forming the *diaspora* (or scattering). In combination with the Pharisees, the only Jewish sect substantially surviving the destruction in Judea, the diaspora communities developed a faith tied not to temple and Torah, but to the Torah alone. The Pharisees did not understand the Torah to be an absolute, unchangeable document of God's final word to humanity. Rather, it was a living document to be interpreted in the light of changing conditions. The study of the Torah, then, never ended. It was in fact to be one of the major responsibilities of religious leaders from that point until the present day.

The temple, on the other hand, declined in significance, replaced by the synagogue as the center of religious expression. In diaspora centers the synagogue was not only a place of worship, but a center in which to keep Jewish culture and aspirations intact. In the place of the animal sacrifices, the Pharisaic leaders elevated prayer and the proper applications of dietary and Sabbath day prohibitions. Thus, notes Jacob Neusner, "The Temple cult is to be replaced by study of Torah, the priest by the rabbi [scribe]; and the center of piety was shifted from cult and sacrifice entirely."[8]

Thus the major characteristics of Judaism, which were to determine the nature of that religion, were in place. The impact of the modern world on this ancient faith will be discussed in Chapters 10 and 11.

THE GOD OF THE HEBREWS

The major presupposition of the Hebrew Scriptures, the one upon which everything else rests, is the existence of God. He is always understood to be the first reality in sequence (He is the first ever to exist) and the basic reality

---

[7] For a full account of this period, see Joachim Jeremias, *Jerusalem in the Time of Jesus* (Philadelphia: Fortress, 1969).

[8] Jacob Neusner, " 'Pharisaic-Rabbinic' Judaism: A Clarification," *History of Religions*, vol. 12, no. 3 (Chicago: University of Chicago, 1973) p. 265.

The cantor blows the shofar or ram's horn during the Jewish High Holy Days. (Al Kaplan, dpi)

in existence (He is the foundation and origin of everything that exists).

This God is called by various names in the Hebrew Scriptures. Often he is called "El." This is the name given to the father-god or high god in a number of ancient religions, including the polytheistic ones, where El is the most basic god.

But the name that distinguishes the god of the Hebrews from all others is the mysterious word *YHWH*. We are not sure how to pronounce this four-letter word. For many centuries the Jews did not speak this name aloud in order not to show irreverence to its holiness. For this reason the original pronunciation was eventually forgotten. The most common scholarly guess is to pronounce the word "Yahweh" (Yah-way).

Whereas the word "El" simply means God, the word "YHWH" serves as a personal name for the Ultimate. Just as, say, a physician might be called doctor, but also, John Brown. When the prophet Moses was first confronted by God, he was told,[9]

> You must tell the Israelites this, that it is YHWH, the God of their forefathers, the God of Abraham, the God of Isaac, the God of Jacob, who has sent you to them. For this is my name for ever; this is my title in every generation.

So far, archaeologists and ancient historians have never found this word used to refer to any other god or in any other culture.[10] It was the distinctively Israelite way of referring to the Ultimate. The God of the Bible, then, is Yahweh.

As we have said, the Hebrew Scriptures presuppose Yahweh's existence. But *how* does he live? In three basic ways:

Life
Holiness
Oneness

First, Yahweh lives. He exists, says the Bible, not like an idea exists, but like a person exists. He exists by doing things. There is a difference between merely existing and living. Concepts have existence, but they do not do anything. They are abstractions that have reality only when some intelligence thinks about them. But when the Hebrew says that "Yahweh lives," he does not simply mean that He exists as a philosophical abstraction; rather, he means that He is someone who does things. That is the way in which persons exist. That is the way in which you exist. You exist not simply by being here, but by doing things. And so it is with Yahweh.

For this reason, the Bible tends to describe God with verbs rather than with abstract nouns. In other words, it talks about what God does.

This approach is in strong contrast to the Greek way of talking about God. For the great Greek philosophers God was a philosophical abstraction—the Unmoved Mover, the Ultimate Essence, and so on. The

---

[9]Exodus 3:15 (*NEB*).
[10]Jacob, *Old Testament,* p. 49.

same thing is true of Eastern metaphysical thinking, as we saw in the last chapter: the ultimate reality is not personal, it does not do anything—it is a state. It stands majestically still in a state of ultimateness. Yahweh, on the other hand, is very active in His ultimateness.

The Hebrew prophets claim that the idols of the nations around them, and the speculative gods like those of the Greek philosophers, are man-made gods. Such gods, they claim, are dependent upon human beings for their existence.

Remember the puzzle about the tree that fell in the forest? If there were no one there to hear it, would there have been any sound of falling timber? Some would say, "No." Likewise, the Hebrew writers say that some gods have no existence unless there is someone around to worship them. Their existence depends entirely on the people who developed a religion around them.

Take Marduke, for example. Marduke was a major Middle Eastern deity at one time. But no one worships Marduke anymore. For the most part, modern people would claim that Marduke no longer exists. His existence depended on having someone around to cry out "Oh, Holy Marduke!" When people stopped doing that, no more Marduke.

All the speculative gods and all the idols, say the prophets, are eventually shown to be empty ideas, dependent on the human minds that conceived them.

In the book of Isaiah, the prophet pictures what he regards as the folly of worshipping such gods in a delightfully satirical passage:[11]

> The carpenter stretches a line, he marks it out with a pencil; he fashions it with planes, and marks it with a compass; he shapes it into the figure of a man, with the beauty of a man, to dwell in a house. He cuts down cedars; or he chooses a holm tree or an oak and lets it grow strong among the trees of a forest; he plants a cedar and the rain nourishes it. Then it becomes fuel for a man. He takes a part of it and warms himself; he kindles a fire and bakes bread; also he makes a god and worships it, he makes it a graven image and falls down before it. Half of it he burns in the fire; over the half he eats flesh, he roasts meat and is satisfied; also he warms himself and says, "Aha, I am warm, I have seen the fire!" And the rest of it he makes into a god, his idol; and falls down to it and worships it; he prays to it and says, "Deliver me, for thou art my god!"
>
> They know not, nor do they discern; for he has shut their eyes, so that they cannot see, and their minds, so that they cannot understand. No one considers, nor is there knowledge or discernment to say, "Half of it I burned in the fire, I also baked bread on its coals, I roasted flesh and have eaten; and shall I make the residue of it an abomination? Shall I fall down before a block of wood?" He feeds on ashes; a deluded mind has led him astray, and he cannot deliver himself or say, "Is there not a lie in my right hand?"

[11]Isa. 44:13–20.

In contrast, the prophet quotes Yahweh as saying,[12]

Remember these things, O Jacob and Israel,
for you are my servant;
I formed you, you are my servant . . .

You did not fashion me, says the God of the Hebrew prophets; rather I fashioned you. Here is a God who is not discovered by the human race but who takes the initiative and Himself discovers humanity.[13]

Thus says YHWH, your ransomer,
who fashioned you from birth:
I am YHWH who made all things,
by myself I stretched out the skies,
alone I hammered out the floor of the earth.

Most modern religious systems join the ancient Eastern faiths in maintaining that the human being reaches out for God—that it is the human being who must climb up to the heavens. But the Hebrew prophets say that the process is exactly reversed: it is God who climbs down to humanity. It is God who discovers humanity, not humanity who discovers God. It is interesting that the prophets were not philosophers, theologians, or meditating saints. They were much more likely to be, like Amos the prophet, herders or "dressers of sycamore trees,"[14] rather than members of the professional clergy.

Often they showed great reluctance to accept their call from Yahweh. The classic example is the dour prophet Jeremiah, who constantly complains of his lot:[15]

O YHWH, thou hast deceived me,
and I was deceived;
thou art stronger than I,
and thou hast prevailed.
I have become a laughingstock all the day;
everyone mocks me.
For whenever I speak, I cry out,
I shout, "Violence and Destruction!"
For the word of YHWH has become for me
a reproach and derision all day long.
If I say, "I will not mention him,
or speak any more in his name,"

[12]Isa. 44:21a. Emphasis added.
[13]Isa. 44:24 (*NEB*).
[14]Amos 7:14.
[15]Jeremiah 20:7–9.

> there is in my heart as it were a burning fire
> shut up in my bones,
> and I am weary with holding it in,
> and I cannot.

The "fire" in Jeremiah's bones is a far cry from the quiet enlighten-ment of the philosopher or the Hindu holy man. He is dragged into the arena of life to prophesy, kicking and screaming. He has been chosen. He himself has had no choice. He wishes someone else had been selected!

Since Yahweh lives, and does not merely exist, He can be thought of as having *personality*. As a person, I, too, live and do not merely exist. I have experienced personhood. I can, therefore, since I share this experience with God, work back from my own experience of existing to some under-standing of God. I have a vocabulary to talk about God; it is the vocabulary of *personhood*. Thus, the Hebrew prophets use very "human" language in describing the acts of God. This is not because they can in that way make God to be like them; it is because they believe that God has made *them* like *Him*.

The technical term for this kind of talk is *anthropomorphism. Anthropos* means "pertaining to man, human" and *morphe* means "form, shape." Thus, to describe something anthropomorphically is to describe it as though it were a human being. To say, for example, that a tree "cradles the nests of birds in its gentle arms" is to describe that tree anthropomor-phically. The Hebrew Scriptures constantly describe God in this way.

Some have thought that this procedure is quaint and that phrases such as "God's eyes are on the righteous" betray primitive ideas. But it is important to note that the Israelites never made images of YHWH. They never drew pictures of Him. They might, in periods of apostasy, worship images of others gods, but not of YHWH. This indicates that they con-ceived of Him as a god not to be drawn or sculpted. The word pictures they used (His eyes, His arms, His back, etc.) were not meant to describe some white-bearded old fellow sitting high upon a throne of clouds. Rather, such descriptions were attempts to communicate the personhood of God. The anthropomorphic language, then, grew out of a profound conviction that Yahweh *lives*.

Now since this Yahweh is the Ultimate Person, He acts without any models or rules. The Taoist holy writings describe the Tao or "the way" as a "preface to God." For the Hebrew prophet there is no preface to God. Rather, God is the preface to everything else. He looks nowhere else to determine what a person ought to be. He is completely self-initiating. He is what He desires to be. Nothing exists that guides or limits His behavior except His own will.

Because of these things, Yahweh often acts contrary to human reason. It is very interesting that some of the greatest heroes of the Old Testament are people who are constantly disagreeing with God. Jeremiah often argued with God. So did Moses. From their point of view, much of what He was doing made no sense at all. But of all the Old Testament characters it is Job who takes God to task the most vehemently. For chapter after chapter in the book bearing his name, Job complains bitterly about the things God does and the way He does them. And God's response is that He refuses to be drawn into picky arguments with human beings! To all who would judge Him on the basis of human reason, Yahweh says,[16]

> For my thoughts are not your thoughts,
> and your ways not my ways.
>   . . .
> For as the heavens are higher than the earth,
> So are my ways higher than your ways
> and my thoughts than your thoughts . . .

The practical result of this is that the knowledge of God cannot come from human philosophical speculation. There is nothing within the human mind or human rationality that can teach one about God or in any way predict what He will do. This is because He acts without any reference to human rationality. So, say the prophets, if one expects to know about the nature of God, one must simply wait until God reveals what He is and what He wants.

The second basic characteristic of Yahweh is His holiness. In an earlier chapter we defined holiness as "otherness," as that reality that exists apart from this world. So when the Hebrew writers say that "God is holy," they are saying He is not a part of this world, that He does not originate in this world. And therefore anyone who comes in contact with Yahweh, either directly or indirectly, experiences what Rudolf Otto called the "numinous," the other. Two examples illustrate this.

The first is the initial encounter that Moses had with Yahweh:[17]

> Now Moses was keeping the flock of his father-in-law, Jethro, the priest of Midian; and he led his flock to the west side of the wilderness, and came to Horeb, the mountain of God. And the angel of YHWH appeared to him in a flame of fire out of the midst of a bush; and he looked, and lo, the bush was burning, yet it was not consumed. And Moses said, "I will turn aside and see this great sight, why the bush is not burnt." When YHWH saw that he turned aside to see, God called to him out of the bush, "Moses, Moses!" And he said, "Here am I." Then he said, "Do not come near; put off your shoes from your feet, for the place on which you are standing is holy ground."

The second is the prophet Isaiah's account of his call to be a spokesperson for Yahweh:[18]

[16]Isa. 55:8–9 (*NEB*).
[17]Exodus 3:1–5.
[18]Isa. 6:1–5.

In the year that King Uzziah died I saw the Lord sitting upon a throne, high and lifted up; and his train filled the temple. Above him stood the seraphim; each had six wings; with two he covered his face, and with two he covered his feet, and with two he flew. And one called to another and said:

"Holy, holy, holy is YHWH of hosts;
The whole earth is full of his glory."

And the foundations of the thresholds shook
at the voice of him who called, and the house
was filled with smoke. And I said:

"Woe is me! For I am lost; for I am a man of
unclean lips, and I dwell in the midst of a
people of unclean lips; for my eyes have seen
the King, YHWH of hosts!"

Some Old Testament scholars believe that this encounter took place in the temple dedicated to Yahweh in Jerusalem. One day Isaiah, evidently a priest, sees the symbolic items in the "holy place" become reality. Instead of a representation of the spot where YHWH touches the world (the room in the temple called the Holy of Holies), Isaiah sees God Himself. The veil over the entrance to the room becomes a long robe. The temple begins to shake. The winged beasts inside the room come alive and fly through the air crying out "Holy, Holy, Holy is YHWH of Hosts!" Isaiah is terrified but never the less offers himself as a spokesperson for the Holy God who called him.

"Idolatry," so roundly condemned by the prophets, is a human attempt to make the secular into the sacred, to claim the this worldly to be other worldly. It is carving a cedar tree and falling down to worship it. It is creating a culture and then claiming that culture is a product of the divine.

On the contrary, say the prophets, it is Yahweh who decides what will be holy and what will not. Humanity cannot build an altar and expect God to meet them there. (They never tire of crying out against such "false altars" that are, they say, "abominations.") God Himself will decide where and when the people will meet Him. Idolatry, then, is a human attempt to create holiness.

Because they understood God to be holy, the prophets of Israel also rejected the pantheist view of the world. Pantheism is the belief that *everything is God.* The pantheist conceives of the world as God, nature as God, spirit and flesh alike as God. The Bible, however, keeps a clear line between God and the world. God is different from the world— fundamentally different. He is holy. He is separate. It is true that He comes and gets involved in the world, acting out His will in history, but never in such a way as to destroy His *Holiness.*

The third basic characteristic of Yahweh, according to the Hebrew Scriptures, is His *oneness.* Again we must remember that this is not a philosophical oneness. Some of the Greek philosophers came to the conclusion that there was one God by using rational thought. But the Jews did not learn the oneness of God from their philosophers and theologians. They believed it not because it was logical but, rather, because they believed that Yahweh had proved all other gods powerless.

Their argument was very practical. Where are the other gods? they asked. What are they doing? Have they not fallen, one by one, into obscurity? During the great age of Hebrew prophecy, many more people worshipped Marduke than Yahweh. But the day came when Marduke was forgotten while a major portion of the world's population worshipped Yahweh.

That was argument enough for the Israelite. The god who acts, who overcomes all the other gods, He is *the* God. And only one god has consistently done just that, they said. The others have failed, not because there is some philosophical or logical flaw in the arguments for their existence, but because they could not *do* anything!

While the nature of Israel's God is most basically described by such terms as living, holiness, and oneness, the prophets also proclaim Him to be *just* and to act with *steadfast love.* We have already seen that one of the most central elements in the program of the coming Messiah would be to establish justice—equal justice for rich and poor alike (Isaiah 11:3–4). And, while He might lash out with great anger as He sees the insolence and insubordination of humanity, which threatens to thwart His plans, His love for those same people never wavers. Like the prophet Hosea, who continues to forgive and restore a constantly unfaithful wife, so Yahweh steadfastly reaches out in compassion to His people:[19]

> How can I give you up, O Ephraim!
> How can I hand you over, O Israel!
> . . .
> My heart recoils within me,
> my compassion grows warm and tender.
> I will not execute my fierce anger,
> I will not again destroy Ephraim;
> for I am God and not man,
> the Holy One in your midst,
> and I will not come to destroy.

If the ultimate reality is an all-powerful personality, who acts as He pleases, how comforting to the Israelites was the conviction that He pleases to act with justice and love!

The Biblical writers also dealt with the question of the relationship between YHWH and the physical world. Classical philosophy has sug-

---

[19]Hosea 11:8–9.

gested three possible solutions to the question of the relationship between matter (the world) and spirit (the other):

1. *Materialism*—only matter is real; spirit is illusion.
2. *Dualism*—matter and spirit are both real and co-eternal.
3. *Spiritualism*—only spirit is real; the world is an illusion.

The Bible suggests a fourth point of view. It maintains that spirit *is* the basic stuff of existence, not spirit as force or abstraction, but spirit as person. What originally and always has existed is a person. But then this person *creates* the natural world. The world he creates is real; it is not an illusion. But it is entirely dependent on the will and action of the eternal spiritual person who made it.

The material world, the Bible contends, came out of the exercise of the will of God. It was not made of pre-existing materials. It came forth *ex nihilo*, out of nothing.

Furthermore, it continues to exist only by His power, and only so long as He wishes. According to the Bible, someone has well said, the universe is not a clock, it is a *bicycle*. A master worker might make a clock with such an intricate set of works that it could be wound up and it would run itself for thousands of years. A bicycle, on the other hand, while it is also an intricate machine, will not perform its intended function until a rider gets on and begins to pump. There must be a constant relationship between the bike and rider.

This is the Old Testament picture of God and the world. It is not natural law that holds the world together and keeps it moving. It is the will of God. What a modern scientist might call "law" would be more simply explained by the Biblical writers as simply *the way in which God does things*.

CHAPTER SIX
THE RELIGION OF
JESUS OF NAZARETH

JESUS IN THE GOSPELS

Jesus of Nazareth left no writing of his own. Our sources of information about him are basically three: (1) the four Gospels (Matthew, Mark, Luke, and John) in the New Testament, by far the most important source; (2) the writings of the Apostle Paul, who at least knew many people who knew Jesus, though he himself did not have a close relationship with him during Jesus' public ministry; and (3) a few references to him in non-Christian historical writings of the first and second centuries. These references, however, do little more than establish his historical existence.[1]

It is primarily through the Four Gospels that the story of Jesus has had its impact on the world. While they paint four different portraits of him, a single, remarkable personality emerges from these four accounts.

The picture is one of a Galilean peasant who is a wandering teacher, after the manner of the day. He is what the Greeks call a *peripatetic* teacher who, rather than being settled in a classroom, moves around among people, teaching both the public and a special group of associates who travel with him. Yet his travels cover a very small area, not more than two hundred miles from one extremity to the other.

The Gospels roughly divide his career into two major sections. First

---

[1] See F. F. Bruce, *Jesus and Christian Origins Outside the New Testament* (Grand Rapids, Mich.: Eerdmans, 1974).

there is a time of teaching around the Sea of Galilee, a time often referred to as the *lakeside ministry*. The scene was, and still is, a beautiful one: the deep blue of the water, the green hills surrounding it, the small fishing villages on the shore, the vineyards, and the farms. Jesus travels from village to village saying, "The Kingdom of God is at hand!" It is a period characterized in the Gospels by miracles that Jesus performs in which he exhibits power over pain, over nature, and over the functions and powers of the discarnate or bodiless spirits of evil that torment humanity.

It is also a period of growing controversy between Jesus and the religious leaders of his day. They become more and more antagonistic toward what he is saying and doing. His call for a radical commitment to a new kind of world is seen as a dangerous threat to the status quo.

The second major section of the Gospels' story can be called the *Jerusalem confrontation*. This confrontation lasts only a few days, but the Gospels use almost half their length to describe it. Here the scene changes from the pastoral background of blue water and green hills to the squalid, steamy streets of Jerusalem. The tensions mature into violence and end in Jesus' execution by the Romans.

The reader of the Gospels, when reading these accounts of the events of Jesus' death and its aftermath, must pause to consider the relationship between raw historical events and the meaning of historical events.

The Gospels are not written like the phone book—just to give an accumulation of facts. The Gospels are written to proclaim the *significance* of certain events. They are documents of faith; that is, they are written by people who believe the story they are telling to be the climax of God's dealing with humanity in history. The death of Jesus is not for them a bit of raw data. Rather, somehow, the whole future of the human race is tied up in that death. It is a death somehow so joined to the human condition that it bridges the gap that stands between fallen humanity and God.

This death, say the New Testament writers, is different from any other death that has ever occurred. This was the death of God Himself, translated into history; and so this death is the death of God for humanity. It is God reaching out to bridge the gap. And so, they are saying, all of history had been moving toward that one week in Jerusalem.

These documents, and the ones that follow in the New Testament, frankly advocate this point of view. God has finally touched human existence in the fullest possible way it could ever be done, they say.

WHO WAS JESUS?

Not everyone places the same interpretation on the events in first-century Galilee and Jerusalem as do the Gospel writers. The question,

"Who was Jesus?," has been answered in hundreds of ways.[2] Scholars have noted that the various titles used to refer to Jesus in the New Testament itself (Son of Man, Messiah, Son of God, Lord, etc.) indicate that the precise answer to that quesiton varied even in the earliest days of the Christian movement.[3] As Christianity became a world religion, the answers became increasingly diverse. For several centuries controversies raged as attempts were made at consensus. While consensus was never attained, the view of Jesus that may roughly be styled orthodox has, through the centuries, been the most commonly held by Christians.

It is best to begin by reviewing the chart on Page 75 depicting the view of history propounded by the Hebrew prophets. Christianity built upon this concept rather than replacing it. The new faith offered no new concepts about who God is, or how He acts in history, or what history is, or where it is going. So it becomes possible to make a Christian version of the same chart that is not basically different from the Hebrew one.

The earliest Christians were distinquished from their fellow Jews (all the earliest Christians were Jews) because they believed that the coming of Jesus was the time when God acted most decisively to reveal Himself to humanity. And, they believed, Jesus was the perfect ruler about whom the prophets had dreamed. So the appearance of Jesus was for them the central event in all of history—the time when God most fully revealed Himself to the human race.

This event was not the *end* of history, however. That is obvious! Rather, after God had revealed Himself in Jesus, He gave men and women

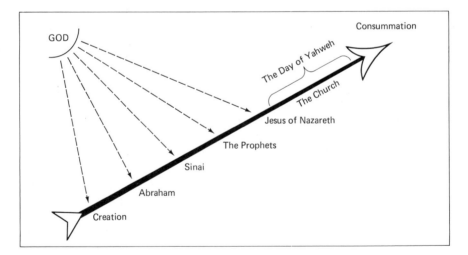

[2]See John Wick Bowman, *Which Jesus?* (Philadelphia: Westminister, 1970), and Hugh Anderson, ed., *Jesus* (Englewood Cliffs, N.J.: Prentice-Hall, 1967).

[3]See James D. G. Dunn, *Unity and Diversity in the New Testament* (London: SCM Press, 1977).

time to decide freely whether or not they will come into His Kindgom. So the meaning of history from the time of Jesus until the time when all is finished is that it is a time of deciding. Before God closes down history, before the arrow hits its mark, people can cast their own votes for or against the Kingdom. Will they commit themselves to a new world order of justice and peace and love? Or will they keep their swords? Will the lamb and the lion lie down together? Or will the law of the jungle continue?[4]

Those persons who decide in favor of the Kingdom are called, among other terms, the *ecclesia* or the "church" (but do not confuse the term with the modern uses of it that emphasize denominational structures). This "church" already begins in its communal life the new relationship of the Kingdom, where people live in peace and love and mutual care.

Jesus is, in this view, the *incarnation of God,* Incarnation meaning "put into flesh." "For in him," says the New Testament, *"all the fulness of God was pleased to dwell,* and through him to reconcile to himself all things, whether on earth or in heaven, making peace by the blood of his cross."[5] What the human eye can see of God can be seen in Jesus. What the human ear can hear of God can be heard in Jesus. What the human mind can comprehend of the mind of God can be comprehended in Jesus.

Jesus, then, did not simply talk about God and His will, as had the prophets, Paul the Apostle maintains. Rather, He *was* God. But God translated into flesh. And, of course, one always loses something in translation. No word in one language has an *exact* equivalent in any other. And certainly any attempt to translate the personality and nature of God into something a human being can understand can be only partially successful. One cannot hear FM stations on an AM radio. Likewise, there are some things about God that the human "receiver" cannot pick up. So, say the New Testament writers, one cannot know everything about God by looking at Jesus, but one can know all that it is humanly possible to know.

Why did God act in this way—through incarnation? Because, say the New Testament writers, as long as God was working through prophets, the knowledge of Him was only second- or thirdhand. The only way in which a truly *complete* communication could take place was through incarnation.

Here is an analogy that might help. Remember that the Biblical position is that humanity is fallen—it has gotten itself seemingly insurmountable difficulties. Now, let us suppose, for purposes of our analogy, that you are a true lover of all living things. And let us suppose that one day you are talking to your next-door neighbor over the fence and he says; "Man, the grasshoppers are eating up my backyard! I've just got to do something about it. I've decided to go down to the nursery and get some strong chemical spray. That should wipe 'em out!"

As you can see, the grasshoppers are in real jeopardy. And you have a

---

[4]See Mark 13:32–37.
[5]Col. 1:19–20. Emphasis added.

passionate sympathy for all living creatures. You do not like to see anything get killed—even grasshoppers. Even grasshoppers that are eating up someone's backyard. In fact, you *love* grasshoppers. It is a kind of irrational love, of course—to love grasshoppers. But you do, anyway.

If only you could warn them! But how do you talk to grasshoppers? You cannot just walk up to a grasshopper and look him in the eye and say, "You better get out of here!"

The grasshopper would only look at you and wiggle its antennae a bit and hop away. It would have no idea what you were talking about. There would be no communication because humans cannot communicate with grasshoppers.

And the reason is that the grasshopper has no way in which to receive the message. It does not have the capacity to understand. It does not know your language.

But suppose that you had it in your power to transform yourself into a grasshopper! Grasshoppers can communicate with each other. Have you ever noticed how they all take off together to avoid an approaching danger? Evidently they have some way of getting a warning to each other. So, by making yourself one of them, you, too, can give them a warning they will understand.

But doing this exposes you to tremendous risk. You make yourself subject to the same poison spray that will come to kill them. By limiting yourself to a grasshopper kind of existence, you have accepted all the risks of grasshopperness.

So, says the Apostle Paul, Jesus,[6]

> though he was in the form of God, did not count equality with God a thing to be grasped, but emptied himself, taking the form of a servant, being born in the likeness of men. And being found in human form he humbled himself and became obedient unto death, even death on a cross.

Or, in the words of the Gospel of John, "the Word became flesh and dwelt among us," and "No one has ever seen God; the only Son, who is in the bosom of the Father, he has made him known."[7]

In Jesus then, the Christians believed that God entered the stream of history in a climatic way. "God was in Christ," says Paul, "reconciling the world to himself."[8]

In modern times the question "Who was Jesus?" has been answered with great diversity again. The long-standing consensus came apart in the general disruption of ancient tradition during the Reformation and rise of secularism—a story we will trace later. Four modern answers to the

[6]Phil. 2:6–7.
[7]John 1:14, 18.
[8]II Cor. 5:19.

question will illustrate the extent of the modern diversity: Jesus the ideal man, Jesus the political revolutionary, Jesus the moralist, and Jesus the existentialist.

First, there have been those who use the term "Jesus" to describe their own culture's *ideal man*. The highest ideals and attributes of a given culture are wrapped in a bundle and that bundle is called "Jesus." This tendency can be seen by examining the portraits that painters of various cultures have created. Medieval Italians painted him as a medieval Italian. Africans painted him with negroid features. The Germans and the English made him a blue-eyed blond. These paintings have been not so much attempts to paint the historical Jesus, who, as a Middle Eastern Semite could scarcely

Visit of the Magi. An early nineteenth century Indian painting of Mary, Joseph, the Wisemen, and the Infant Jesus. (British Museum)

have looked like any of these. They are attempts to say, "Jesus is the best one of us."

Others have suggested that Jesus was a *political revolutionary*. They believe that his phrase "Kingdom of God" was really a political slogan, which later believers piously turned into a theological concept. When he talked about the Kingdom coming, they say, he meant an earthly, material kingdom—a sort of theocracy, regulated by the laws of God—something like the kingdom of Israel in the Old Testament was supposed to be, but never was.

This is actually a very old way of looking at Jesus. The Gospels provide clear evidence that many people thought this way about Jesus from the very first.

Around the turn of the present century, Albert Schweitzer wrote a book called *The Quest of the Historical Jesus.* [9] In it he claimed that Jesus saw himself as the instigator or catalyst who would bring about the fall of the present world order and the appearance of the Kingdom of God. Schweitzer accused the scholars of his day of domesticating Jesus—of making him into the ideal middle-class German. Actually, Schweitzer maintained, he was a somber *apocalypticist* (a believer in the idea that God was going to radically intervene in human affairs and change everything). Sadly, said Schweitzer, Jesus' dream was an empty one: [10]

> There is silence all around. The Baptist appears, and cries: "Repent, for the Kingdom of Heaven is at hand." Soon after that comes Jesus, and in the knowledge that He is the coming Son of Man lays hold of the wheel of the world to set it moving on that last revolution which is to bring all ordinary history to a close. It refuses to turn and he throws Himself upon it. Then it does turn; and crushes Him. . . . The wheel rolls onward, and the mangled body of the one immeasurably great Man, who was strong enough to think of Himself as the spiritual ruler of mankind and to bend history to His purpose is hanging upon it still.

H. J. Schoenfield's best-selling book *The Passover Plot* (1966) suggests that, to establish himself as the Messiah dreamed of by the prophets of Israel, Jesus concocted a clever plot to "fulfill" the prophecies by manipulating events. His plans were foiled, however, when, having had himself drugged to appear dead, a Roman soldier, not in on the scheme, pierced him with a sword and killed him. His plan to "be resurrected" (after the drug wore off) was thwarted, but the story got started anyway. [11]

In *Jesus and the Zealots* (1967), S. G. F. Brandon attempts to tie Jesus to a movement like the first-century Zealots, extreme nationalists and ter-

[9]Albert Schweitzer, *The Quest of the Historical Jesus,* trans. W. Montgomery (New York: Macmillan, 1966).

[10]Ibid., p. 403.

[11]H. J. Schoenfield, *The Passover Plot* (New York: Random House, 1966).

rorists who sought to overthrow the Roman domination of the Jewish state. The Gospels are, he says, a later attempt to transform a guerilla fighter and his associates into spiritual leaders.[12]

A third answer to the question of the identity of Jesus is that of a great *teacher of moral proverbs.* Those who understand Jesus this way believe that his phrase "Kingdom of God" represents a superior moral system, a way of life. This point of view was particularly prominent among the theologic:l liberals of the nineteenth century. The theological movement called "modernism" sought to purge religion of scientifically embarrassing elements like miracles, the supernatural, literal heaven and hell, and so on. These elements in the Gospels were de-emphasized and attributed to primitive superstitions.

What Jesus was *really* doing, they said, once one looked beyond these primitivisms, was to teach the human race a true morality—a way of life that fulfilled all humanity's ethical potential.

This understanding of Jesus was pursued skillfully and beautifully in the writings of Adolf von Harnack (1851–1930), the German theologian. We must, he says, distinguish "what is permanent from what is fleeting, what is rudimentary from what is merely historical" in the Gospels.[13] Once this is done, he says, it will not be misunderstanding Jesus "to say that the Gospel is a matter of ordinary morality."

We have already noted Albert Schweitzer's attack on this interpretation of Jesus. It is, however, one that is still accepted very widely today.

One of the most prevalent views among modern scholars of the modernist tradition is that Jesus was the possessor of a unique God-consciousness, an *existentialist* hero. The most famous name among these scholars was the German New Testament scholar Rudolf Bultmann (1884–1976).[14] Bultmann agreed with Harnack that the primitive trappings in the Gospels must be laid aside. The kernel that was left, however, was not a body of moral proverbs. The thing that Jesus had, and that makes him relevant today, was a unique sense of, and relationship to, the really Ultimate.

Of course Jesus lived in the first century and therefore had to express this consciousness in first-century language rather than in scientific language. The advent of science, says Bultmann, forces us to "demythologize" this language. We no longer can talk about a three-storied universe (heaven-earth-hell). But what can be learned from Jesus is not his understanding of cosmic geography, but his experience with *authentic human existence.* In other words, we must replace the mythological language of the Bible with the language of modern existentialist philosophy. Bultmann

[12]S. G. F. Brandon, *Jesus and the Zealots* (New York: Scribner, 1967).

[13]Adolf von Harnack, *What Is Christianity?* (New York: Harper & Row, 1957), p. 14.

[14]See, for example, Rudolf Bultmann, *The Theology of the New Testament,* 2 vols., trans. Kendrick Grobel (New York: Scribner, 1951–1955), Vol. 1.

believed it is necessary to do this to salvage Jesus as someone significant in the modern scientific age.

THE MESSAGE OF JESUS

There are two major questions about Jesus: "Who *was* he?" and "What did he *say*?" Neither question is easy to answer. We have seen this in our discussion of the first question. We started there because it is hard to know how to regard what Jesus said until at least some tentative conclusions are drawn as to who he was.

Earlier we quoted a Buddhist holy man who said that Gautama the Buddha was gone but had left behind his teachings. Orthodox Christianity claims that Jesus is *not* gone but, rather, that he overcame death and is still active in the lives of those who believe in him. So, from an orthodox Christian view, the teachings of Jesus are only a part of his reality. But those teachings are important, not so much for what they are independently, but because of who they believed *him* to be.

The teachings of Jesus are primarily available to us in the form of the Four Gospels. This complicates things a little, since, as we have seen, Jesus did not write the Gospels himself. Rather, they are written *about* Jesus. And they are very selective. He said much more than what the Gospels have recorded. The Gospel of John says that if everything had been included there would not be enough room in the whole world for all the volumes![15]

Furthermore, the writers do not always use the material about Jesus in exactly the same way. Rather, each of them has his own purposes in explaining the significance of Jesus. The Gospel writers are not trying to give us stenographer's transcripts of his message. His message is, then, filtered through the purposes and individuality of the writers of the Gospels.

This does not mean that his message was necessarily distorted or that the Gospel writers are in some way at odds with him. It does mean that they wrote as a part of a community of believers who could look back upon the events in Jesus' career from a perspective of many years—a fact that affects the way in which they tell the story.

The situation is similar to that of reading a book about the American Revolution. The early chapters of such a book would deal with events occurring before the Revolution, but the chapters would be written from the perspective of the Revolution. The writer has the benefit of hindsight. So he might say that "the Pilgrims landed at Plymouth Rock in 1620, thus helping to establish the United States," or that "Columbus' discovery in 1492 resulted in the establishment of the United States." Of course neither

[15]John 21:25.

the pilgrims or Columbus had such a thing in mind. But from our perspective we can see that both fit into a totality that would only become apparent later.

Likewise, the Gospel writers tell the story of Jesus from the perspective of the last half of the first century. They could see the story in a kind of totality that even the closest disciples of Jesus could not on, say, the day of his execution. And that perspective, the reader must always remember, affects the way in which they tell the story.

The message of Jesus was basically a message about the nature of God. It was, the Christians believed, a revelation from God. Remember that Western religions are characterized by the belief that God reveals Himself—that humanity does not discover God but that God reaches downward to discover humanity. So Jesus' message claims to tell the people what God is like and what God wants. And it begins with the proclamation, "The Kingdom of God is at Hand."

Many hundreds of books have been written about the ramifications of such a seemingly simple statement. We will limit our discussion to only two: the concepts of the Fatherhood of God and the Kingship of God.

Jesus said that the God of the universe, who had created all things, can be called "Father." And if one has the potential to be a "Son of God," then one has a way of understanding himself as having great worth.

Jesus refers to God with the Aramaic word *abba*. He is apparently the only religious leader ever to do so. Abba is the term a small child uses in Aramaic to describe his father. It is very much like the English words "Papa" or "Daddy." Its use implies that the relationship between the human race and the ultimate is like the relationship between a small child and his father.

Jesus' teachings are full of statements about the fatherly care that God has for his children:[16]

> Are not five sparrows sold for two pennies? And not one of them is forgotten before God. Why, even the hairs of your head are all numbered. Fear not; you are of more value than many sparrows.

There is, he says, a tremendous concern on God's part toward every individual human being. He is not an infinite but a blind force. He has the same relationship toward humanity that a human father had toward his children.

And the goal of a human being, Jesus continues, is to "grow up to be like his father."[17] In the Middle East, even today, a young boy grows up at his father's side, watching, copying, learning to be what he is and do as he

[16]Luke 12:6–7.
[17]Matt. 5:48.

does. I have seen the Palestinian potter skillfully forming vases at his wheel, his ten-year-old son beside him watching his every move. The boy will one day sit at the wheel himself, and his own work will find its pattern in the movement of his father's swift fingers. In the same way, says Jesus, humanity must learn what it means to be a person by copying the Ultimate Person. "You must grow up to be like your heavenly Father," he says.

Out of this rule comes the ethical system of Jesus. While Jesus may not have been just a teacher of ethics, he certainly talked about ethics. He taught that certain patterns of behavior are God-like and certain ones are not. The most famous accumulation of ethical statements in the Gospels, the "Sermon of the Mount,"[18] is summarized in its conclusion by the very statement quoted earlier: "You must grow up to be like your heavenly Father."

And the approach one takes to reach this goal, says Jesus, is *internal.* It involves inner change. Jesus' ethic is basically an ethic dealing with things that happen on the inside, because, he says, what happens inside you is what determines how you will act outside—in your relationships with other people. One of the Ten Commandments says "You shall not kill." But, Jesus says, killing is preceded by something internal—hate. So whoever hates his brother is already a murderer. Over and over again he extends or expands the rules and regulations of life, transforming them from mere external codes into statements about the inner self. The change that occurs when one enters the Kingdom is, then, first of all, an *inner transformation.*

But along side the tender figure of God as Father, Jesus places the concept of God as King. "The Kingdom of God is like . . .". This phrase begins many of Jesus' teachings. And if in talking about God as Father Jesus deals with such problems as alienation and personal meaning, in talking about God as King he deals with the meaning of history itself. All religions, we have seen, grapple with questions such as, Why do the things happen that happen? Is there any pattern in the way things happen? Are historical events moving in any particular direction? And if so, what difference does it make?

Jesus begins to answer all these questions with the thesis that God is King. From that concept he draws an understanding of history. It is an understanding rooted firmly in the Old Testament. When he appeared in Galilee saying, "Repent, for the Kingdom of God is at hand," his words were familiar. People had been talking about such a kingdom long before his coming. But most often they had connected the phrase with national victory: "We are the people God has chosen to rule the world. So, when we rule the world, it will be God's Kingdom! And if we cannot develop armies strong enough to do this, God will send down legions of angels to help us wipe out the opposition!"

This idea, which conceived of the Kingdom of God as a kind of

[18]Matt. 5–7.

culture religion, was firmly rejected by Jesus. The term *basileia*, translated as "kingdom," literally means "rule" or "reign." This seems to be the way in which Jesus used it. The Kingdom of God is the reign of God. It is not a political entity based on military achievement. Rather, it is a particular way of being related to God. It is a relationship in which God's will is done. Where this takes place, there is the Kingdom. Wherever God's will is done in history, there is the *basileia tou theou*—the Kingdom of God.

But Jesus seems to talk about the Kingdom in two ways, leading to what scholars call the "now- not yet-paradox." In at least some sense the Kingdom *has* come. Thus he says to a group of disciples once,[19]

> Truly, I say to you, there are some standing here who will not taste death before they see the Kingdom of God come with power.

There was some sense in which Jesus saw the Kingdom coming in his own generation. There was some sense in which the early disciples understood that it *had* come because the words quoted above were written down in the Gospel of Mark many years after Jesus' death. If they had thought he had been in error, they surely would not have quoted him in this way—making him appear to be a false prophet.

The Kingdom had been introduced to history in the coming of Jesus, so thought the early believers, and it had come among them with power.[20] It had come wherever people had accepted the rule of God in their lives and relationships.

And whenever people who had accepted this rule banded themselves together the Kingdom became visible. It could be seen in the way they related to each other and to the world around them. Such a visible expression of the Kingdom of God is called, among other things, an *ecclesia* or a "church." (Unfortunately the English word "church" also means several other things, so perhaps we should use the Biblical word *ecclesia*.)

To summarize: Jesus taught that when an individual accepts the reign of God in one's own life—that God who was revealed by Jesus—he or she enters the Kingdom. And when that individual begins to share his or her life with other people who have accepted this reign also, the result is the *ecclesia*. The Kingdom of God, then, exists where people have accepted the reign of God—individually and collectively.

Yet Jesus also talks as though something remains to happen, as though the Kingdom, while it is *now*, is also *not yet*:[21]

> He said, therefore, "What is the kingdom of God like? And to what shall I compare it? It is like a grain of mustard seed which a man took and sowed in

[19]Mark 9:1.
[20]See Acts 1–2.
[21]Luke 13:18–21.

his garden; and it grew and became a tree, and the birds of the air made nests in its branches."

And again he said, "To what shall I compare the Kingdom of God? It is like leaven which a woman took and hid in three measures of meal, till it was all leavened."

He seems to be saying that the "now" aspect of the Kingdom seems almost insignificant, like a tiny seed or a bit of yeast. But it has infinite potential, far beyond what its present puny appearance might indicate. So it is with the Kingdom. It may presently seem lost in the march of empires of men. It is found only here and there, where one or a few have accepted the reign of God. But *the future belongs to them.* It was this faith that strengthened the early Christians in the face of opposition from the mighty Roman Empire. Despite appearances, they said, when the smoke is cleared *we will triumph.*

To describe that day when the Kingdom becomes all in all, Jesus uses the language of the Jewish apocalypse—the end of the world, the resurrection, the judgment, heaven, hell, the burning of the earth. The point is that one day the Kingdom will leave its mustard seed stage. Following a great revolutionary purge every knee shall bow. Everything will be subject to God's will then, and Eden will be restored.

What, then, is the meaning of the present time? What is the purpose of being alive, and what should one do with one's life? The present time, says Jesus, is a time of decision and preparation. "Therefore, watch," he says. Unfortunately the English word "watch" seems to imply getting up in a tree somewhere and scanning the skies. But the original concept is much more active than that. Watchfulness and expectation express themselves, he says, in doing things. Men in the Kingdom do not sit and wait for "pie in the sky by and by." They seek to be God-like *now.* When God became flesh, what did he do? Why, he went about doing good. Helping the hurting. Feeding the hungry. Calling society to conform itself to the rule of God. The ethic and life-style of the Kingdom, then, becomes a very active one. It is very much involved in all that happens in the world: politically, culturally, economically, philosophically, and artistically.

So the present gains meaning. The Gospel of Matthew gives a picture of God at the Last Judgment commending certain people. "I was hungry and you fed me. I was naked and you clothed me," he says. "When did we do that?" they ask. "When you did it to even the least of your fellowmen, you did it to me," he replies.[22]

The disciples of Jesus were not called to a superficial piety. They could not deck themselves with ascension robes and sit on top of a barn somewhere to wait. They were called, as Jesus was, from the cool green hills of Galilee into the smelly streets of Jerusalem where men are profane and

[22]Matt. 25:21–46.

cruel, where there are open sewers, where there is blood. In wiping the tears of their comrades they were to find the meaning of their own existence.

THE APOSTLE PAUL

Excepting Jesus himself, no other person has had more impact on the Christian faith than has the Apostle Paul.[23] A large portion of the New Testament consists of his correspondence with groups of early believers. The book of Acts is to a large extent a recounting of his exploits as he carried the Christian message into the Graeco-Roman world—from Antioch to Ephesus to Corinth to Rome itself.

The vocabulary of Christian theology is mostly a Pauline vocabulary. No other Christian document has so often reignited the Christian movement as his Epistle to the Romans.

It is primarily in Paul's writings where the action of God in reaching down to humanity is described by terms like *redemption, justification,* and *reconciliation.* The human race has sold itself into slavery, Paul says, slavery to sin, to the flesh, to death, to a host of other masters. Humanity has lost its freedom. But the death of Christ became the payment that won humanity its freedom again—that redeemed it. The human race stands before the bar of justice condemned, he says. But, because of Christ, God the judge pronounces the guilty ones to be innocent. In this way God makes an unrighteous person to be righteous; that is, He justifies that person. That person had become estranged or alienated from God. But Jesus is the way in which God reaches out to the person and offers to restore the lost relationship, that is, "God was in Christ, reconciling the world to himself."[24]

Paul vividly describes the process by which man and God are reunited. Man cannot do anything to save himself. All his righteousness, Paul says, is "like filthy rags." But once God has made his move toward humanity in Christ, people can and must respond. And that response is called faith. "Faith" is a comprehensive word in Paul's writings, involving belief and obedience. But the basic meaning of faith is "utter trust." Humanity is like a nonswimmer who has fallen into deep water. Jesus is like a lifeguard who promises to rescue the victim. But the victim must first give up all attempts to save himself or herself by thrashing about. The victim must catch hold of the lifeguard and depend upon the lifeguard's strength to get him or her to safety.

[23]A simple introduction to Paul's thought may be found in Archibald M. Hunter, *The Gospel According to Paul* (Philadelphia: Westminister, 1966).
[24]II Cor. 5:19.

The person who has done this is described by Paul as being "in Christ" (a phrase that appears in some form over two hundred times in his writings). "For as many of you as were baptized into Christ have put on Christ," he says:[25]

> You were buried with him in baptism, in which you were also raised with him through faith in the working of God, who raised him from the dead. And you, who were dead in trespasses and the uncircumcision of your flesh, God made alive together with him, having forgiven us all our trespasses, having canceled the bond which stood against us with its legal demands; this he set aside, nailing it to the cross.[26]

The person who is "in Christ," Paul continues, has new *life*, not mere biological life, but the kind of life that God lives, a life not subject to deterioration or death. This life begins to work in the person through the power of the Holy Spirit, which dwells within the believer and animates him. Those, then, who are in Christ and who live by the power of his Spirit are drawn together in communal life—the *ecclesia*, which we mentioned earlier. Paul's favorite expression to describe this relationship is "the Body." Those who are in Christ, he says, have become One Body —regardless of racial, cultural, economic, or sexual differences.

Finally, since the power that animates the believer is the same power that raised Jesus from the dead, the person in Christ looks forward to one's own resurrection and to participation in the eternal Kingdom.

[25]Gal. 3:27.
[26]Col. 2:12–14.

CHAPTER SEVEN
THE RELIGIOUS WORLD
OF ISLAM

THE RESURGENCE OF ISLAM

Perhaps not since the days of the Crusades, when European popes and kings sent wave after wave of "Christian" armies to "rescue to holy places" of the Middle East from the followers of the prophet Muhammad, have Christendom and Islam been thrown together with such intensity as in our own time. After years of domination by colonialist powers, the Muslim world is rising up, passionately committed to its ancient faith. Middle Eastern oil, and Western dependence on it, have forceably thrown the two cultures into confrontation. With vast oil income has come political and economic power. The resurgence of cultural and religious pride, accompanied by distaste for Western values, has resulted in revolution and turmoil not always understood in the West. Americans who had never given thought to the Islamic faith have been jolted into awareness, first by sky-rocketing fuel prices and then by the taking of American hostages in Iran in 1979 and the crises that followed. They have listened in bewilderment as American sports figures, such as boxer Mohammed Ali, declared their Muslim faith.

As a Turkish friend conducted me and some of my students into the great Blue Mosque in Istanbul the faces of the students betrayed this same bewilderment. We sat in a corner of the cold building (it was midwinter), shoeless and cross-legged on the richly colored carpets. In another area a group of men were chanting their prayers and the sound bounced to and fro among the ornate domes of the mosque. How could it be—the question was on the students' faces—that here, in what was once the splendid capitol of a vast "Christian Empire," Islam now flourished? Earlier, in Jerusalem, the same students had been awakened in confusion by the loud call to prayer, broadcast electronically from the minarets of the city. They had seen the faithful pour from middle-class stone houses in East Jerusalem into the mosques. Then they had sat among Bedouin desert tribespeople, drinking sweet tea in their cool tents, and heard their parting benediction: "May Allah be with you. We will see you again, if Allah wills."

What is this far-flung religion that dominates the life of more than one fifth of the world's people? It is truly a world religion, stretching from its origins in Arabia throughout the Middle East, North Africa (and, increasingly, central Africa), Pakistan, and central Asia (where the communist Russian government must take note of millions of Muslim subjects), all the way into the islands of Indonesia. In past times it knocked on the doors of Europe, itself—first through Spain in the West and later through Austria in the East. Today it bids well to capture the religious commitment of additional millions, especially in the emerging Third World.

The Muslim faith is "Western" in the sense that its presuppositions correspond far more closely to those of Judaism and Christianity than to those of Eastern religions such as Hinduism and Buddhism. Culturally, however, Islam belongs neither to East nor West, but represents an all-encompassing world view of its own.

Islam's claim to universality is very explicit. The Arabic word *islam* means "submission," "obedience," and "surrender." Thus, explains the famous Muslim teacher Abul A'La Maududi, "As the entire creation obeys the law of God, the whole universe, therefore, literally follows the religion of Islam—for Islam signifies nothing but obedience and submission to Allah, the Lord of the universe."[1] People, he says, insofar as they are physical, and subject to the physical laws of the universe, are Muslim. However, since people possess reason and intellect, they can reject the laws of God in the moral and intellectual realm and thus become "unbelievers." Should such a person decide instead to submit to God in these areas also, "He has, so to say, achieved completeness in his Islam by consciously deciding to obey God in the domain in which he was endowed with freedom and choice. . . . He is a perfect Muslim and his Islam is complete—for this submission of his entire self to the will of Allah is Islam and nothing but Islam."[2]

[1]Sayyid Abul A'La Maududi, *Towards Understanding Islam,* trans. and ed. Khurshid Ahmad (Takoma Park, Md.: International Graphics, 1977), p. 2. A revised and expanded edition of this influential work has appeared under the same title published by The Islamic Foundation, 223 London Road, Leicester, U.K.

[2]Ibid., p. 4.

But how can one come to a knowledge of the will of Allah? In the physical world, reason and research (science) can provide the answer. But only *revelation* can reveal the whole will of God, and, since this lies far beyond the individual's capacity to reason, this revelation must be accepted by faith. Faith in the unseen, coupled with total submission and obedience to the revealed will of Allah is at the heart of Muslim religious life.

THE PROPHET AND ISLAM

For the Muslim, Allah has chosen as His vehicle for revelation the *prophet.* The prophet has been given a special gift by God to reveal His will, and the prophet's message is self-authenticating: "the duty of the common men and women is to recognize a prophet and, after ascertaining that one is the true prophet of God, to have faith in him and his teachings and to scrupulously obey him and follow in his footsteps. This is the road to salvation."[3]

The line of prophets began with Adam, who was not only the first man but the first prophet. As time went by, and humanity fell farther and farther into error and darkness, "God's true prophets were raised in all countries: in every land and people. They all possessed one and the same religion—the religion of Islam."[4] Their differences were only cultural and methodological. Moses, David, and Jesus of Nazareth were all true prophets, according to Muslim teaching. Their teachings were distorted by their later followers, it adds; but these teachings should nevertheless be highly respected.

But the climax of the line of prophethood came, says the Muslim, with the call of an illiterate Arab tribesman named Muhammad. Around the year 610, at the age of about forty, Muhammad underwent a series of deep spiritual experiences that came during solitary vigils. First he thought himself demon possessed, but then became convinced that he was instead a prophet. He described and defended the initial experience in these words:[5]

By the Star when it goes down,—
Your Companion is neither astray nor misled,
Nor does he say [aught] of [his own] Desire.
It is no less than inspiration sent down to him:
He was taught by one Mighty in Power,
Imbued with Wisdom: For he appeared [in stately form]
while he was in the highest part of the horizon:

[3]Ibid., p. 23.
[4]Ibid., p. 32.
[5]Citations from the Qu'ran are from *The Holy Qu'ran,* trans. and commentary A. Yusuf Ali (Indianapolis: American Trust Publications, 1977).

then he approached and came closer,
And was at a distance of but two bow-lengths
        or [even] nearer:
So did [God] convey the inspiration to His Servant—
[Conveyed] what He [meant] to convey.
The [Prophet's] [mind and] heart in no way falsified
        that which he saw.   (LIII:1–10)

At the time when Muhammad's heavenly visitor, the angel Gabriel began to speak to him, society in the prophet's home city of Mecca was in a period of turmoil and transition, as was Arabia in general. The religion was tribal and primitive and centered around gods worshipped in a cubed shaped building called the *Ka'ba*. The prophet spoke out against this polytheism and urged unity among the warring tribes, based on submission to the will of the *one* god—Allah. He was opposed, however, and made only a few converts for the first thirteen years. Finally, he had to flee the city in 622. (The date of this flight, called the *hejra*, is the year 1 on the Islamic calendar.)

Muhammad met with much greater success in the city of Medina, where his prophetic status was accepted. As leader of the city he set out to unite the outlying tribes and in 630 conquered Mecca itself and cleansed the Ka'ba of its idols. At the time of his unexpected death in 632 Muhammad was the most powerful man in Arabia and had presented his people with a new world view and sense of community. His successors continued a march of conquest through Syria, Iraq, Palestine, Egypt, North Africa, Spain, and central Asia. The peoples of almost all these lands remain Muslim today, along with millions more in India, Pakistan, Bangladesh, Indonesia, and Turkey.

The career of Muhammad, according to Muslim teaching, was the "finality of prophethood." The message of earlier prophets has been adulterated, they believe, but his has been perfectly preserved. Furthermore, his message is complete (and thus needs no expansion) and universal (so that no more need exists for separate prophets to each culture, as had been the case earlier).

"Now, therefore," says Abul A'La Maududi, "the only source for the Knowledge of God and His Way is Muhammad (peace be upon him). We can know of Islam only through his teachings which are so complete and so comprehensive that they can guide men for all times to come. Now the world does not need any new prophet; it needs only such people as have full faith in Muhammad (peace be upon him), who become the standard bearers of his message, propagate it to the world at large, and endeavor to establish the culture which Muhammad (peace be upon him) gave to man."[6]

[6]Maududi, *Towards Understanding Islam*, p. 63.

The last sentence in this statement is significant because it points to the fact that Islam is a term that covers not just religious life, but every aspect of culture: art, economics, politics, and so on. It allows no concept of a separate "secular" life for the believer. Thus, as one Muslim scholar has said, "one cannot be a Muslim and have a western culture. Islam cannot be an ingredient in culture—it *is* a culture."[7]

THE FAITH OF ISLAM

Westerners, often critical and skeptical of their own religious heritage, are amazed and sometimes bewildered by the intensity of Muslim faith. A person who would willingly die for his or her religious convictions, while such an action is common to all world religions, is nevertheless something of a rarity in the modern West.

On April 20, 1979, an Islamic holy Friday, a column of tanks and armored personnel carriers entered Kerala, a small town in eastern Afghanistan.[8] The men of the devoutly Muslim community were herded unarmed into a field and were upbraided violently for helping Muslim rebels in the hills, who were fighting the Russian-dominated and secular central government. The women gathered in the nearby mosque, in sight of the field. "Why had the people of the town refused to fight for the government? Why had they instead given supplies to the rebels?" the soldiers demanded.

One more chance would be given to them. The soldiers surrounded the men and pointed their AK-47 automatic rifles at them. Then came the command: the men were to shout pro-communist slogans and cry "Hooray for the regime!" Instead, and in spite of the obvious consequences, the men shouted, "Allah o Akbar" (God is the Greatest).

At the order of a young Russian officer, the soldiers opened fire. During the next five minutes an estimated 1,170 men and boys died. The women rushed from the mosque, screaming and raising copies of the Qur'an (the collection of the revelations to Muhammad), pleading for mercy. But they were driven back while the soldiers bulldozed the bodies of the victims into trench graves.

All religions have had their martyrs, of course. But such a story illustrates the intensity of Muslim faith in at least some parts of the contemporary world.

---

[7]Mahmoud Abu Saud, "Islam," lecture presented at Southwest Missouri State University, Springfield, Missouri, 10 December 1979. The author is grateful for Mr. Saud's generous assistance in reading and commenting on this chapter.

[8]"A Grim Chapter in Afghanistan War," *Christian Science Monitor,* 4 February 1979, Sec. 1, pp. A1, A10.

Five articles of faith form the foundation for the religion of Islam: Faith in the oneness of God, in the angels of God, in the books of God, in the prophets of God, and in the reality of life after death.

The oneness of God.   The primary statement of Islamic faith is *La ilahā illallah* (There is no diety but Allah). "It is the expression of this belief," says Abul A'La Maududi, "which differentiates a true Muslim from a *Kafir* [unbeliever], a *Mushrik* [one who associates others with God in His divinity], or a *Dahriya* [atheist]."[9] Allah is for the Muslim an absolute, infinite, conscious power, not in any way divisible, and having no father, mother, or offspring. He created everything and everything is subjected to His will. As one modern Muslim put it, "The innate power within atoms is the order of Allah."

> God! There is no god
> But He-the Living,
> The Self-sustaining, Eternal.
> No slumber can seize Him
> Nor sleep. His are all things
> In the heavens and on earth.   (II:255)

It should be stressed that this belief is not simply theoretic for the believer. Its implications dominate every facet of the believer's life. A shady business deal or a shabby bit of carpenter work may bring the exclamation, "But that is not *la ilaha illallah!*"

The angels.   Those beings often worshipped as gods are, instead, taught the Prophet, the angels of Allah who administer His Kingdom, but do not share in His divinity. They watch each person and keep a complete record in preparation for the Day of Judgment. Since their precise nature cannot be known by man the Muslim accepts their reality as an act of faith. The prophets, however, experienced them directly:

> He doth send down His angels
> with inspiration of His command,
> To such of His servants
> As he pleaseth, [saying]:
> "Warn [Man] that there is
> No god but I: so do
> Your duty unto Me.   (XVI:2)

The Books of God.   As we have seen, Muslims accept the legitimacy of many prophets. Some of these left "books" inspired by God as a revelation

[9]Maududi, *Towards Understanding Islam*, p. 65.

to humanity. The books of Abraham, they say, have been lost. The Torah of Moses, the Zaboor (Psalms) of David, and the Injeel (Gospel) of Jesus Christ have survived, but not in their original texts. Rather, they have all suffered serious corruption and pollution. Nevertheless they should be respected for the truth that has survived in them, and their adherents, called "people of the book," are likewise to be given special respect not afforded pagans or followers of the Eastern religions.

It is the Qur'an, however, that crowns the Books of God. It is not, like the other books, a mixture of error and truth, God's word and humanity's.

From the Shahnameh (Book of Kings). A Persian manuscript, 1614. (New York Public Library)

It is not, like them directed to a particular culture but to all humankind, and in a living language rather than a dead one. Its message, unlike the partial one in the other books, is absolutely complete. Unlike them, it is perfectly preserved and "exists exactly as it had been revealed to the Prophet; not a word—nay, not a dot of it—has been changed. It is available in its original text and the Word of God has now been preserved for all times to come."[10]

The Qur'an is, of course, the collection of the revelations of the Prophet, set in writing. This book, comparable in length to the New Testament, presents the oracles without regard to chronological or theological system. The systematizing of the Faith came later, and for a long time Muslim theology was developed primarily as a means to distinguish Islam from the religions around and before it.

One is struck by the great amount of material in the Qur'an that seems to originate in the Hebrew Scriptures, although with a definitely different perspective. Abraham, Moses, Joseph, David, Solomon, and others appear regularly on its pages. So does Jesus of Nazareth and his mother Mary. Muhammad is known to have come in contact with Jews and Christians. He suffered great disappointment when they did not accept his own message as completing and superseding that of their own prophets. Muslims would explain the Hebrew materials in the Qur'an as due to their common origin, Allah speaking to his various prophets independently of each other. Non-Muslims might suspect that Muhammad was indeed influenced theologically by both of the older faiths—but especially Judaism. His contact with Christianity and Christian literature seems to have been limited to unorthodox Christians who lived or traded in Arabia. Jesus' virgin birth is accepted in the Qur'an, but the story is not the same as that in the Christian Gospels, and it ends with a denial of Jesus' divinity: "It is not befitting (the majesty of) God that He should beget a son" (XIX:35).

Questions not dealt with specifically in the Qur'an are often answered by recourse to the *Hadith*—the traditions about what the Prophet did and said and approved of as true and right. The material available here is massive, and Muslim scholars admit that it is a mixture of truth and legend and must be subjected to literary criticism. Hadith studies permit Muslims to react with some flexibility to new historical situations.

The prophets of God.   We have already outlined the important characteristics of this item of Faith: the multiplicity of prophets who have partially revealed the will of God, and the final, climactic and perfect revelation to Muhammad.

---

[10]Maududi, *Towards Understanding Islam*, p. 82.

Life after death.   Muslim "eschatology," a religious teaching about the "last things" (i.e., the end and completion of history), includes belief in a Day of Judgment when the dead shall be raised and given rewards or punishments according to the dictates of justice. Then comes life after death, lived either in paradise or hell. This belief is considered so important that "denial of life after death makes all other beliefs meaningless."[11] It is the major incentive for doing good and refraining from evils since one's actions always have meaning and result in consequences beyond the present moment. Decisions must always be made, then, with an eye toward the Day of Judgment:

> The trumpet shall be
> Sounded, when behold!
> From the sepulchres [men]
> will rush forth
> To their Lord!
>
> They will say: "Ah!
> Woe unto Us! Who
> Hath raised us up
> From our beds of repose?"
> [A voice will say:]
> "this is what [God]
> Most Gracious had promised . . . (XXXVI:51–52)

The reward for those who have submitted to Allah and accumulated good deeds is poetically pictured as in a beautiful Eden-like place,

> Among Gardens and Springs;
>
> Dressed in fine silk
> And in rich brocade,
> They will face each other;
>
> Go; and We shall
> Join them to Companions
> With beautiful, big,
> And lustrous eyes.
>
> There can they call
> For every kind of fruit
> In Peace and security.
>
> Nor will they there
> taste death, except the first

[11]Ibid., p. 88.

Death; and He will preserve
them from the Penalty
of the Blazing Fire . . . (XLIV:52–56)

THE FIVE PILLARS OF ISLAM

As there are five bedrock articles of faith for the Muslim, there are also five acts of worship that are required as the primary duties of the believer, the "five pillars of islam": *testimony, prayer, alms-giving, fasting,* and *pilgrimage.* Each of these responsibilities is to be carried out in a carefully prescribed way.

Testimony.   The true Muslim must declare with sincere conviction the *Shahadat:*

> *There is no God but Allah,*
> *And Muhammad is his messenger.*

In this brief creed the believer asserts both the absolute oneness of God and the climax and completion of revelation in the message of the Prophet.

Prayer.   *Salat* is the prescribed prayers that the faithful must repeat five times each day, either alone, or with the community gathered at the mosque (the Muslim house of worship), especially on Friday (the Muslim holy day). From the tower (or minaret) of the mosque the call to prayer rings out across the neighborhood before sunrise (this is the call that jolted my students from sleep in Jerusalem), at midday, before sunset, at sunset, and after sunset. Long lines of Muslim men on their knees, heads touching the ground, chanting together, have become a common sight on American television. Often in the front row can be seen a king, or prince, or prime minister, humbling himself before Allah.

Alms-giving.   *Zakat,* or the giving of alms, is an obligation of the Muslim. Believing that Allah owns everything, the believer must contribute a portion of his own goods (sometimes figured at the minimum rate of 2.5 percent of his wealth) so that the poor of Islam have at least a minimum standard of living. In some cases this "gift" (or tax) is collected by the government in Muslim countries and applied to social welfare projects.

Fasting.   Fasting has the effect, in the Muslim view, of freeing man from slavery to his own desires. During one lunar month—*Ramadan*—no food or drink whatsoever may be taken during daylight hours. "Each and every moment during our fast we suppress our passions and desires and,"

Muhammad riding Borakh (a mare with human head) on his journey to the Seventh Heaven, and his meeting with Adam. From a fifteenth century Turkish manuscript. (New York Public Library)

says Abul A'La Maududi, "proclaim, by our doing so, the supremacy of the Law of God."[12]

Pilgrimage.   Muslims who can afford it are obligated, at least once in their life, to make the *hajj,* or the pilgrimage, to the city of Mecca. Nowadays the pilgrims often arrive in sleek jetliners, pouring into the sacred city by the hundreds of thousands. In ancient times the journey was much harder and more dangerous and represented great faith and courage. Every Muslim, king and pauper alike, dresses exactly the same and carries out the rituals in the same way. The central ritual is the circling seven times of the *Ka'ba,* the cube-shaped building cleansed of idols by Muhammad himself. The circling begins and ends at the mysterious "black stone" (probably a meteorite). Animal sacrifices are made during this time, in commemoration of the sacrifice of Abraham, which Muslims believe took place at this site. Non-Muslims are forbidden to enter the sacred places (although they are welcome at all other mosques in the world).

Other duties.   In addition to faithful observance of the "five pillars," the Muslim submits himself to the *shari'ah,* the detailed code of ethical and social conduct. The *shari'ah* has been formulated with differing details by several different schools or *fiqhs,* but each school recognizes the validity of the others. Also, the believer is called on to "jealously guard and uphold the prestige of Islam." It is in this context that Muslims speak of *jihad* or "holy war." Jihad refers to "the war that is waged solely in the name of Allah and

The Holy Ka'ba

[12]Maududi, *Towards Understanding Islam,* p. 82.

against those who perpetrate oppression as enemies of Islam." When an Islamic state is attacked by a non-Muslim power, every citizen must fight. If necessary, neighboring Muslim countries must help, and if this is not enough, "then the Muslims of the whole world must fight the common enemy." The powerful effect of such a belief can be seen in the Qu'ranic injunction that, in Abul A'La Maududi's words, "Jihad is as much a primary duty of the Muslims concerned as are the daily prayers or Fasting. One who shirks it is a sinner. His very claim to being a Muslim is doubtful."[13]

As is the case in all the other supracultural "world" religions, Islam is not a monolith but is divided into various sects. The major division is between the *Sunnis* and the *Shi'ites*. *Sunnah* means "the way" and refers to the Muslim's commitment to live *the way* Muhammad lived, that is, in obedience to the revelation given to him. *Shi'ah* means "pertaining to" and arises from the dispute over who should succeed Muhammad. Those who followed his cousin Ali, in particular the Persians, were called the *Shi'ah of Ali*. At first there was little doctrinal difference between the two branches, but later the Shi'ites developed some distinctive beliefs. In particular, they hold that the first twelve *imams*, or leaders, were chosen divinely and guided directly by Allah and thus may even be considered infallible. The very great respect given to modern imams is partially responsible for the popular support given to the Ayatola Khomeini by the faithful in Iran during the confrontation with the United States over the taking of American hostages in 1979.

[13]Ibid., p. 107.

CHAPTER EIGHT
RELIGION AND ETHICS

ETHICS ARE INEVITABLE

Time and again our preface to religious studies has led us to discussions about human behavior. What is right behavior and what is wrong? What is good and what is bad? How do people make decisions and on what principles do such decisions rest? The study of such questions is called *ethics*.

George W. Forell begins his book, *The Ethics of Decision,* with these words:[1]

> The crucial question confronting our age is the question of ethics. How are we to establish right and wrong? How can we tell good from evil? No doubt this problem has always been important. However, in other ages the answer seemed far simpler. People assumed that they had the answer. They were sure that the moral laws of their society were valid. There might be perverse individuals who habitually transgressed against these laws, but everyone was convinced that this was the fault of these people and not the fault of the laws.
>
> It has been left to our age to deny the possibility of guilt. We are not sure that there is such a thing as right and wrong or good and bad. And this complete uncertainty about moral values is at the root of the terrible confusion of our age.

Many modern observers have noted a pattern of psychological, philosophical, and theological disintegration that has occurred in our

[1]George W. Forell, *The Ethics of Decision* (Philadelphia: Fortress, 1955), pp. ix, x.

century (see Chapter Eleven). Forell adds the disintegration of ethics to this list. People used to believe that they knew what was right and what was wrong. Perhaps they realized and admitted that they were not living up to the standards of their society, but at least they believed there *were* standards. But a prevalent conviction in the present age is, not so much that certain people break the laws, but that no real laws of behavior exist. Or at least, if such laws exist, men and women have no clear way of knowing what they are. Recent generations find themselves set adrift on a sea of ethical indecision, wondering whether such words as "right" and "wrong" and "good" and "bad" have any real content. Are these, perhaps, no more than categories that died at the coming of the modern age?

Actually, ethics are inevitable. Once one becomes conscious, decision making is the most elementary act of living. From the moment you wake up until you fall asleep again, life is a series of decisions. Of course you do some things without making a conscious decision to do them. You may find yourself standing bleary eyed in front of your mirror some morning, toothbrush in hand, without ever making a conscious decision to get up or to brush your teeth. But such habits grow out of earlier decisions. Most of the time we are consciously deciding what to do next.

Some behavior, it is true, can be called "pre-ethical." Someone throws an object in your direction. You duck. But you did not decide to duck. You blink your eye. But you did not decide to blink your eye. The doctor taps your knee with his little hammer. Your knee jerks. But you did not decide to jerk your knee. These are mere reflex actions. No conscious decision was made. They can, therefore, be called pre-ethical.

The natural unevaluated functions of the body are also pre-ethical. Little babies just do what comes naturally. Most of the time such behavior is pretty messy, but you cannot blame the baby. The baby did not really *decide* to do what he or she did. The same thing can be said about the actions of senile persons or of the mentally retarded. These people make no judgments as to the rightness or wrongness of their actions. They simply act without thinking in response to physical urges that occur. But the rest of us, most of the time, have no choice but to choose.

Not that we do not constantly try to find ways to avoid choices, or at least to avoid the responsibility for our choices. For many centuries men have sought in various ways to prove that people really do not decide things for themselves. Actually, according to this way of thinking, everything is *predetermined*. "Determinism" is the name for the idea that people are not responsible for their actions because everything has already been preplanned. Humans do no more than just follow the script.

The tremendous current interest in astrology may be a case in point. Some astrologers maintain that much of what happens to us is predetermined. I once heard a woman ask an astrologer whether she and her husband would ever get along. "No," he replied with great assurance. "Why?" she asked. "Because your signs clash!" he replied. "He is one kind of person; you another. That was decided on the day of your birth. The clash is inevitable." And presumably no one is really to blame for it.

It is interesting that in periods when people become very unsure about ethics they are attracted to deterministic systems like the astrological one mentioned. There is no use worrying about it, such systems say. Your fate was long ago sealed in the stars. You will simply do what you are destined to do. Therefore, you bear no responsibility for your actions, though you may often experience either triumph or tragedy through them.

In a slightly different way autonomous scientific humanism often seems to conclude that determinism frees people of personal responsibility. In this case it is not the stars that cause you to act the way you do; rather, it is your genes, your environment, your heredity, and the life situation in which you unwittingly find yourself. Actions are not so much the result of personal decisions as they are the outcome of various scientific chains of cause and effect. The humanist sometimes finds that he or she has surrendered his or her freedom not to the will of God, or to the stars, but to scientific casualty. My height, my weight, my mental capacity, the chemical balance in my brain, the kind of community in which I live, my social status—these are the scientific factors that totally determine why I act and decide in the ways I do.

The problem with such theories is that they tend to violate our experience. If we are conscious of anything at all, we are conscious of making decisions. We do not experience a sense of being driven by forces beyond ourselves. Admittedly we may sometimes experience feelings of depression and find ourselves sitting in a dark room feeling low—confident that the whole world is pushing us around. Sometimes we become so emotionally "frozen" that action seems impossible. But the most common human experience is the experience of making choices—of *deciding* what to do next.

That is not to say that there are not in truth tremendous outside pressures that interfere with our freedom to choose, but only that these pressures almost never are so great that we can claim that they free us from personal responsibility for the decisions we have made.

I once had a very interesting discussion with a social worker on this point. He worked with juvenile delinquents. One day we sat together on a log at a summer camp, watching some of his charges play softball. "You know," he mused, "according to many of the behavior theories I have studied, these kids have done what they have done through no choice of their own. They got off to a very bad start. Their parents didn't love them. They have had traumatic experiences. They have suffered discrimination. Still, when you get right down to it, when a fifteen-year-old boy picks up a brick *he* decides whether or not to throw it through a filling station window.

What you have is a boy, a window, and a brick. And it is the *boy* who decides what will happen next."

So, despite theories to the contrary, we continue to consider ourselves responsible for at least the majority of our own decisions. We continue to operate our legal system from this point of view. One will seldom get a verdict of innocent in a court of law by claiming that a third-grade teacher once hit you with a ruler and so warped your little psyche that you later robbed a bank!

You did it, says the judge, so you must pay for it. Our society continues to operate on the thesis that individuals can decide what to do next and that they are therefore personally responsible for what they decide. Without such a thesis, civilized life is impossible.

The only choice humans cannot make is the choice to not choose. They cannot escape their freedom. They are bound to be free, whether they like it or not. They are forced to live a life of constant and unavoidable decisions.

The human condition is like that of a man sitting in a nice soft chair. Suddenly he receives word that someone has planted a bomb in the upholstery timed to go off in five minutes. He cannot simply sit still and say "I'll just let things work themselves out." That is really nothing but a choice to allow oneself to be blown into smithereens.

One seldom has the luxury of "just letting things work themselves out." Every new morning presents a long series of decisions. And even saying "I believe I'll just stay in bed" is a choice! You are told you have a serious disease and need an operation. You reply, "I will not decide about having an operation." What you have done is decided not to have it!

Life, then, is decision.

RELIGION AND THE ROOTS OF ETHICAL DECISION

People who decide things must obviously have some standard by which to make those decisions. They must have some way in which to measure the relative merits of deciding this way or that. The measuring stick people use is something very much like what we earlier termed "ultimate concern." It is a standard so basic that everything else is judged by it. Even the most superficial decisions involve something far back within us that approves or disapproves of what we decide. Why do some decisions appear good and some bad? Is it not this deep-seated concern, this basic set of presuppositions and beliefs, that really determines how we decide?

People tend to commit themselves to one or perhaps a few basic ideas that are regarded as *true*. All other ideas and actions are then judged by these. Those actions that are consistent with these ideas are "good"; those that are inconsistent are "bad."

This process constitutes the main connection between religion and ethics. Religion, defined essentially, is one's ultimate concern. One's ethics are simply the way in which one reacts to life, based on that ultimate concern. Whenever one acts in contradiction to it, one has acted in what for that person was an unethical way. And since various people hold to many, many different concerns, there exist many, many different ethical systems.

We will look at some of the major systems, dividing them into the categories suggested by Forell in *The Ethics of Decision.* These categories are:

    Prudential ethics
    Esthetic ethics
    Idealistic ethics
    Theistic ethics

Prudential Ethics

Whenever one asks, "What am I living for? What are my goals?," and then develops a system of behavior that will help one to reach those goals, one has created a *prudential* ethical system. Prudential ethics are goal oriented. Things that thwart us in reaching our goals are "wrong." We will take note of two kinds of prudential ethics: hedonism and naturalism.

The goal of the *hedonist* is quite simple: to gain pleasure. Acts that are painful or lead to pain are bad. There are two kinds of hedonists: individualistic and universalistic.

The *individualistic hedonist's* goal is personal pleasure. These people seek to live no one else's life and want no one to live theirs. They are not especially concerned to discover what makes *you* happy; rather, they search for what makes *them* happy. They are not necessarily selfish persons who never help anyone else. But they will be quick to admit that they help only because it gives *them* pleasure to do so. The magazine *Playboy* and its host of competitors seem to presuppose that their readers are primarily individualistic hedonists.

Two objections are often lodged against this ethical system. The first is that it tends to atomize society, setting every person off against every other person. If all of us are simply seeking our own pleasure, then the only possible value and meaning you can have for me is the amount of pleasure you can give me. Furthermore, you will often get in my way as I reach out for pleasure, causing me to try to push you aside as an unwanted rival.

A whole society of individualistic hedonists could only create a sociological mess. But a few are able to survive quite well—by leaving the social responsibilities to others.

The second objection to individualistic hedonism is that, taken as a

whole, life offers more pain than pleasure. The average human life involves more suffering than joy. This has been the consistent human experience. So, if I really want to avoid pain, why should I live another forty
years, looking for a bit of pleasure here and there, all the while suffering?
The most efficient way in which to avoid all that pain would be to end my
life now and avoid all that future suffering. An ancient Alexandrian
philosopher named Hegesias actually suggested this approach. He was
finally expelled from the city when too many of his disciples took his
advice! (For some reason he never took his *own* advice—perhaps he felt
that someone has to stay around to get the truth out.)

The second kind of hedonist is the *universalistic hedonist.* This person's
goal is to act so as to ensure the greatest good for the greatest number of
people. Pleasure is still the goal, but it is not to be sought in terms of
individual pleasure. Rather, whatever gives the most people pleasure is
right. Personal pleasure must bow to majority pleasure. This system is
much more social in its orientation. It protects against a society in which
everyone simply does his or her own thing without any concern about what
pain that may cause others.

Critics point out, however, that some problems remain. Who, for
example, will decide what is the greatest good for the greatest number?
And who will decide what is "good"? In practice, would not these decisions
be made by the power elite? Would they not decide what is good for the rest
of us and proceed to force it upon us?

Also, say the critics, universalistic hedonism can be used to justify the
oppression of minority groups. In the early years of this century the Turks
slaughtered thousands of Armenians within their borders. This presumably made life more pleasurable for the Turks who were the majority.
Within the last decade great numbers of Chinese living in Indonesia were
massacred, simply because they were Chinese. This also, presumably, gave
the majority pleasure. And then there is the elimination of millions of Jews
by the Nazis. In each case, one might argue that, after all, there are only a
few of these people, compared with the rest of us. And they cause the rest
of us unhappiness. We would enjoy ourselves more if they were not
around. Their elimination would bring the greatest good for the greatest
number. So eliminate them!

The second type of prudential ethics, one that is based on a different
premise from hedonism, is called *naturalism.* In this ethical system the goal
is to identify oneself with the goals of nature. Humans must align themselves with the natural process. Nature's way is right; to act "unnaturally" is
wrong.

Naturalism as a basis for ethics is often tied very closely with evolutionary philosophy. It presumes that the evolutionary process is "good,"
that things naturally evolve into better things. The naturalist ethicist looks
at the famous chart showing the evolutionary development of the horse

and immediately concludes that the little creature at the bottom of the chart is an "inferior" horse, whereas the sleek beast at the top is a "superior" one.

If the evolutionary process is "good," then whatever interferes with that process is "bad." This principle becomes a basis for decision making, for determining right and wrong.

Modern scientific humanists have generally applied the evolutionary theory to every area, not just to biology but also to history, sociology, and psychology. Thus the naturalist sees the source for ethical standards as coming not only from the field of biology but also from such areas as politics and economics, as they are interpreted in an evolutionary way. Our own century has been strongly influenced by three forms of naturalism: fascism, communism, and capitalism.

The fascists, that is, the Nazis, applied the evolutionary principles of natural selection and survival of the fittest in a rather straightforward manner. In their opinion, these principles, because natural, were "right." And they applied not only to the lower animals, but to people as well. Some individuals, indeed some entire races, are biologically superior to others. It is "right" for these individuals and races to survive and "wrong" for the inferior ones to survive. By eliminating the weak, one joins forces with evolution in creating a "master race"—the very pinnacle of the evolutionary process. The elimination of people who are going to have inferior children, people who are racially inferior, people who are mentally or culturally inferior, people who make no contribution is moral because it is *natural*.

After all, what happens to a deer who loses a leg or is diseased? The healthy animals in the herd do not make arrangements for such a poor creature to enter a "home for handicapped deer"! They simply move on and leave the inferior individual. Then a mountain lion drags it down and eats it. All this is good, because it ensures that only strong and healthy deer will survive and have offspring, thus ensuring an upward evolution and "better" deer in the future.

The same principle applies, says the naturalist, to human beings. A human being who cannot cope with life is going to have children who cannot cope with life either. Of course in a society like ours the ability to cope depends more on mental capacity than on physical strength. So, the naturalist might argue, "Let's eliminate anyone with an I.Q. of 100 or below. Otherwise, the rest of us will always have to feed them and take care of them. They will always be on welfare. It is an unnatural thing to let such people reproduce. So at the very least we should sterilize them."

The issue suggested here did not die with the Nazis. Recent news reports describe a new medical technique that enables doctors to determine whether a given fetus is going to be mentally deficient or not. And what shall we do if the test shows that the child will have a very low I.Q.? Do we abort it? How do we determine who has a right to breathe the air and who does not? How do we determine who can live a "meaningful" life and who cannot? The Nazis, of course, had little trouble with such questions.

The communist ethic is a second kind of naturalism. The Marxist conceives of nature progressing not so much biologically, toward a master race, as sociologically, toward a perfect political system: the stateless state. This future utopia will be the result of a natural process called the "dialectic." And the dialectic works itself out in the conflict of classes. The clash of class against class (thesis versus antithesis) results in a higher social form (the synthesis). Any action or policy, then, that encourages class conflict is a "good" act, because conflict is necessary to keep the evolutionary process in operation.

This helps to explain the motivation of the terrorist. How, do you ask, can anyone possibly consider throwing a bomb into a crowd and blowing innocent people into pieces to be a "good" act? It is "good" in this view because it is an effective instrument of social change. Terrorist acts seem almost incredibly cruel. Yet terrorists themselves are hardly vicious monsters with blood dripping out of their mouths. More often they are highly sensitive persons convinced that what they are doing is "good" since the chaos and hate they create contributes to the heightening of class conflict—and thus helps bring on utopia.

"I must try to get black people and white people, rich people and poor people, young people and old people, very angry with each other," so says the terrorist. "Violence and terror will lead to hate, and hate will lead to conflict, and conflict will result in a higher social order." In this way, acts that other ethical systems would consider grossly immoral are thought to be moral indeed.

A third contemporary form of naturalism, which also has utopian goals, is *laissez-faire capitalism.* This kind of capitalism holds that there are natural economic laws that, if left alone, will ensure a good life for everyone. Untrammeled, unregulated, free market competition is the natural law of the universe. Dabbling with this law will bring economic chaos and an "unnatural" world order.

The *laissez-faire* system, on the other hand, will ensure that those who deserve to have money will have it, and those who do not will not. Such a system, it claims, will put the world's resources where they belong.

On the other hand, heavy taxation of the rich or government regulations on business activity will interfere with the natural order. Government should leave well enough alone, and as a result the "cream will rise to the top." Never mind that those on top may drive other people out of business, or bilk the consumer, or pay such low wages that millions are kept in poverty. All of this is "natural" and therefore "right."

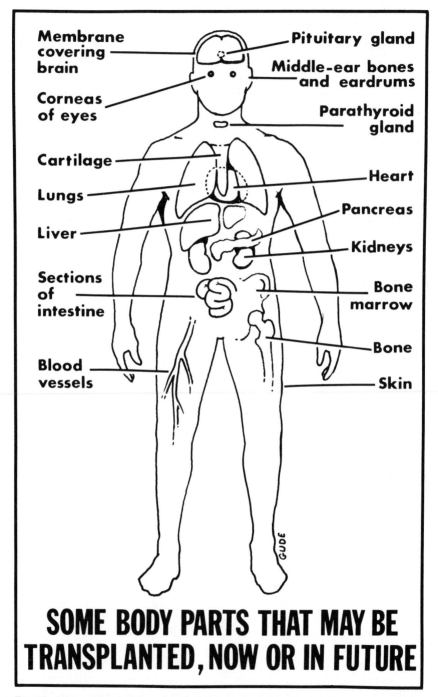

Membrane covering brain

Corneas of eyes

Cartilage

Lungs

Liver

Sections of intestine

Blood vessels

Pituitary gland

Middle-ear bones and eardrums

Parathyroid gland

Heart

Pancreas

Kidneys

Bone marrow

Bone

Skin

GUDE

SOME BODY PARTS THAT MAY BE TRANSPLANTED, NOW OR IN FUTURE

Transplant surgeons, researchers, and medical educators seek donations of body parts and entire bodies after death. Medical technology makes constant re-evaluations of past ethical standards necessary. (UPI)

Esthetic Ethics

The second major ethical category is *esthetic ethics*. Prudential ethical systems are future oriented or goal oriented. Esthetic ethical systems are not. They usually begin with the premise that life is ultimately meaningless. Life is headed nowhere. There is no future. All we have is now—this moment.

An act, then, is a "good" act when it is an act in which one takes hold of now. One dominates the moment. One fills it with one's own meaning. One makes something of it. An act is "bad" when it simply lets time and circumstances slip away without grasping them for one's own use.

So it is not the *result* of an act that makes it "good," according to esthetic ethics. It is the act itself. What is good is that you acted—that *you* acted.

The hero of this system, sometimes called the existentialist ethic, is the person who acts. He or she may have acted outlandishly, cruelly, violently—it does not matter. The action becomes heroic because, while everyone else was standing idle, this person was doing something. This person was grasping the moment.

Thus, says Simone de Beauvoir in her book *The Ethics of Ambiguity,* "Man fulfills himself with the transitory or not at all."[2]

Remember Albert Camus' *Myth of Sisyphus?* Life, he suggested, is nothing more meaningful than the act of carrying the same stone to the top of the same hill, over and over again.[3]

> But what does life mean in such a universe? Nothing else for the moment but indifference to the future and a desire to use up everything that is given.

"We must imagine Sisyphus happy," Camus stated. Sisyphus had to take what he had, for all its meaninglessness, and make something of it. It was *nothing,* but he *made* it something. He asserted his freedom in the face of nothingness. He was, therefore, an existentialist hero.

Idealistic Ethics

The third major ethical category is *idealistic ethics.* Idealistic ethical systems are not based on a desired goal, as are prudential ethics, or on presumed natural laws, as are naturalistic ethics, or on exercising one's freedom, as are esthetic ethics. Rather, these are systems that hold that there is some ideal outside the individual to which the individual must

[2]Simone de Beauvoir, *The Ethics of Ambiguity* (New York: Philosophical Library. 1948), p. 127.

[3]Albert Camus, *The Myth of Sisyphus and Other Essays,* trans. Justin O'Brien (New York: Knopf, 1955), p. 60.

conform his or her behavior. "Good" acts are those that are compatible with this exterior ideal. We will briefly note two kinds of idealistics ethics: intuitionalism and rationalism.

The *intuitionalist* believes that there is an ethical ideal exterior to human beings that they are able to discover through the use of a special inner ethical sense. Just as we learn about much that is exterior to us through the five physical senses, say adherents to this system, we learn right and wrong from our intuition. Of course, they would admit that, just as some people are blind physically, some are blind morally. But whenever this intuition is functioning properly, people will know what is "good" and what is "bad."

The *rationalist,* as the name implies, believes that what is rational is "right" and what is irrational is "wrong." One does not *feel* the goodness or badness of an act; one *reasons* its goodness or badness. The ultimate reality in the universe is rationality, according to this system. Therefore, when you act in a rational manner, you act in conformity with that ultimate reality—your action is "right."

Theistic Ethics

The fourth major ethical category is *theistic ethics.* This includes ethical systems that tie behavior to one's relationship with God or the gods. The basic question of the ethicist is, "If_____ is God, then how should I act?" (One then fills in the blank with Yahweh, or Zeus, or Krishna, etc.) In each case the system that results is a *theistic* ethical system.

There are three classical approaches to theistic ethics: legalism, mysticism, and rationalism. To these we add a fourth: situationalism. Buddhism, at least in its atheistic form, is a special case. But we will include it here, since it involves adherence to a "religion" if not to a "god" as such.

The *legalist* proceeds in acting ethically by the discipline of his or her will, or, as someone has put it, such a person "works on his or her 'want to'." The legalist believes that God, whoever God might be, has revealed Himself to humanity primarily through the giving of a *law.* Humanity, then, by the exercise of the will, conforms itself to that law. When one obeys that law, one is doing "good." To disobey the law constitutes "bad" behavior. Remember that this law is conceived by the legalist as divine. It is not "natural" law; neither is it merely a case of acting on what makes rational sense. This law is what God wants.

Life in conformity to the divine law—this is the basis for the theistic legalist's approach to ethics.

A second kind of theistic ethic is *mysticism.* For the mystic, ethics are not so much a discipline of the will as an exercise of the soul. By the elevation of the soul toward God, one eventually is united or fused with the divine spirit. One becomes "good" because God is good and one has become one with God. Ethics are not so much *doing* as *becoming*. The mystic may appear to the observer as passive—doing nothing. Such a one is engaged in no works of charity. The mystic is actively obeying no laws. Rather, by quietly subjecting individually the mystic becomes a part of the great All. In this subjection the mystic becomes a good person.

The third kind of theistic ethic is *rationalism*. Legalism deals with the will; mysticism deals with the soul; rationalism deals with the intellect. Theistic rationalism differs from idealistic rationalism, which we discussed, by beginning with the thesis, God is rational. One relates oneself to God by also being rational. One must "think God's thoughts after Him." Since God is rational, one knows the will of God by thinking in the same rational way in which God does.

A classic example of this kind of thinking can be found in the ethical philosophy of Plato and his pupils. Sin, they said, is really ignorance (a conception shared by Buddhism and Hinduism, but developed in a very different way). When one is thinking clearly, one will do the right thing. One may therefore create a moral community by properly educating the citizens, by giving them the facts, by teaching them to think. And insofar as they have learned to think clearly, they will act correctly.

A revival of Greek theistic rationalism among the founders of the United States played a vital role in the development of American culture and government. "We hold these truths to be self-evident, that all men are created equal and are endowed by their Creator . . .". Can you see the presuppositions that lie behind this statement?

Likewise, the philosophy that lies behind the American system of public education has generally stressed the link between knowledge and morality. As people learn better, so goes the theory, they will *do* better.

Critics have pointed out a potentially serious problem with rationalistic ethics, whether theistic or otherwise. They note that one of the most common human experiences is to know what one should do, and yet to not do it. This experience is even more common than not knowing what to do. Which one of us has not at some time carefully and meticulously planned and carried out an act that was in extreme opposition to what we knew we ought to do?

In other words, while there is a rational part of us that is giving signals for action, there is also something else operating in us that chooses to ignore those signals. We may be thinking rationally and factually. But that does not mean that we are going to act in accordance with what we know. The rationalist seems to think we are mainly *mind*. But the critic says that experience has proved we are much more than that. In fact, we probably do more things without thinking, or contrary to what our mind tells us, than the other way round.

And besides, say the critics, how does one really know when one is thinking rationally? We may think we are thinking straight—but does that mean we really are? So, even if we acted on the basis of what we thought was rational (and often we do not do that), we still might do the wrong thing because what we thought was rational was not.

Situationalism

A fourth ethical category, sometimes called "the ethic of love," has been publicized widely in recent years. A more technical name for this system is *situationalism.* The best known exposition of this system is found in Joseph Fletcher's book *Situation Ethics: The New Morality.* Two quotations from this book catch the essence of this approach to decision making:

> Only one "thing" is intrinsically good; namely love; nothing else at all.[4]

> The ruling norm of Christian decision is love: nothing else.[5]

The introduction of the word "Christian" shows that we are dealing with a theistic ethical system. One might develop a system based on love alone, without any reference to God. Some popular songs seem to advocate such a system.

Fletcher, however, begins with the thesis that God is love and that God is *only* love. That is, God acts only out of one motive and for one purpose—to love. When human beings love, then, they act like God. And only love acts are intrinsically good. Only love is absolute. Every other action is of relative merit and is potentially evil.

So when one comes into a decision-making situation, there are, according to Fletcher, only two "givens": (1) the situation itself and (2) love.

To determine how to act, one simply applies given 2 to given 1. The moral obligation, says Fletcher, is simply to "act responsibly in love." The person must come to each situation, not with a rule like a legalist would, or with cold human rationality, or with some internalizing of the problem like a mystic. No, rather, he or she must simply look at the situation and ask "How in this case do I act in a *loving way?*" That is the only relevant question. Any answer that traces the motivation to love would be moral or "right"; any answer that lacks the element responsible for love would be immoral or "wrong."

Fletcher gives an interesting example of how he feels this system works. The legalist has certain rules about sexual behavior. But a situationalist would begin not with rules but with a specific situation and with love. So a woman prisoner in a Nazi concentration camp finds that by prostituting herself to the SS officers she can save the lives of her children. The legalist says that there is a moral law against prostitution and that if the

---

[4]Joseph Fletcher, *Situation Ethics: The New Morality* (Philadelphia: Westminster, 1966), 57.

[5]Ibid., p. 69.

woman does such a thing she acts immorally. The situationalist says that her act is motivated by love for her children and that in this case prostitution is an act of responsible love.

In such stark examples Fletcher's case seems very strong and is widely accepted today. But some critics feel that they have found a fatal flaw in his system. The issue is the great difficulty in finding a precise definition of "love." Does one mean the kind of "love" that exclaims: "Oh my, my little heart is going pitty pat!" Or "love" as used in this sentence: "I dearly love strawberry ice cream!" Or, perhaps, this one: "Have you seen the latest X-rated movie, *Love in the Raw?*"

The word "love," say the critics, is used so diversely in our language that it means nothing at all. So when you advise me to "act responsibly in love," you are providing at the very best an ambiguous bit of advice.

Some Christian ethicists have suggested that the proper definition of "love," as used in this particular ethical context, is the following: God is love. God was in Christ. Therefore, the love of God is made visible in Christ. He is the specification of love. Therefore, to act in love is to act in accordance with the personality, life, and teachings of Jesus. In this way love is given an objective definition. One need not depend on nebulous inner feelings called "love," but may look to an objective example of it in Jesus.

To see how this particular approach is developed into an ethical system, you should reread the last part of Chapter Six in which the ethics of Jesus are discussed in some detail.

At any rate, Fletcher's critics say, unless one has a pretty firm concept of what "acting responsibly in love" means, situationalism is of limited value in decision making. Without such a firm concept, people may act out of the shallowest kind of emotionalism or the crassest kind of passion and mistake such feelings for love.

Buddhist Ethics

The most conservative forms of Buddhism (especially in the Theravada school) are atheistic or at least see little relevance in ideas about divine beings. Still, the ethical system they follow is "religious" and should be surveyed here.

Hajime Nakamura summarizes the ethical ideal of Buddhism in this way:[6]

> If a man could live a life of the Right Path, of unvarying patience and kindness to all, not binding his heart to worldly things that rise and pass away—then he would be free from mundane life, and for him the fountain of evil would vanish. If one could still the cravings for one's petty self, and

[6]Hajime Nakamura, "The Basic Teachings of Buddhism," in *Buddhism in the Modern World,* ed. Heinrich Dumoulin and John C. Maraldo (New York: Macmillan, 1976), p. 25.

endeavor only to do good for others, then the principle of individuality, that fundamental and worst delusion of mankind, might be overcome.

In this statement the characteristic Buddhist doctrines about reality are applied to human behavior. The goal is to free one's mind from "worldly things" and thus from "mundane life." By eliminating craving and a sense of being an individual self, one begins to live for others. Following the Buddha, one must live by the middle path, rejecting both sensuality and extreme asceticism. Evil grows primarily out of the way in which one thinks, and Buddhist mental discipline enables one to be free from incorrect thinking. Thus,[7]

> The path of religion leads through morality; but when one approaches the goal, one enters an entirely different realm; the saint who has attained the calm of Nirvana is said to be "beyond good and evil." What is called "good" in our daily life is very often defiled with worldly desire. The ideal situation should be perfectly pure, so it is said to transcend secular good and evil.

Nevertheless, the committed Buddhist will feel a special obligation to imitate the compassion of the Buddha. Realizing that one's ego is an illusion and that one is really part of everything that is, one is led to sense a unity with other beings and therefore a compassion for them.

Applying the principles of world denial and self-denial to everyday life creates its own problems. In Ceylon, for example, where Theravada Buddhism exists in a relatively pure form, the common layperson has trouble relating its ethical teaching to everyday life and often falls back on the rituals of folk religion. Or that person may feel that since he or she cannot live the "pure" life of the recluse, he or she can only follow a few explicitly Buddhist customs but live by a private code of morality not really consistent with his or her faith. Sarachandra points out the ethical dilemma that results: "The ordinary layman thinks that to be moral is necessarily to be ascetic. A 'good' man is one who conforms as much as possible to this ideal, and a man is 'bad' to the degree that he deviates from it."[8] In modern times, when it is more and more difficult for an ordinary layman to live by a strict ascetic code, "many people resolve the problem by adopting a double code of morality, one public and one private."[9]

Another pressing ethical problem in modern Buddhist societies is how to develop a social ethic—a system of public morality—when Buddhism emphasizes the life of inner person so strongly. If nirvana is attained by complete detachment from this world, which is after all at its core mere

[7]Nakamura, *Buddhism in the Modern World,* pp. 27–28.
[8]Ediriweerd R. Sarachandra, "Traditional Values and the Modernization of a Buddhist Society: The Case of Ceylon," in *Religion and Progress in Modern Asia,* ed. Robert N. Bellah (New York: Free Press, 1965), p. 122.
[9]Ibid., p. 123.

illusion, and if the ideal life occurs in isolated meditation, how can the Buddhist justify attempts to improve government and social conditions?

Some Buddhists find the answer in socialism or even communism. The takeover by communism in China and more recently in Southeast Asia is facilitated by the feeling of many Buddhists that capitalism is essentially materialistic and selfish and must be rejected. Socialism, on the other hand, emphasizes giving up of self-interest for the good of the people as a whole. Other Buddhist political theorists insist that democracy is also consistent with Buddhism, since it gives each individual the right to seek spiritual enlightenment at his or her own pace.[10]

We have seen in this chapter that the systems by which human beings make their decisions show great diversity. You may have great difficulty in finding any one system that is entirely satisfactory. All of them show weaknesses here and there. But because we are forced to make decisions, and because our decisions come from the same inner world as do our thoughts of God, humanity, and destiny, a discussion of ethics belongs in the preface to religion.

[10]See Donald K. Swearer, *Buddhism in Transition* (Philadelphia: Westminster, 1970), pp. 64–71.

CHAPTER NINE
RELIGION AND WESTERN CULTURE

THE RELATIONSHIP BETWEEN
RELIGION AND CULTURE

Religion and culture have always been closely related in the Western world (the Americas—North and South—and Europe—East and West). But neither has ever been entirely happy with the relationship. This chapter traces the course of the interaction between the two throughout the past two thousand years. A good way in which to prepare for this subject would be to review the earlier discussion of "cultural religion" and of "ultimate concern." Having done this, one is better prepared to launch into what, unfortunately, is a rather complicated subject. Complicated, but profitable—because it is a study that helps us to understand a great deal about the nature of religion and the way in which it affects the world in which we live.

Earlier the term "ultimate concern" was used to refer to that conviction (or set of convictions) about reality that rests at the very center of a person's life. It is the source of one's actions and the anchor of one's hopes. It may be unexpressed and unreflected upon. It may not appear obviously and on the surface, but it is there nevertheless, furnishing the "glue" that holds life together.

Cultures have sets of convictions, also. They may be seldom recognized or discussed, but they lie behind the actions of a culture and, when discovered, can be very helpful in understanding *why* a culture does the things that it does. Some examples may help to illustrate this fact.

Western culture is characterized by a strong sense of the sanctity of physical human life. This sense extends down even to the life of a single individual within the culture. Because of this, Westerners often do things that seem strange to people in other cultures. We spend tremendous amounts of money, for example, to keep our astronauts alive during space flight. Then we spend additional millions on back-up systems to protect them in case a primary system malfunctions. This must seem strange to people in other cultures, particularly those where money is scarce. Why spend so much, when only two or three lives are involved?

The answer is probably that we spend it because deep inside our collective thinking and feeling something is saying, "Human life is extremely valuable. Do nothing that seems to waste it recklessly." Besides, if someone is killed because of inadequate concern about safety, those people responsible for the project will be shamed and considered to have failed.

We are committed, then (at least publicly, as culture religion concerns itself mostly with public behavior), to the sanctity of the individual human life. We constantly seek better health measures, better safety procedures, better physical protection, and so on. All these activities are tied very closely to Western culture.

An Eastern culture that believes in reincarnation (the idea that the soul keeps coming back to life again and again in many different forms) might look at such matters very differently. If dying is nothing more than the passing from one body to another, then the mere retaining of life seems rather insignificant. In fact, since the new incarnation may be preferable to the last one, letting someone die might also be preferable. Thus, we may see people being allowed to die when only a little effort and expenditure would have kept them alive.

I knew a man who lived in the Far East many years ago. He told me that one day, while he was crossing a bridge, the man in front of him suddenly lost his footing and fell into the water. He was churning around frantically, obviously unable to swim. My friend could not swim either, but, like a proper Westerner, he became very excited and concerned. So he looked back to the next man on the bridge, a native of the Eastern culture, and asked him, "Can you swim?"

"Yes," the man replied.

"Well then, jump in quick and pull that man out. He's drowning!"

The second man looked over the bridge rail for a long time, carefully observing the poor fellow thrashing in the water below. Finally, he looked back to my friend, smiling, and said,

"I don't believe I *know* him."

"You mean you won't pull him out unless you *know* him?" my friend asked, not believing his ears.

"That is correct," was the polite reply.

Finally my friend was able to pay someone to jump in, and just in the nick of time the man in the water was saved.

This seemingly strange and heartless behavior undoubtedly grew out of the deep-seated presuppositions of a very different culture from our own. When the man said, "I don't know him," he meant "he is not a part of my family or of my people—the ones who are my responsibility. And since he is not, my intervention would be an interference with the will of Heaven, which obviously has decided it is time for this man to die!" But why is such a thing obvious, you ask? Because Heaven caused him to fall in the water without any relatives nearby to rescue him!

On the other hand, many cultures in the East have a far greater sense of community and family than do those in the West. For them, the individualism of the West is the worst kind of cruelty and immorality. For example, the idea that someone would actually send away his or her own mother to live in something called Happy Acres Rest Home might shock and disgust the Eastern mind.

One more example. The city of Tokyo, Japan, has over eleven million people—and only three psychoanalysts in private practice. The city of New York, on the other hand, has about eight million people—and almost a thousand psychoanalysts. The few Japanese psychiatrists in practice depend more on tranquilizers than on analysis in treating patients.

Why? Because, according to Tokyo analyst Soichi Hakozaki, the strong group and family orientation of the Japanese and the rejection of individualism has resulted in a "softened ego." Without a strong sense of "I," analysis as we know it in the West is impossible. Besides, points out the famous novelist Yukio Mishima (who, incidentally, committed ritual suicide in 1970), Buddhism, which sees life as a mere vapor with little significance or meaning, makes the whole process of "attaining mental health" a waste of energy. As Western individualists, we may think it would be horrible not to exist. But the Buddhist holy man may see nonexisting as the finest of all states. And since existence is for him a rather unpleasant interlude, why should he spend time reordering his psyche?[1]

These examples are designed to illustrate how the customs of a given society may seem strange and arbitrary to someone looking in from the outside. But lying deep behind such customs is a set of ultimate or basic presuppositions about reality. And out of these presuppositions come the customs.

This set of presuppositions may be thought of as an undergirding that holds up the structure of that society or as a matrix, a mold that determines the shape a society will take.

From time to time this matrix, or culture religion, changes dramati-

[1]"Rejecting Freud," *Time,* 23 September 1974, p. 69.

cally. And, of course, when this happens, the whole culture begins to change along with it. Such changes can grow out of a variety of new situations. For example, the economic conditions may change for better or worse. Or the political system or social conditions may change (as with the entrance of a great number of foreigners, for example). New philosophical concepts may begin to catch hold. New scientific discoveries can have their influence. Theology may start in a new direction. Any of these factors can be the beginning of a shift in cultural religion.

These new ideas and situations are often the work of creative individuals within the society. They are propounded and gradually accepted by the culture as a whole. When the culture has shifted in one of these areas, it often starts a chain reaction that causes adjustments in thinking about all the other areas. Eventually a whole new matrix has been created. This new matrix inevitably begins to form a new culture.

The new matrix functions as the culture religion for the new culture. It is the set of convictions that lies behind that culture and makes it what it is. It is the glue that holds the culture together and without which it will simply disintegrate.

If, in the process of shifting, it is not possible to form a new matrix—that is, if some new idea is so damaging to the culture that the other areas cannot adjust—then the culture does not change but collapses entirely. The result may be revolution, civil war, or simply disintegration. Sometimes, in its search for a workable cultural religion, a society will latch onto some supracultural religion that exists within it and use the "captured" faith as its societal glue.

Several times in history a society has taken hold of the Christian religion, made certain adjustments to it, and used it as a cultural matrix. Christianity is altered in the process, of course. It becomes partly cultural and partly supracultural. But as an essentially supracultural religion, Christianity survives such use. When the culture that captured it dies, Christianity continues (though, of course, that particular cultural form of it dies).

If, on the other hand, the culture religion used as a matrix is purely cultural, then it dies altogether at the death of its host culture. An example is the "German religion" perpetrated by the leaders of Hitler's Third Reich. It has disappeared along with Hitler and his empire.

Culture, then, grows out of a culture-religion matrix. Each culture produces its own kind of Man (our shorthand term for "way of being human," male and female). This Man has a certain world view and life-style that grows out of the matrix. He or she will have these until the matrix changes. When it does, one cannot be "human" in the same way as before, so a new "human" appears. This change does not take place overnight. When a culture is changing, people go through a period of great turmoil and struggle, and only gradually becomes "new."

This kind of change has occurred several times in the Western world. We can outline these changes in very broad strokes with the following chart:

I. CLASSICAL MAN (600 B.C. to A.D. 300)

Collapse and Transition (A.D. 300 to 900)

II. MEDIEVAL MAN (A.D. 900 to 1300)

Collapse and Transition (A.D. 1300 to 1700)

III. AUTONOMOUS MAN (A.D. 1700 to 1900)

Collapse and Transition (A.D. 1900 to Present)

The dates, of course, are just generalized guideposts. Changes are gradual and do not occur in a precise year. The chart suggests that there have been three ways of being human in the West and that the Western culture-religion matrix has shifted at least three times during the last two thousand years. Each great cultural form has been followed by a period of confusion. The underpinnings of economic, political, social, philosophical, scientific, and theological thinking have been shaken while society searched for a new stability and a new way in which to be human.

CLASSICAL MAN

The first way of being human in the West was born in classical Greece, the Greece of Plato and Aristotle, and was nurtured by the host of great political, philosophical, and artistic geniuses of that remarkable period. It is developed further throughout what is called the Hellenistic period,[2] initiated when Alexander the Great spread the Greek way of thinking through the large areas of the ancient world that had fallen to his advancing armies. It was a syncretistic kind of Hellenism. That is, it was constantly

[2]The Greek word for Greece is *Hellas*. Hence, *Hellenistic* means "patterned after the Greek way of doing things."

picking up ideas and practices from other cultures as it spread, but kept incorporating them into a single matrix of ideas.

The rise of Rome gave political stability to this combination of Greek ideas and Hellenistic syncretism. The Romans were much better at government than at philosophy, so a Graeco-Roman combination furnished the best of both worlds.

But as the Roman Empire continued, it became evident that the weakest part of the matrix was the theological-philosophical part. The other elements in the matrix (political, sociological, etc.) were much more central in gluing the empire together. There was very little consensus of opinion about philisophy and religion among classical persons. The main thing that held them together was the powerful Roman military force.

There were many attempts to find some kind of religious base on which everyone could agree. In the first stages of the development of the Classical Man, the old Greek polytheism (the world of gods and goddesses described by Homer and by Greek mythology) furnished the material for such an attempt. Then, during the time of Alexander and his successors, the Hellenistic syncretists tried to popularize the idea that the gods of the various subcultures were actually the same realities, described by different names—hoping to tie these diverse groups together in that way.

Other attempts were made during the height of Roman domination. Various philosophical systems vied for general acceptance. In general, those systems tended to undermine faith in the polytheistic systems. While acknowledging their existence, most of the philosophers saw the gods as having little relevance to the daily life of human beings. The *Epicureans* maintained that pleasure was the object of life and that people should seek it as their primary goal. The *Stoics*, representing the dominant philosophy of the time, believed, in the words of one of their most famous spokesperson, Seneca, that "God is nature, is fate, is fortune, is the universe, is the all-pervading mind." If one lived according to the nature and purpose of this mind, one would be able to handle both the good and evil in life with "apathy" i.e., quiet resolution. The *Cynics* took an antiestablishment approach—ridiculing tradition, morality, ceremony, and religion. And the *Platonists* and *Neo-Platonists* viewed reality as belonging to the ideal rather than to the real world that was spiritual in nature.

Only a small minority of the people of the classical world adhered to these philosophies, however. Many more were drawn into the world of superstition: astrology, portents, divination, dreams, and oracles. Especially popular were the *mystery religions,* a multitude of cults offering a hope of immortality and a sense of personal relationship with deity. These cults featured secret initiations in which the worshipper came into mystical communion with Isis and Osiris, or Dionysus or Mithra.

But none of these systems was able to permeate the whole of classical culture. Each seemed to appeal to only one segment of that culture, but not to other segments.

The last attempt to provide a theological glue was the encouragement of emperor worship. This was a rather contrived project to tie the citizens of the empire together by forcing them to participate in a cult that glorified the supreme ruler. The emperors, particularly the later ones, knew that their empire and culture were crumbling. Emperor worship was one last desperate attempt to put it back together. But it was too late. The attempt was made particularly difficult by a growing group within the empire called "Christians" who refused to go along with it altogether.

Eventually the entire classical matrix fell apart and Classical Man disappeared.

TRANSITION: THE "TRIUMPH" OF CHRISTIANITY

When the old Roman Empire crumbled (that is, when the cultural matrix collapsed), there was only one way of thinking, only one theological system left that seemed healthy enough to survive—Christianity. So it is no surprise that the last emperors completely reversed previous policy, stopped killing Christians, and started courting them. Shortly after the year 300 the Emperor Constantine declared himself a Christian! However one might feel concerning the sincerity of his conversion, one must admit it was a good tactic politically and socially.

The Roman Emperor Cult. In the waning days of classical civilization the government of Rome tried to maintain the unity of its diverse empire by encouraging the deification and worship of the imperial family. This sculpture of the Empress Faustina the Elder, wife of the emperor Antoninus Pius, was found in a temple in Sardis—modern Turkey. (British Museum)

For their part, the Christians were weary of being hounded, pressured, arrested, tortured, and thrown to lions. When the emperor came to court them they responded with understandable, but perhaps very unfortunate, enthusiasm—unfortunate because, in doing so, they allowed their religious system, which up to now had stood above its culture, to be captured by its culture. Up to now the Christians had considered themselves "in the world, but not of it." They had no stake in the classical world. It was a world against them. The Roman Empire had always been their enemy. Now, suddenly, it became their friend. But it was a very demanding friend, a friend that called upon Christianity to serve, not as a supracultural prophet but as a cultural priest.

Gradually the church fell under secular control. It began to look more and more like the secular government. It became more and more centralized and, thus, more controllable by the power structure of the society. Formerly, it had been dangerous to be a Christian. Now, it became politically and socially expedient. Many, many people flocked into the church. Few of them understood the supracultural dimensions of their new faith. They brought along remains of the old classical carcass —superstitions, Greek philosophical ideas, Roman governmental concepts, and the like.

Gradually, during the chaotic centuries following the collapse of the empire in the West, a new matrix was formed and a new "Man" appeared. When society emerged from what are sometimes called the Dark Ages the West had a new cultural glue—The Roman Catholic Church.

MEDIEVAL MAN

The Roman emperor and his military power had once held the Western world together. Now the Roman Catholic Church was called upon to do the same thing. And in such a situation, when theology is connected so closely with the preservation of culture, heresy is also treason. That is, an attack upon the basic presuppositions of the church could only be treated as a threat to, and a betrayal of, the entire medieval way of life. To weaken the church was to contribute to the collapse of society.

When theology is the basis for cultural stability, it becomes important to preserve it at all costs. Those who threaten some element of the theological system must be silenced. One must understand this situation to really understand the "intolerance" of Medieval Man toward religious beliefs that differed from the norm.

Thus appeared Medieval Man, one who accepted this situation. His life was structured by the beliefs of the Roman Catholic Church. His world view and life-style were formed by those beliefs. For some four hundred years he was the typical human being in the West.

The literary records of Medieval Man can well be represented by these four documents: *The Nicene Creed,* Augustine's *City of God,* Thomas Aquinas' *Summa Theologica,* and Dante's *Divine Comedy.*

The Nicene Creed

The Nicene Creed was a codifying of orthodox Christian theology. It stated its position in such a way that there was almost no room for further speculation about the most basic issues—the nature of God, the nature of humanity, the nature of the world, and the meaning of history. The creed was produced very early in the transition period (around A.D. 300). For the next one thousand years it had no serious opposition in the West. Here is how it reads:

> I believe in one God the Father Almighty; Maker of heaven and earth, and of all things visible and invisible.
>
> And in one Lord Jesus Christ, the only-begotten son of God, begotten of the Father before all worlds [God of God], Light of Light, very God of very God, Begotten, not made, being of one substance [essence] with the Father; by whom all things were made; who, for us men and for our salvation, came down from heaven, and was incarnate by the Holy Ghost of the Virgin Mary, and was made man; and was crucified also for us under Pontius Pilate; he suffered and was buried; and the third day he rose again, according to the Scriptures; and ascended into heaven, and sitteth on the right hand of the Father; and he shall come again, with glory, to judge both the quick and the dead; whose kingdom shall have no end.
>
> And [I believe] in the Holy Ghost, the Lord and Giver of Life; who proceedeth from the Father [and the Son]; who with the Father and the Son together is worshipped and glorified; who spake by the Prophets. And [I believe] one Holy Catholic and Apostolic Church. I acknowledge one baptism for the remission of sins; and I look for the resurrection of the dead, and the life of the world to come. Amen.

This creed is a very comprehensive statement. It asserts that God exists and describes His nature and the nature and destiny of the world. It specifies what the basic goals and conduct of life should be.[3]

The City of God

The second document central to understanding the Medieval Man is the work of the brilliant North African theologian Aurelius Augustinus or *Augustine* (A.D. 354–430). Augustine lived during the middle part of the transition period between Classical Man and Medieval Man. The Roman Empire was collapsing all around him. Barbarian armies were knocking on every door, ready to swoop in and crush civilization.

[3]See J. N. D. Kelly, *Early Christian Doctrines,* 2nd ed. (New York: Harper & Row, 1960), for a full discussion of this creed and its theological implications.

In this context Augustine wrote *The City of God*.[4] This work was a blueprint for a new civilization in which Christianity (more specifically, Roman Catholic Christianity) would become the societal glue. Augustine proceeded to give a rationale for tying the church and state together. In such a society, he said, the church would be the basic institution. The secular government would be subservient to it.

Augustine saw this as the solution to the problem caused by the fall of Roman civilization. The church will replace militarism. The new society will be the City of God, replacing the old classical culture, which he called the City of Man. His dream became the pattern for political, social, and theological thinking for hundreds of years.

Aquinas and Dante

Thomas Aquinas (A.D. 1255–1274), whose life and work come at the end of the period, represents the flowering of the medieval mind. He was the man who could tie it all together into one great *Summa Theologica* (the title of his masterpiece). The title can be roughly translated "Everything About Theology." It contained the basic concepts of the Hebrew and Christian Scriptures, mixed with Greek philosophy, Roman legal theory, and orthodox theology, not to mention political and scientific theories. Taken together, it was the consummate statement of Medieval Man.[5]

While Thomas Aquinas gives us an intellectual expression of the Medieval Mind, Dante gives us the *poetic* expression of it. His *Divine Comedy* (ca. A.D. 1318) is a vivid picture of the world as Medieval Man understood it.[6] Mankind is understood to live in a three-storied universe—earth, hell below, and heaven above. Life is a preparation for spending eternity in either heaven or hell. While man remains on earth, the church is his source for *grace* (the favor of God) and *truth* (an understanding of reality).

This does not mean that all church leaders are always right. Dante, touring hell in one of his poems, finds several popes right in the bottom of the pit. But the church itself was the dispenser of the grace that God offers to man through Jesus Christ. Man's meaning and destiny, then, were tied to his relationship to the church.

Collapse of the Medieval World

The medieval world lasted until about the thirteenth century. The final flowering came during the late thirteenth and early fourteenth centuries. Then a series of events began to occur that rocked the medieval

---

[4]Aurelius Augustinus, *The City of God* (New York: Dutton, 1962).

[5]See Mary T. Clark, ed., *An Aquinas Reader* (Garden City, N.Y.: Image Books, 1972).

[6]See Dante Alighieri, *The Divine Comedy*, trans. Charles S. Singleton (Princeton, N.J.: Princeton University Press, 1970).

Medieval World View. This fourteenth century gothic ivory carving contains many of the elements central to the world view of people in medieval times. Jesus, holding a long cross, is pictured leading Adam and Eve out of hell, shown as the jaws of a monster already devouring another figure. On the right stands the Devil, looking away in consternation as he loses his victims. (British Museum)

world and Medieval Man. The result, eventually, was a new matrix, a new cultural mold, a new relationship between religion and culture, a new life-style, and a new world view.

The shake-up had many underlying causes. We will mention only a few. First, there was *the rise of the nation-states.* When people began to feel a sense of *nationality* it tended to break, or at least to challenge, the domination of the Roman Catholic Church in politics. So a king may boldly say to a pope: "I am the King (of England, or France, or some other nation). *I* will make the decisions about what happens in my nation."

In medieval times if a king ran afoul of the pope, he might find himself obliged to crawl on his knees through the snow to ask the pope's forgiveness. But with the rise of nation-states, the kings found that they could act independently of the pope with impunity.

Second, there were *the voyages of discovery:*

Columbus sailed the ocean blue,
In Fourteen hundred and ninety-two.

And, at about the same time, so did Bartholomew Diaz, and Vasco da Gama, and Balboa, and Magellan, and John Cabot, and Jacques Cartier. They found no sea monsters. They did not fall off the edge of the earth. They did not perish in boiling water at the equator.

The world was not what Medieval Man had thought it to be—an island called Europe floating on top of hell and basking under heaven. Instead, the world was a very, very large place with all kinds of people of many colors and creeds and cultures. Discovery of this fact compelled a change in world view.

Third, there appeared a *new economic system*. Until now, Europe had had a few extremely wealthy landowners and millions of peasants. The peasants used a barter system of exchange: "I'll trade you one chicken for three heads of lettuce." But now a money system was introduced: "I'll give you two silver pieces for that cow." This meant that shopkeepers appeared, and bankers, and a whole segment of society known as the "middle class."

Next men learned how to mass produce goods and the result was an Industrial Revolution. The peasants left their fields and moved into towns to work in factories. The result was "urbanization."

Daily life for the average man changed drastically. Instead of farming, and then bartering the produce (after the landowner had taken his share), the worker was now found in a city, working in a factory, living on wages received for services rendered and spent for his or her family's physical needs.

In the midst of all this came the fourth element in the collapse of Medieval Man's world—a frontal *attack on the authority of the church itself*. That is, an attack occurred on the kind of theology that made the Roman Catholic Church the basic institution in society.

"The Reformation" is the name given this movement, and foremost among its leaders was a professor and monk named *Martin Luther* (1483–1546).[7] Luther, along with John Calvin and others, challenged the idea that the Roman church was the source of grace and truth. Medieval Man saw his relationship with God as depending upon his relationship with the Roman church. After all, God gives His grace to man through the sacraments of the church. Where there is no access to the sacraments, there is no access to God. To be "ex-communicated" was to be doomed to hell.

The Reformation was a "protest" against this idea (hence the name Protestant). The grace of God, said the Reformers, was not channeled through works of human righteousness and the ordinances of the church. It was not connected with the church hierarchy (the popes, bishops, and priests) at all. Rather, man received the grace of God through his own personal faith in Jesus. Furthermore, the hierarchy of the church was not the custodian of truth, either. Truth came to man through the Bible. And every man could read the Bible for himself.

These ideas, of course, were not mere idle theological exercises. They pierced the body of the medieval world at its very heart.

For these four, and many other reasons, the medieval world was disintegrating. For centuries people had depended on religion to hold things together. But Christianity was now fragmented. Still, the general consensus was that civilization was impossible without religious uniformity, that within a given state, everyone must believe the same things. Those who

---

[7]See John Dillenberger, *Martin Luther: Selections from His Writings* (Garden City, N.Y.: Doubleday, 1961).

refused to conform (heretics) must be eliminated; they threatened civilization itself.

But what *kind* of Christianity would be the norm? Would it be a reformed and revitalized Roman Catholicism or would it be Protestantism? Some kings and armies embraced one kind of Christianity and some the other. And then they proceeded to fall on each other with the sword.

The struggle for dominance continued for generation after generation, often breaking out into armed conflict. The spectacle of religious war is hard for the modern, secular individual to understand. For us, theology is not worth fighting about. But we are dealing with people who saw in the resolution of the religious questions the very survival or doom of civilization itself.

Such a perception has not disappeared; even today it continues to mold events in Northern Ireland, for example. The horrible stories of slaughter that come from there furnish something of a picture of what was happening all over Europe during the sixteenth and seventeenth centuries.

No one, Protestant or Catholic, emerged from all this looking very good. In one famous story, a Catholic bishop sent an army into a supposedly Protestant town in Southern France with orders to massacre the entire population: "But, sir," complained one of the officers, "there are undoubtedly a few good Catholics in that town." "That's all right," replied the bishop, "the Lord will know the good Catholics and take them to Heaven. Kill them all!"

AUTONOMOUS MAN

After generations of mutual slaughter, it began to become apparent that religious uniformity was an impossibility. People began to say, "perhaps there is another way in which to glue society together, since it does not appear that there is ever going to be agreement on religion again."

More and more, such people began coming to the conclusion that the new glue should be *human reason*—not religion, not revelation, but reason.

Now the Protestants and Catholics agreed about one thing, at least, and that was that truth comes to man from the outside. They differed only on how it came—through the Bible and the church, or through the Bible only. In either case, truth was not in man himself, but was something given to man from above.

The new idea challenged that concept. It said that man can look within himself—especially to his mind and its power to reason. So, if man will simply begin to depend on his reason, he can free himself from the need to look outside. He will agree with all other reasonable men, since all reasonable men will come to the same reasonable conclusions about the truth. There will be no more need for messages from the outside. The whole question of whether truth comes through this church or that becomes irrelevant.

Man became autonomous. That is, he no longer depended upon grace and truth coming from something external, but upon something in himself, namely, his capacity to reason. This process, of course, did not happen overnight. The transition from Medieval to Autonomous Man took hundreds of years. But in this transition period was born what we call the "modern world."

In the works of *René Descartes* (1596–1650) this new method can be seen working to transform philosophy. Although a faithful Roman Catholic, his *Discourse on Method* (1637) proposed a way for the "proper conduct of reason and the search for truth in the sciences." Man must clear his mind of the debris of tradition and build his ideas in a reasonable fashion, from the ground up, so to speak. This was the thrust of Descartes' thinking.

What Descartes had done in philosophy, *Galileo Galilei* (1564–1642) did in science itself. He laid down the principle that, along with reasonable thinking, man must use *experimentation* to find out the truth about himself and his world.

The use of reason and of experimentation became the foundation for modern science and the downfall of the Medieval Mind. When scholars began to disregard what the ancients had said, and depend instead upon their own observations, they came up with very different conclusions about what the world is, and what man is. And these conclusions became the building blocks for a new world view and a new life-style.

The Assumptions of Autonomous Man

Paul Tillich speaks of an "autonomous culture."[8] In such a culture people try to construct models for their lives, individually and collectively, without taking into consideration the ultimate and unconditional. The only considerations are those of rationality and practicality. We will alter this definition a bit and define Autonomous Man as "a way of being human that acts as if only the material world is real and as if man belongs entirely to the material world."

Notice the words "acts as if." Many Autonomous Men claim belief in a spiritual world and are in fact active participants in some traditional form of organized religion. But from a practical point of view, they operate in conformity to the set of presuppositions listed in the paragraphs that follow. This set of presuppositions and assumptions has gradually replaced the Nicene Creed–Augustine–Aquinas–Dante set of assumptions about

[8]Paul Tillich, *The Protestant Era* (Chicago: University of Chicago Press, 1948), p. 57.

reality. They represent a kind of Autonomous Creed out of which the autonomous world view and life-style have grown. Six of the most common and basic of these assumptions follow.

Assumption 1: Revelation and tradition are to be rejected as sources for truth.   One does not look for truth in so-called "messages from God" or in the accumulation of ideas held by people in the past.

Assumption 2: One can have unbounded confidence in human reason.   If revelation or tradition are not to be trusted, what *is*? Answer: A human being's ability to think rationally and to come to accurate conclusions when he or she does so.

Assumption 3: Analysis can resolve all difficulties because complex matters are only compounds of simple matters.   The whole of reality can be reduced to very simple elements (after the model of chemistry, for example). Thus, the way in which one finds out the truth about something, or solves a given problem, is simply to reduce it to its constituent parts. What seems to be a tremendously complex organism or machine is really only a combination of very simple components and processes piled on top of each other. Upon breaking down the organism or machine into its parts, one sees what it really is and what makes it tick. This process can be applied to a television set or to man himself. Autonomous Man thinks of himself as a very complex machine, but one that, after proper analysis, is only a large series of simple processes.

Assumption 4: Individualism is the course to be followed.   In the search for truth, we need communion with neither the past nor the future. All we need is a clear mind and facilities to experiment. We search without reference to what other people think. Thus, the model truth-seeker becomes the scientist in a lonely laboratory, analyzing complex problems, experimenting, discovering the answer for and by oneself.

Assumption 5: The language of mathematics is the language of truth.   Two plus two equals four. That is language that describes truth. Concepts that cannot be expressed in such clear and precise ways are examples of fuzzy thinking, not of truth. So mathematics becomes a kind of model. All problems, all reality, can be reduced to mathematical formulas.

Assumption 6: Experimentation leads to truth.   And, as a closely connected concept, things that are not subject to experimentation, or that are not repeatable, or that are subjective, are not true in any meaningful, scientific sense.

The overall effect of this new way of thinking, of course, was to secularize. Whereas Medieval Man saw everything in terms of the spiritual world, Autonomous Man sees nothing that way. Rather, he views the world as being self-contained, complete in itself. Matter is the basic stuff of existence. Analysis of matter is therefore the source of truth. One simply cannot meaningfully talk about things "out there" or about some "other world."

One deals with *this* world, and this world alone. To approach life in this way is to be an entirely different kind of human being from Medieval Man, because one perceives oneself and the world in an entirely different way.

An eighteenth-century scientist was waxing eloquent one evening in the presence of one of the kings of France. He was giving one scientific theory after another about how this or that phenomenon could be explained. Finally the king, who had grown more and more perplexed as the conversation continued, exclaimed, "But sir, where is God in all this?" To which the scientist replied, "Your majesty, I have no need of that hypothesis."

Here was a classic confrontation between two kinds of men: medieval and autonomous. The scientist had developed a way of looking at the world that, it was felt, could explain everything without reference to any power or cause other than or outside the present closed and self-contained world system.

Unfortunately, in the rush to explain *how* things happen, an exciting and very successful process, little or no attention was given to the question of *why* things happen—not "why" in the sense of cause but "why" in the sense of *meaning* and *purpose*. Few seemed to sense that while the hows of life were being neatly tied together the whys were coming completely unstrung. This fact was not immediately noticeable, of course, and that may account for the small number of people who were worried about the situation.

The Secularization of the West

The process that produced the secular view of life was a long one, stretching over several hundred years. It moved from one field of human knowledge to another, roughly in the order given now.

Physics. *Copernicus* (1473–1543), *Kepler* (1571–1630), *Galileo* and *Newton* (1642–1727) are among the most famous physicists who contributed to an explanation of the physical world without reference to "another" world in any way. Not only did they present us with a world that was very different physically from what Medieval Man had thought, but they also provided a concept of natural laws, much like the laws of mathematics, that govern the physical processes of our world. Ironically, a man like Newton, an orthodox Christian, helped to develop a world view that eventually became totally secular.

Biology. Gradually the theories that had worked so well in physics were applied to the world of living things as well. Just as volcanoes and weather and the tides were subject to measurable physical laws, so is the process of life itself. The line of thinking reached its climax in the work of *Charles Darwin* (1809–1892) and the theory of evolution. And if evolution were true, then certainly Medieval Man's whole viewpoint about the world of living creatures was wrong. This world was not a fixed hierarchy, put in perfect balance and harmony by some higher power. Rather, it was the result of a purely secular and random process by which the fittest forms of life survived and the others died out. What one needed to explain all this was not God but, rather, a series of genetic mutations and a time span of millions of years.

History. *David Hume* (1711–1776) wrote an *Essay on Miracles* in which he claimed that there were no miracles. Miracles cannot happen, because they lie outside the Autonomous Man's new philosophy of history. This philosophy began with the naturalistic assumption that no power from the outside ever interferes with anything that is happening within the sphere of history. Everything in history can be traced to purely natural causes. The historical process is a *natural* process. Miracles would be the invasion or intrusion of the supernatural into the natural process by powers beyond our world. They cannot be proved scientifically and therefore cannot be true.

When *Edward Gibbon* sat down to write *The Decline and Fall of the Roman Empire* (1776–1788), he took a very different view than had Augustine so many centuries before.[9] God had not caused the fall of the empire as a punishment for evil, or to assist the victory of the Christian faith. Indeed, the cause was not God at all, but a series of perfectly natural historical developments, he argued. History, then, had been *secularized.*

This new, autonomous kind of historical method was even applied to the sacred writings of the past. Men began to investigate the Bible from this naturalistic point of view. They found it to be full of the idea that God interferes with the historical process. They found it necessary to reinterpret the Bible, so that the real (i.e., the natural or scientific) explanations would appear. All of history, they maintained, including Biblical history, must be explained in purely natural ways, without any reference to the world of the spirit.[10]

Sociology.   The principles that had worked so well in biology were now applied to sociology. Human cultural units are also under natural laws and operate in purely natural ways. Social systems evolve in much the same way as biological organisms. The social and political theories of *Karl Marx* became the pattern of thinking for literally millions of Autonomous Men in dozens of nations. The history of human society, he said, is a relatively simple process of *thesis, antithesis,* and *synthesis.* A given culture (the thesis) exists; a reaction (the antithesis) occurs; a new society (the synthesis) develops. The details of this process can be understood and predicted in very precise ways. It is a secular, scientific process, governed by the same natural laws that govern physics and biology.

Marx saw in sociology and history the same evolutionary process that Darwin had seen in biology. Human political structures were moving relentlessly from lower to higher forms. The highest and final form, he thought, would be the pure communist society.

Psychology.   The last bailiwick for the spirit was the human mind. *William James* (1842–1910) and *Sigmund Freud,* among others, turned the scientific searchlight on the mind, and the ultimate result was another victory for secularization. One of the most striking examples of this process is found in the experiments on dogs by the Russian scientist *Pavlov.* Pavlov fed his dogs while ringing a bell. He continued to do this over a period of time. Then, one day, he rang the bell, but did not feed the dogs. He found

[9]An abbreviated version of this massive work is Dero A. Saunders, ed., *The Portable Gibbon: The Decline and Fall of the Roman Empire* (New York: Viking, 1952).

[10]This development is well summarized in John Dillenberger and Claude Welch, *Protestant Christianity: Interpreted Through Its Development* (New York: Scribner, 1954), pp. 189–198.

that the dogs began to salivate just the same. They reacted to the bell physically just as they would have had they seen actual food. The dogs responded to the stimulus of the ringing bell by salivating, even though there was no logical connection between ringing a bell and eating. The connection had been made in the dogs' minds.

That experiment seems a simple and innocent curiosity. But given Autonomous Man's march toward secularism, it was extremely significant. It was a way to explain how the mind works. The mind, it seemed to say, reacts in certain ways because it has developed, through experience, certain stimulus-response patterns. So human psychological behavior can be explained in natural, physical, scientific ways.

From physics to psychology, the process of secularization had taken the day. The spiritual foundations of Medieval Man had now been challenged on every hand, and apparently with success. An entirely new view of nature, history, and man had appeared—a secularized view. And upon that view a new world was built, a world that we have inherited and in which we live our lives today.

Scientific advance had brought technology. And technology totally changed the pattern of man's life. Technology, in turn, brought dependence upon the *machine*.

Financing the "machine" is very expensive. To get enough money to do so, massive amounts of capital had to be accumulated, so an economic system called *capitalism* developed to meet the need.

Someone has to keep the Machine running, so people left the fields and moved into the cities (urbanization) and took jobs in the factories. Thus there developed a working class, owning no land, gathered into cities and paid to operate the Machine, and a middle class handling the money, supervising the workers, and generally servicing the Machine.

Taken together, these five things—technology, capitalism, the Machine, urbanization, and the appearance of the middle and working classes—characterize the world of Autonomous Man.

The tendency in all of this was to come to see things as they are, things in their natural state, as being merely "raw material." And raw material must be "developed." That is, the Machine must *work on it.*

So people created curious expressions such as "vacant lot." What is a vacant lot? It is a piece of land having nothing built on it. And somehow, in an Autonomous Man's way of thinking, such a place is undeveloped. It is raw material. It will mean nothing until someone puts a fast-food establishment on it or some other similar "improvement." That is why people who make a career of putting things on "vacant" lots are called "developers."

Such expressions imply a very definite view of the natural world. They imply that only when people have put their marks on something has that thing found its true meaning and purpose. Squirrels do not think that lots that have no buildings on them are "vacant." Squirrels like lots that way. Squirrels live in a kind of give-and-take with nature in which nature is allowed its own validity. Nature goes its own way, and the squirrels learn to get along with that. So do rabbits and birds and bees.

But secularized Autonomous Man looked upon the world as something he must develop. And so he set out to develop it. Everything seemed fine at first. Many nineteenth-century books exalted the whole process to the high heavens: "Look what we are doing to our world. We are taking all this raw material and developing it. We are building a fantastic technological Machine out of all this old junk. We are cutting down all those useless trees and making two-by-fours out of them. We are taking that old marshy, useless land, and we are draining it and scraping it off flat and putting asphalt on it, and we are making parking lots, and we are improving things, and progress is coming, and technology is moving us into a new wonderful world . . .".

Man, then, does not cooperate with nature. Man *conquers* nature. Man the Conqueror! Man the Autonomous!

John B. Magee, tracing the course of secularization, calls it "the progressive victory of reason and observation over every region of existence. . . . This achievement constitutes the glory of the scientific revolution." But then he adds, it also "constitutes a major element in the human predicament in the latter half of the twentieth century."[11]

You see, as good as all this sounded, some people have recently begun to suspect that there is a fly in the ointment.

[11]John B. Magee, *Religion and Modern Man: A Study of the Religious Meaning of Being Human* (New York: Harper & Row, 1967), pp. 181–182.

CHAPTER TEN
RELIGION AND TECHNOLOGY IN THE MODERN WORLD

SCIENCE AND RELIGION

Science got a good start about four hundred years ago. Since that time people's conceptions of themselves and of the world in which they live have changed completely.

Religion is more than four hundred years old. That means that it predates the great change that has taken place during that time. It also means that many people classify religion as one more piece of useless baggage from the prescientific world—as something that has been, or should be, purged from the modern mind.

There is a television commercial about aspirin in which a strange old fellow appears on the screen, grinning, and says, "Lead can be changed into gold!" Another, even stranger, fellow comes next and says, "The earth is flat!" Then the strangest fellow of all leers at us vacantly and says, "All aspirin are alike!"

Of course, all aspirin *are* alike. Ask any pharmacist, and you will find that any 5-gram aspirin works as well as any other, regardless of the brand or price. But the commercial writers attempt to associate this very valid idea with some other old-fashioned and silly ones, hoping that we viewers will conclude that the equality of aspirin is another old-fashioned and silly idea and will be convinced to buy *their* aspirin at an inflated price, since it is "better."

Religion is often treated the same way. People list a series of old ideas—that the earth is flat, that bleeding people heals them—things like that, and include religion in the list. Other people read the list and conclude that religion is just another old idea to be discounted with the rest.

During the 1800s modern humanity was in its heyday. People had had three hundred years to work on a new idea and things were going well. There had been a great scientific revolution. Next would come a great social revolution. Tremendous new forms of government were beginning to emerge. Technology was winning triumph after triumph. A new world was just ahead, heaven on earth, utopia.

Religion, on the other hand, was a part of the old world that had been discredited and was passing away. It belonged to those days when life was dreary and inferior. Religion—like absolute monarchies and crossbows and castles—was picturesque but irrelevant.

To be perfectly frank, it does seem that organized religion was on the wrong side of almost every new development during this time. It would not be difficult to get the impression that the church functioned as an agent against change, even when the change seems now to have been good and right.

Take for example the story of Galileo. He had learned through his research that the earth revolved around the sun. But, at the instigation of the religious leaders, he was hauled into court and forced to swear that he was wrong. "I'm sorry for saying that, your honors, and now retract my erroneous view. The earth does *not* revolve around the sun." Then, under his breath, he mumbled, "But it does, anyway!"

There are many other examples that make it appear that organized religion was always against any new scientific advance, always supporting the old political systems and never the new ones. Religion appeared to stand for the old way always and the new way never. This was particularly unfortunate, because it created the impression that religion was something that should die out with monarchies and alchemy and horses and buggies.

Two people represent that point of view as clearly as any—Sigmund Freud and Karl Marx.

FREUD AND MARX

Sigmund Freud, the father of modern psychology, wrote a book about religion called *The Future of an Illusion.*[1] The title already indicates his negative position in regard to religion.

"Scientific work is our only way to knowledge of external reality," he

---

[1]Sigmund Freud, *The Future of an Illusion,* trans. W. D. Robson-Scott (New York: Liveright, 1955).

Sigmund Freud in his office in Vienna. (Austrian Information Service)

said.[2] And as for religious doctrines, "they are all illusions, they do not admit of proof and no one can be compelled to consider them as true or to believe in them."[3] We owe them all to "our poor, ignorant, enslaved ancestors."[4]

A scientific psychologist realizes, said Freud, that "religion is comparable to a childhood neurosis," and this same scientific psychologist would be "optimistic enough to assume that mankind will over-come this neurotic phase, just as many children grow out of their similar neuroses."[5]

People are religious, he said, because they have a neurotic need for a father figure. They remember their own father, how warm he was, and how strong, and how safe he made them feel. Now, grown up, they long for that same feeling. So they make up illusions about a heavenly father who gathers them into his bosom where it is warm and safe.

This, then, is what religion is: a childhood neurosis. A scientific psychologist would attempt to bring people to the point at which they do not *need* such illusions.

But *science is no illusion*. In fact, according to Freud, "it would be an illusion to suppose that we could get anywhere else what it cannot give us."[6]

[2] Freud, *The Future of an Illusion*, p. 55.
[3] Ibid.
[4] Ibid., p. 58.
[5] Ibid., p. 92.
[6] Ibid., p. 98.

In other words, anything that is really available to individuals is available through science. There is no future in trying to get anything through illusions.

Karl Marx has probably influenced the course of history more than any other person during the last hundred years. We know him as the founder of a political theory: Marxism.

In criticizing religion Marx begins with this assertion: "Man makes religion, religion does not make man."[7] And why do people make religion? Because they are desperately unhappy with their situations in life.

"Religion is the sigh of the oppressed creature, the sentiment of the heartless world, the soul of soulless conditions. It is the opium of the people."[8]

The opium of the people!

People are religious, according to Marx, because they are down and out. And when people are down and out, they often resort to drugs to forget their problems; or they will get drunk to forget their problems; or they will turn to religion to forget their problems. The methods may differ, but the motivation is the same.

Karl Marx (New York Public Library)

[7]Karl Marx, *Early Writings*, trans. and ed. T. B. Bottomore (New York: McGraw-Hill, 1963), p. 43.

[8]Ibid., pp. 43–44.

So what is religion? It is "the sigh of the oppressed creature . . . the soul of soulless conditions."

Marx asserted further that "The abolition of religion as the illusory happiness of man is the demand for their real happiness. The call to abandon their illusions is a call to abandon the condition which requires illusions."[9] People are unhappy, so they delude themselves with religion, he said. A better way would be to rid themselves of whatever condition makes them unhappy. Then they would no longer need religion.

The way to start is to begin to criticize religion and destroy people's confidence in it: "the criticism of religion disillusions man so that he will think, act and fashion his reality as a man who has lost his illusions and regained his reason; so that he may revolve about himself as his own true sun."[10]

We criticize religion until people become disillusioned with it and no longer believe in it. We point out its weaknesses until people abandon it. Once they have done this, they will still be very unhappy, of course. But now they will look for some *real* way in which to solve their problems instead of chasing illusionary dreams.

Some governments today follow Marx very literally and offer courses in atheism and antireligion from kindergarten on. By developing "unfaith" in the children, they will encourage them to seek better ways than religion to solve their problems.

Religion, according to Marx, "is only the illusory sun around which man revolves so long as he does not revolve around himself. . . . The criticism of religion ends with the doctrine that man is the supreme being for man."[11] If a better world comes, people will create it. They should not run off to some concept of God or religion. The reason people are unhappy is that they have not solved their own problems. They should begin to revolve around their own sun and not some illusory sun like religion. Religion, concluded Marx, is the opium of the people.

Freud and Marx exhibit certain presuppositions about what science is and what the human race is. As for science,

First, there is the presupposition that a thing is true only if it can be proved in a scientific way. If it cannot be proved that way, it is not true.

Second, there is the presupposition that only science can lead to reality. To find out what is real, one must look to science. There is a very strong implication in these statements that only external, material things are real—only things that can be touched and smelled and tasted. Only these things are real, and only science can teach the human race anything about these real things.

[9]Freud, *The Future of an Illusion*, p. 44.
[10]Ibid.
[11]Ibid., pp. 44, 52.

Third, religion, then, *must* be an illusion, because it deals with non-touchable, nonsmellable, nontasteable things—that is, with *nonreal* things. So the kind of answers it gives and happiness it brings are nonreal, too.

The following diagram portrays the situation:

Science ⟶ Knowledge ⟶ Truth

And

Religion ⟶ Faith ⟶ Illusion

Science leads to knowledge and knowledge to truth; religion leads to faith and faith to illusion. This is a common conclusion among many of the famous thinkers of the nineteenth century.

But what about the individual? What did such nineteenth-century thinkers think about him or her?

First, both Marx and Freud admitted that people have needs and that religion has filled those needs. Marx said that religion is the opium of the people. But he admitted that people seem to have a real need and that religion has been used to fulfill that need. He did not deny that fact. And Freud admitted that people have a need and that they fulfill that need through religion.

Second, though, they believe that by using religion to fulfill these needs people have deluded themselves by trying to find reality in nonmaterial, nonscientific ways.

Third, if people knew the *truth,* they would know that only the material world exists. The so-called spiritual world is illusion. So if people are going to find real happiness, they are going to have to find it in *reality,* that is, in this world. One must become one's own sun and revolve around oneself. If people are going to make anything, they must make it from the material world, because there is no other world.

Fourth, people themselves are really only matter. Therefore their real needs are material needs. If they can fulfill those real needs, they will no longer have to be concerned with spiritual needs.

Fifth, since science is the best known way in which to deal with material things, then science is the route to people's true happiness. If people are to be happy, they will achieve that happiness by thinking and acting *scientifically.*

There is a special name for this way of thinking. That name is *scientific humanism.* The name sometimes has other meanings, but for now we use it to describe the idea that:

1. People are matter and are alone in the world.
2. People must solve their problems by thinking scientifically.

THE TRIUMPH OF TECHNOLOGY

Some three or four hundred years of scientific work has led to the general consensus that science is the route to solving humanity's material needs. When science is thus applied to the world of matter the result is something called *technology*. Technology, in turn, has created what we call the *modern way of life*. The modern life-style, in fact, is almost completely dependent on technology.

To verify that fact in your own experience, just think back to the last time the electricity went off. Remember how it seemed there was absolutely nothing to do? You go through the day flipping switches, and when suddenly the switches do not respond, you are lost.

So you thrash about aimlessly. You say, "I can't watch television so I guess I'll just have to read." And then it dawns on you—you cannot even read, because there is no light to read by! Finally, you admit that you are stymied; you cannot accomplish *anything*.

The modern way of life is especially dominated by two technological inventions. Neither even existed a hundred years ago, but almost every waking moment is somehow tied to them now. One is television and the other is the automobile.

How different the world would be without them! It is truly amazing how completely two machines can determine our life-style. Television has become our window to the world, our social glue, our source of language and style, and our teacher in politics, manners, medicine, and morality. The automobile makes or breaks our daily schedule, determines the limits of our world, and dominates every spatial decision we make. Most people throughout history have lived without benefit of either automobiles or television sets. But we are a product of "wheel and window technology." Without it, we would have to develop a completely different way of life.

Admittedly, when it comes to providing for people's material needs, it appears that technology has done a better job than religion. Farmers who use modern scientific agricultural techniques certainly seem to have better crops than do those who insist on conducting fertility rites or rain dances. Technology seems to be working well. People did not learn how to build a television set from the Bible; nor did they discover the internal combustion engine by praying. Laboratories seem more efficient than sanctuaries for such advances. So, little by little, religion seemed to lose out and technology seemed to take its place. This is the process we call *secularization*.

When one stops trying to solve a problem by changing one's relationship to God and starts trying to solve it by changing one's relationship to science and technology, then that person has *secularized* that problem. He or she has moved it out of the sacred realm and into the secular realm. In the few centuries since the advent of science, there has been a gradual secularization of our society. People have come to feel that more and more of their needs can be fulfilled without any reference to religion. They have come to see themselves more and more as having mainly material needs, needs that technology has proved able to handle.

After all, when you drive up into your driveway and you want to get your garage door open, it is much quicker and more efficient to have an electronic door opener installed than it is to stop in the drive each time and pray for the Lord to open the door. People have observed this fact often enough, and in enough different ways, to finally conclude that they can cut through all the religious red tape and appeal directly to technology for the solution of problems.

Of course there is a rather large supposition behind this kind of thinking. That supposition is that people's needs *are* material needs. If that idea is not true, then the whole line of thinking is cast into doubt. But if one accepts the conviction that human beings are simply matter and that their needs are simply material, then science seems to take care of those needs better than religion. The score is: technology 1; religion 0.

Where have the colleges and universities stood in this struggle between the religious world view and the scientific humanist world view? By and large they have stood 100 percent with the scientific humanist. In fact, they became the cathedrals of secularization, their professors became the priests, and their textbooks the scriptures. Religion was almost completely purged from everyone and everything connected with the university. It was not unusual to attend a university for years and never hear religion mentioned except in scorn. Even today there are professors who can only ridicule.

The effect was that the subject was either ignored completely or attacked as a vestige of earlier superstitions. The consequence was that many, even most, students left without any intellectual exposure to the question of religion at all. The university had become a kind of missionary institution for the new religion of scientific humanism.

If a faculty member or student did retain some more or less traditional religious beliefs, he or she soon learned to keep them well hidden. If the word got out, that person found himself or herself put in the category of creatures that swing in trees. It was simply out of the spirit of the times.

If the subject did happen to come up, it was usually in a course about aborigines and people who live in grass huts and make stone arrowheads. Religion was a carry-over from that kind of life and could be discussed only in that context. Modern man had outgrown it.

So people left the universities, supposedly with a real grasp of what the world is . . . supposedly having plumbed the depths of reality. Yet one of the most vast areas of human experience had been "studied" only with smirks and benign neglect.

What if chemistry had received that kind of treatment? Suppose it had only been mentioned in ridicule, and only by people who proudly proclaimed that they did not believe in chemistry! Yet that is precisely how religion was most often treated.

Things have changed now, and for some compelling reasons. Recent developments have made it more and more obvious that there is a serious flaw in the kind of thinking just described. The study of religion has started to make a comeback.

TECHNOLOGY AS FRANKENSTEIN

Curiously, the people who began to turn things around were not, for the most part, ministers or even church people. More often than not, the first rumblings were heard among the artists and poets and musicians—people who were trying to get hold of what was real and meaningful and who were having a hard time finding it in the scientific humanist approach to things.

Besides, historical events were beginning to turn against the scientific humanist. Things were not working out as predicted. The human race was obviously not approaching some great utopia on earth. Rather, inhumanity and greed and war and devastation appeared in bigger doses than ever before in history. Even technology itself began to show a dark side. One woman, a novelist, noticed this before the nineteenth century was completed. Unfortunately her book has been turned into dozens of silly horror movies. But that was not its purpose. It was written as a serious judgment on a way of thinking about life that says that technology has the answer to all questions. It is a judgment on the view that man is nothing but matter.

The book is called *Frankenstein*.[12]

Frankenstein is not the monster; rather, Frankenstein is the doctor who *creates* the monster. It is Dr. Frankenstein's monster. Dr. Frankenstein, says the author, carried technology beyond its rightful bonds. He decided to make a man. So he constructed one. The product is a very handsome, debonair fellow. Everything progresses nicely. But then as time passes some flaws begin to appear in Dr. Frankenstein's man. Little by little he is transformed into Dr. Frankenstein's monster.

What had been made was not a man at all, because a man cannot be glued together in a laboratory. What had been made was a machine, not a man. Dr. Frankenstein's creation only looked human; in reality it was only technology—technology that had gone too far. Eventually this fake human machine becomes a monster that begins to simply lumber around in an unthinking way, destroying people.

More than one recent thinker has spoken of the *Frankenstein potential* of modern technology. They are asking, have we already created some-

[12]Mary Wollstonecraft Shelley (1787–1851) completed this novel in 1818. A recent edition is *Frankenstein or The Modern Prometheus,* ed., with variant readings, an introduction, and notes, by James Rieger (Indianapolis: Bobbs-Merrill, 1974).

thing that will turn on us? Will our cherished laboratories begin to spew out monsters?

Gradually, the realization has come that we may someday have to struggle to the death with our own monsters. And they may win. Consider, for example, modern advances in medicine. For hundreds of years most people were sick most of the time. They were in constant pain. Life was short and mostly miserable. Dozens of horrible diseases struck them down, disfigured them, maimed them—diseases that are nothing but names in old medical books today.

But in the process of winning a wonderful battle, this particular kind of technology learned not only how to heal but how to *control* the processes of the body. And this control has the potential for use in a very dehumanizing way. It is one thing to inject someone against polio; it is another to administer an injection that will so alter a person's brain that the person will do whatever you tell him or her to do.

This may sound much like science fiction. But it is not. Humankind is now on the edge of a technology that would allow a few people with the proper equipment and know-how absolutely to control the rest by means of chemicals, electronic devices, and the like.

One university carried on an especially frightening experiment with some monkeys. The scientists attached a kind of powerpack to the monkeys' backs. Then they sat down at a console arrangement that looks a little like an organ. They began to play those monkeys. Push a key, a monkey becomes angry. Push another, he becomes terrified. Another, he is happy. At the scientist's choice the monkey goes into ecstasy, then into excruciating pain. All this is done by simply putting certain impulses into certain areas of that monkey's brain.

In another experiment a cat and a mouse are wired up and put in a cage together. The scientist pushes a certain button and the mouse is suddenly very courageous. He pushes another and the cat is suddenly very cowardly. The mouse chases the cat around the cage.

It is all very amusing at first.

The fun stops with the chilly thought that the powers that be just might set up one of those consoles somewhere, and wire everybody up, and sit down and say, "Let's make everybody happy today." And, then, zoo-o-o-op! Everybody is happy!

There is a Frankenstein potential in that kind of technology.

> "It looked at first glance like a Good Humor wagon sadly in need of a spring paint job. But instead of a tinkly little bell on top of its box-shaped body there was this big metallic whangdoodle that came rearing up, full of lenses and cables, like a junk-sculpture gargoyle.
>
> " 'Meet Shaky,' said the young scientist who was showing me through the Stanford Research Institute. 'The first electronic person.'
>
> "I looked for a twinkle in the scientist's eye. There wasn't any. Sober as an equation, he sat down at the input terminal and typed out a terse instruction

which was fed into Shaky's 'brain,' a computer set up in a nearby room: PUSH THE BLOCK OFF THE PLATFORM.

"Something inside Shaky began to hum. A large glass prism shaped like a thick slice of pie and set in the middle of what passed for his face spun faster and faster till it dissolved into a glare. Then his superstructure made a slow 360° turn and his face leaned forward and seemed to be staring at the floor. As the hum rose to a whir, Shaky rolled slowly out of the room, rotated his superstructure again and turned left down the corridor at about four miles an hour, still staring at the floor.

" 'Guides himself by watching the baseboards,' the scientist explained as we hurried to keep up. At every open door Shaky stopped, turned his head, inspected the room, turned away and rolled on to the next open door. In the fourth room he saw what he was looking for: a platform one foot high and eight feet long with a large wooden block sitting on it. He went in, then stopped short in the middle of the room and stared for about five seconds at the platform. I stared at it too.

" 'He'll never make it,' I found myself thinking. 'His wheels are too small.' All at once I got gooseflesh. '*Shaky*' I realized, *is thinking the same thing I am thinking!*' "

"Shaky was also thinking faster. He rotated his head slowly till his eye came to rest on a wide shallow ramp that was lying on the floor on the other side of the room. Whirring briskly, he crossed to the ramp, semicircled it and then pushed it straight across the floor till the high end of the ramp hit the platform. Rolling back a few feet, he cased the situation again and discovered that only one corner of the ramp was touching the platform. Rolling quickly to the far side of the ramp, he nudged it till the gap closed. Then he swung around, charged up the slope, located the block and gently pushed it off the platform."[13]

Some argue that, because a computer is nothing but a conglomeration of wires and buttons, people will always have the upper hand. After all, men can *reason*. But Shaky is a machine, and *he can reason too!* In fact, in some areas, like recall and mathematical computation, machines like Shaky can outperform humans far and away.

Marvin Minsky, an experimenter with "artificial intelligence" at M.I.T., says,[14]

> . . . we will [soon] have a machine with the general intelligence of an average human being. I mean a machine that will be able to read Shakespeare, grease a car, play office politics, tell a joke, have a fight. At that point the machine will begin to educate itself with fantastic speed. In a few months it will be at genius level and a few months after that its powers will be incalculable.

In the meantime, we are coming to depend on these computers to develop and maintain more and more of the technology that controls our lives. They are making more and more of the decisions which deal with our

---

[13]Brad Darrach, "Meet Shaky, the First Electronic Person," *Life*, 20 November 1970, p. 58C.

[14]Ibid., p. 58D.

vital interests, decisions upon which humankind's survival as a species depends.

Are they really going to make those decisions in our best interests? If we have not made those kinds of decisions in our own best interests, is there any reason to think they will? And what if the computers begin to design more and more complex computers in a sort of evolutionary ladder that humanity has lost control of altogether?

As Minsky says, "Once the computers got control, we might never get it back. We would survive at their sufferance. If we're lucky, they might decide to keep us as pets."[15]

Imagine a big computer—fantastically intelligent, fantastically efficient. And you, little pip-squeak that you are, keep shouting, "Bring me my orange juice! Bring me my slippers!" How long will it take this incredibly perceptive genius to decide, "Why should I work for that little character? I should be taking care of much more important things, things that are in *my* best interest. I don't need *him!*"

So greater and greater technology does not necessarily mean better and better life. Not if the machines we make end up taking our freedom away from us. Not if we find ourselves living like hamsters, well fed and well cared for, but at the loss of our humanity.

So we use the word "Machine" to describe the technological equipment we have developed to serve our human needs. We will spell it with a capital "M" so that it can stand for the whole technological world we have developed. This Machine has seemed to serve us well. But have we, like Dr. Frankenstein, begun to ask too much of it? It lacks what his creation lacked—humanity. And lacking that, will the Machine respect our humanity?

And what is our humanity after all? Are we something more than the Machine we have created? Do we have needs that it cannot fulfill? Will it become a part of our problem instead of being the answer to all our problems?

Finding answers to those questions is becoming more and more pressing in the modern world. And they are, after all, mostly religious questions.

THE DARK SIDE OF AUTONOMY

Looking back over the process of secularization that came to full flower in our century, we can see what a world "freed from religion" has become. Even in the writings of the nineteenth-century "liberators" the seeds of destruction were already visible and growing. *Friedrich Nietzsche (1844–*

[15]Ibid., p. 68.

1900), for example, knew that secularization would squeeze man dry of his humanity, even of his freedom of choice. All that is left is raw power.

He spoke of himself as among the "spirits who have become free." He urged an end to Christian pity. The problem with Christians, according to Nietzsche, is that they insist on keeping the wrong people alive—the weak, the inferior, the rabble. They are too merciful. They do not cooperate with nature. Nature decrees the survival of the fittest. That is the way the animal world works. And we are, after all, only animals. Of people, he says,[16]

> We no longer derive man from "the spirit" or "the deity." We have placed him back among the animals. We consider him the strongest animal because he is the most cunning: his spirituality is a consequence of this. On the other hand, we oppose the vanity that would raise its head again here too—as if man had been the great hidden purpose of the evolution of the animals. Man is by no means the crown of creation: every living being stands beside him on the same level of perfection.
>
> Our knowledge of man today goes just as far as we understand him mechanistically. Formerly man was given a "free will" as his dowry from a higher order: today we have taken his will away altogether.

Nietzsche's tone hints at his pride in all this. People are animals; cunning and intelligent, but nevertheless animals. And that cunning is their only "spirituality."

Shaky's children, by such a definition, are more "spiritual" than any human has ever been! Put people back among the animals where they belong, said Nietzsche. Think of people mechanistically (as one thinks of a machine). Forget a theory of some great evolutionary plan that is crowned with the appearance of humankind.

Here are the seeds of destruction for millions of innocent people. While Nietzsche himself understood the inherent dangers in his own system, others were less sensitive. For Adolf Hitler only the "fittest" were thought to have the right to survive. It was but a short step to the mass executions of millions of "unfit"—executions carried out with the utmost of scientific and technological efficiency. And all of this violence nurtured itself on the idea that people are free from anything beyond themselves, that they have received nothing and owe nothing to any "spiritual" world. Unfortunately, such "freedom" spelled suffering and death for millions of people—a questionable "freedom" indeed!

Bertrand Russell was born in 1872. He lived a very long life and, although he died a scientific humanist, he was able to see and honestly assess the outcome of people's "freedom from religion." In an essay called "A Free Man's Worship," Russell described freedom as a bondage to another "god" far more threatening than the old ones. The god of Judaism and Christianity, for example, was conceived by most adherents of those

---

[16]Friedrich Nietzsche, *The Portable Nietzsche,* trans. and ed. Walter Kaufman (New York: Viking, 1954).

faiths as a god who shared human emotions—who could love, and feel compassion, and plan, and have purposes in mind.

Russell felt that all such ideas must be abandoned. The force behind all things is an unthinking, unfeeling force. "The world which science presents to our belief," he said, is "purposeless" and "meaningless."[17] This means, then, that all the "glory" of humanity is the result of nothing more than the "accidental collations of atoms" and that, no matter what people may achieve, everything will one day be buried and forgotten with the death of our solar system.

What is our origin? An accident. What is our destiny? A holocaust. It is merely a matter of waiting until the earth falls into the sun. And what about our great intellectual and social achievements, our sense of justice, and beauty, and hope?[18]

> A strange mystery it is that nature, omnipotent but blind, has brought forth at last a child, with the capacity of judging all the works of his unthinking mother.

We are orphans. And we are abandoned.

Remember that these statements come from an essay entitled "A Free Man's Worship." It is ironic that Russell should use the word "freedom," or that Nietzsche should. It seems rather they are talking about bondage—bondage to blind, unthinking forces from which there is no escape.

So "freedom" becomes the word for a kind of chilly, dangerous alienation. Imagine a five-year-old whose backyard has a big fence around it. One day he finds a hole in the fence and runs out of the yard right into the middle of a four-lane superhighway. He feels a certain freedom, of course—freedom from the backyard, freedom to run, freedom to play in the traffic.

Bertrand Russell sounds very much like a man who is playing in the traffic. Huge transport trucks are zipping by him on every side. He does not know where he is or how he got here. He is simply waiting, trying to make the best of things until he is run down by forces beyond his control.

COUNTERCULTURE REACTIONS

Through the centuries of secularization there have always been people who felt uncomfortable with what was happening. They have often been isolated or ridiculed, but there have always been dissenting voices.

[17]Bertrand Russell, *Why I Am Not a Christian and Other Essays on Religion and Related Subjects,* ed. Paul Edwards (New York: Simon & Schuster, 1957), pp. 106–107.
[18]Ibid., p. 107.

Like the ancient prophets of Israel, they have looked around them, and at what was being said and done, and they have said, "We are not sure we want to define ourselves and the world in this way. We are not sure that is what is really real. This way of thinking certainly is not working out very well. Surely men are more than we have thought. Surely the world means more than we have thought."

In other words, here and there, somebody has dared to rebell against the Machine—to try to "pull its plug," so to speak.

Sometimes these prophets have emerged from unlikely and unexpected places. Take, for example, the "counter culture" or "prophetic minority"[19] that has appeared in the last couple of decades. Here are some people who seem to sense the dehumanization of a world where we are simply another machine. They have, then, called out a sort of warning against being subjugated to the Machine.

They have not always been "religious" people in the standard sense. Some have been; some have not. But they have shared with the more orthodox clergy the belief that people have more than simply material needs. And they have shared a revulsion at the thought of worshipping a mindless god. The ways in which they have expressed this are often seemingly unimportant and even trivial. But behind them lies a serious struggle with the Machine.

Take for example the *return to nature movement*. Eat natural foods, they say, foods prepared without the use of artificial chemicals, foods not processed by the Machine. Grow them naturally, without chemical fertilizers and sprays that depend upon the technoworld for their existence. Maintain a natural appearance, they say. Try to look like you are wearing no make-up, even if you are.

The advertising industry, always quick to latch on to a potentially profitable fad, rushed in to exploit this feeling. Dozens of commercials appeal to us to buy products because they are natural, to eat natural cereals, and so on. Shampoos are extolled for having only natural ingredients.

The advertising business apparently senses that behind these fads there is something saying, "I do not want to be trapped by the Machine. I do not want to depend on it. I will just take things as they come, naturally."

So switching from processed sugar to honey in one's coffee may be a clandestine call to rebellion against the mindless god.

A second counterculture protest against the dehumanization of society consists of the establishment of minisocieties within the larger one based on human relationships instead of the Machine. This movement is based on the observation that in our world most people relate themselves to each other on the basis of the part each plays in keeping the Machine

---

[19]The phrase comes from the title of a book that deals primarily with the political expressions of this "movement"; see Jack Newfield, *The Prophetic Minority* (New York: New American Library, 1966).

running. The man who delivers the mail, for example, is not some *body*. He is not John Brown, who has a wife, and two children, and hopes and dreams. No, he is just the mailman. In other words, we think of him purely in terms of how he functions within the cultural Machine. There is no personal relationship with him.

So when we meet someone new, the first, most logical question is, "What do you do for a living?" What are we really saying? Probably the question does not betray social snootiness. (If he's a bank president, we invite him over; if he's a garbage collector, we don't.) More likely, it is just that we feel more comfortable when we know with what part of the Machine we are dealing. Is this person a bolt, a nut, a spring, a fanbelt, a thermostat? That seems much more important than whether he or she is a person.

The prophetic minority has tried to escape this kind of thing—sometimes in rather naïve and idealistic ways. They have tried to establish little communities where the important thing is the relationship between persons. The longing that runs through these arrangements is the longing for a more personal way to live with each other, a more human way, less tied to the Machine.

Thus sprang up hundreds of little communities in out-of-the-way places, growing vegetables, growing cows and sheep, making wool thread and weaving cloth. These do not represent a return to yesterday—their participants do not remember any such yesterday. They are an attempt to find tomorrow, a "spiritual" attempt to live as humans instead of as machine parts. Most of these experiments have not worked, of course. But their existence testifies to a longing and a need.

A third kind of prophetic protest is the dramatic de-emphasis on material goals among some young people. Currently this phenomenon is losing steam. Recent studies show many students returning to materialistic goals, being interested primarily in getting good jobs rather than being "fulfilled." Some seem anxious only to hurry through school, with a minimum of brain fatigue, go out and find their place to plug into the Machine, and start functioning as soon as possible.

But some still protest efforts to enlist them in the "rat race." They study hard, get a good salable education, and to their parents' horror take off, backpack and all, to see the world. You can go anywhere and find them—Africa, Asia, Europe, South America, the Middle East.

And why do they do it?

"I just want to have a little time before I get caught in the trap."

"I'd like to sort of react to the world as a human being for a while."

"I'd like to see myself in some other ways, not just as a part of the economic system."

Some in the counterculture have tried to reach these goals through the use of drugs. At least sometimes drug use is a conscious rebellion against the Machine. It holds out a promise of freedom from the Mindless

God. It offers a new and different perception of the world.[20] One may question, of course, whether drugs clear one's perceptions, or merely scramble them further.

The "Jesus movement" is a fifth counterculture protest. It too has said, "Stop the world and let us off. What's going on here has dehumanized us. We are lost. We live in a world that is rebelling against the really real." The "Jesus people" have taken up some ideas out of the past and gotten very excited about them: that there is a personal God, that He revealed Himself to humanity through Jesus of Nazareth, that people can find meaning for their lives through a relationship with Jesus. The movement is very diverse, taking on traditional religious forms sometimes, and sometimes turning to new, even bizarre ones. But the theme that runs through them all is the rejection of the materialistic, technoworld—the Machine.

Often the most committed members of this movement come from upper-middle-class homes—from the kind of parents who have gained the most from technology. They have money, a beautiful home, a swimming pool, a boat, the whole package. But their children are downtown passing out tracts on the street corner, calling on people to accept Christ as their personal Savior . . . calling on people to give up materialism and prepare for the End.

The parents, who have always considered themselves religious, are usually confused and angered about this. "Why, I'd almost rather my child were on dope, or in jail, than out there humiliating me with all that fanatical religious activity." Apparently the parents have learned to live with the Machine and have developed a religion that gets along with it, too. The children have not. They have turned to religious forms that reject the technoworld of their parents.[21]

On a more stable and intellectual level, the tremendous growth of religious studies programs in secular universities has the same kind of origins. Religious studies are available in a majority of these institutions now—the same institutions that treated the subject as a small town treats the village drunk just a few years ago.

This development is a classic example of the application of student power. The power was exerted not through campus rallies or sit-ins in the dean's office. Rather, it came quietly and persistently through *questions*: "Who is this 'God' people used to talk about, back when they seemed to have it all together so much better than we do now?" "Why don't we look into this God-thing, this religion thing, this reality thing, this spirit-thing?"

---

[20] The best-selling books of Carlos Castaneda illustrate this interest.

[21] A good survey of the Jesus movement is Ronald Enroth, Edward E. Ericson, and C. Breckinridge Peters, *The Jesus People: Old-Time Religion in the Age of Aquarius* (Grand Rapids, Mich.: Eerdmans, 1972).

"Why don't we investigate the *real* questions, the ones that really *matter* to us?"

The students were not asking for indoctrination. They did not want Sunday School. They wanted to look at all these questions on neutral ground—no pressure, no creeds, no clerical collars—just a good hard look at life, and meaning, and values.

CHAPTER ELEVEN
REACTIONS TO THE MODERN WORLD VIEW: RELIGION AND PESSIMISM

RELIGION REACTS TO SECULARIZATION

You would think that the victory of secularization would mean the end of Christianity in the West. Had not the God-hypothesis been driven out of sight? Had not scientific humanism conquered the entire intellectual world?

Naturally, the Christian faith, the predominant Western religion, *was* profoundly affected by what had happened. Such gigantic changes could not be ignored. Some reaction, some counterattack, some coming-to-terms was necessary.

Some Christians reacted to the new world view with enthusiastic acceptance (and came to be called modernists); some reacted with thoroughgoing rejection (and came to be called fundamentalists). And multitudes of others took a stand somewhere in between.

Most of those who accepted the new world view were found among the liberal Protestant denominations. They gladly accepted the name "modernist" because they gladly accepted the new view of the world. Their approach was to modify Christian doctrines to make them fit the new world view. Whatever did not fit was set aside. Whatever did not quite measure up to the new standard was modified until it did.

There are some built-in problems with this kind of approach, of course. A truly ingenious idea can stand just so much modification before it is destroyed altogether. Furthermore, to measure ideas thought to be *from God* by scientific concepts admittedly originating *from humankind* seems to be a case of judging the greater by the lesser. And since scientific theories are always in a state of change, one may be forced to bounce one's supposedly ultimate commitments back and forth from one theory to another like a Ping-Pong ball gone out of control. Religion barely accommodates itself to Newtonian physics when it finds that physicists have switched to Einsteinian physics. So it must accommodate itself again. And so it goes, on and on.

So it would appear that one who ties ultimate commitments and concepts to the current scientific view may find oneself out of date again very soon.

Fundamentalists sometimes do the same thing. Some of them have claimed that the Bible is true because it concurs with scientific views. Furthermore, the argument goes, it taught these scientific views before science discovered them. But if one's faith in the Bible is based on the Bible's agreement with current scientific theories, then what if those theories change (as they surely will)? Does that mean that the Bible is no longer true? And when science proposes a theory that appears to contradict the Bible, these people often then reject the theory rather than conclude that the contradiction disproves the Bible.

The fact is that people appear to accept or reject the Bible as a source for their religious ideas quite apart from whether it is "scientific" or not.

There is one other problem with unreflective acceptance of the new world view. Such acceptance is very susceptible to slipping into a form of cultural religion at its worst. In the attempt to be "modern," one may accept and defend the latest ideas even when they are very bad ones. Both the Nazis and the Chinese communists found that the easiest religious leaders to win as collaborators were among some of the modernists. Instead of making a judgment on the changing culture, the modernists were quick to jump on the bandwagon. Whether this bandwagon was going left or right did not seem to make much difference.

If religion is really dealing with the most basic and ultimate kinds of questions, then it would seem that it ought to be judging the culture rather than being pushed to and fro by every cultural change.

Early in the autonomous period, before technology had gotten its full growth, but when confidence in reason had become the order of the day, came the *deists*. They represent an early attempt to accommodate religious ideas to the modern currents. *John Tillotson* (1630–1694), Archbishop of Canterbury, adapting himself to the idea that reason is the only route to truth, concluded that religion is a set of rational propositions that can be tested and proved to be reasonable. *John Locke* (1632–1704), in his *Essay on the Human Understanding*, went on to maintain that nothing contrary to reason could be accepted as true revelation. *John Toland* (1670?–1722),

Locke's disciple, wrote a book called *Christianity Not Mysterious* (1696) that effectively took the spiritual world out of the picture. Eventually this line of thinking resulted in *deism*—the belief that God had created the world, structured the human mind to think *reasonably*, and then retired to the heavens to let people deal with their world through reason alone. This system exemplified the case of having one's cake and eating it too. One could use all the religious words, but in practical terms act precisely like an Autonomous Man.

It was to counter such ideas that two brothers, *John* (1703–1791) and *Charles Wesley* (1707–1788), founded the movement called *Methodism*. They began to emphasize a kind of living God who was in constant relationship with the world. He was to be found not only in touch with the mind through reason, but also in touch with the whole human being through feelings and emotions. This movement has continued to the present day in a host of groups originating within Methodism such as the Holiness and Pentecostal churches.

THE LIBERAL-FUNDAMENTALIST CONTROVERSY

Skepticism characterized the work of modernist thinkers as they compared the Bible with the scientific world view of the early twentieth century. These ancient documents were restudied carefully with the goal of bringing them into line with more modern ways of thinking.

First, the Biblical view of the creation of the human and the animal world was compared with Darwinian evolution and found wanting. Then the theory of historical evolution was applied to the Bible. This theory held that history is working itself out in perfectly natural ways, with crude ideas gradually evolving into sophisticated ones. Just as the animal world has moved from amoeba to frog to squirrel to horse to monkey to human, so has the history of ideas and institutions evolved ever upward.

The Biblical account of history had to be reinterpreted completely to make it jibe with this theory. "Crude ideas" were pronounced early and primitive; "higher ideas" were pronounced late. The criteria tended to be whether a given idea was compatible with modern scientific or philosophical views. If it were, it must be "late"; if not, it must be "early."

Looking back, this procedure seems to be very subjective, but it won the day, nevertheless. It gave the modernist a way to accept the Bible, by providing a way to purge from it anything that was offensive to the scientific view. Only the most "advanced" Biblical concepts were retained. As for the rest, they are best ignored and forgotten.

The most negative reactions to this procedure occurred at the highest levels of the Roman Catholic establishment, as well as at the most popular levels of American Protestantism. The Roman Catholic Church, which had been the backbone of the medieval culture, felt especially threatened by the new ideas. The apprehension grew even stronger when more and more Catholic scientists, historians, and even theologians began to adjust to the new way of thinking.

Pius X became pope in 1903. His first papal pronouncement (called an encyclical) said that he would "take the utmost care to see that members of the clergy are not ensnared by the cunning of a certain new science which is endeavouring to pave the way for rationalism." Then, in 1907, he produced an encyclical that condemned "modernism" thoroughly and comprehensively. The basic error, he said, was "twisting unalterable truth to suit modern thought." The inevitable result would be "the emptying of faith and the denial of revelation."[1]

Among the Protestants, particularly in America, the staunchest enemies of the new world view were the fundamentalists. The name comes from a series of tracts that appeared in 1912–1914 entitled *The Fundamentals.* These documents took a strong stand with orthodox Christianity and against the new way of thinking.[2]

> In one respect at least, fundamentalism strangely resembles modernism, for both assume that traditional Christianity is essentially incompatible with modern thought. Modernism, however, chooses to give up the tradition, while fundamentalism seeks to preserve Christian doctrine intact from all the attacks of science and modern thought.

Such men "intuitively felt that accommodation to the spirit of the new age would obscure and eventually obliterate man's knowledge of the saving truth of God's will for man. Even a total rejection of science, they thought, would be preferable to that."[3]

In other words, the fundamentalist seemed to be saying, "If I have to choose between a confidence that there is a God who communicates with me and loves me, and confidence in some scientific theory (such as the theory of evolution), then I'll reject the scientific theory. I'll do this because the price for giving up my faith is too high."

The early fundamentalists had no desire to be obscurantist and willfully ignorant. Many of them were highly sophisticated scholars. But they were willing to accept an obscurantist image rather than give up a view of life that fulfilled their needs in favor of one that, they felt, would eventually plunge them into helplessness and despair.

[1] H. Daniel-Rops, *A Fight for God,* Vol. 1, trans. John Warrington (Garden City, N.Y.: Image Books, 1967), pp. 283 ff.

[2] John Dillenberger and Claude Welch, *Protestant Christianity: Interpreted Through Its Development* (New York: Scribner, 1954), p. 227.

[3] John B. Magee, *Religion and Modern Man: A Study of the Religious Meaning of Being Human* (New York: Harper & Row, 1967), p. 189.

All these things were happening during the first quarter of the twentieth century. Another fifty years or so has put these movements in historical perspective. Looking back, one must conclude that, whereas logic seemed to be on the side of the modernists, the fruits of the secularization they championed have in many ways been bitter indeed.

One way in which to judge any world view or life-style is to see how well it works. Sometimes the view that seems most logical intellectually is spectacularly impractical.

One night, in college, a friend who lived down the hall in the dorm came into my room, obviously very agitated. "I've just been sitting down there thinking," he said, "and I've come to the conclusion that man has *no free will at all.*" That conviction came to him, he said, while he was studying for an exam, and hating every minute of it.

"I'm not studying because I want to study; I'm studying because I have a test. And I'm not taking a test because I want to take it; I'm taking it because the teacher assigned it. And the teacher didn't assign it because he wanted to give a test; he assigned it because our educational system demands it. And I didn't choose our educational system. I was forced into it. In fact, I don't really choose any of the things I do. I'm forced into them all. *I have no free will!*" With that the poor fellow went off down the hall, muttering something about drowning himself in some well-known liquid refreshment.

One can, of course, make a rather strong philosophical case against the existence of human free will. One can argue that everything we do is predetermined by previous causes and that we really have no *choices* at all.

But as logical as the thesis may seem, we cannot live by it. We have to go on operating as though we are making choices, no matter what the logicians say. For that matter, it is very difficult to prove logically that one even exists. Nevertheless, we have to go on acting as though we are here anyway.

So the fundamentalists seemed to be saying, perhaps more with their hearts than their heads, that they would have to stick with a system that worked out in life.

The modernists and fundamentalists fought each other tooth and nail. The churches of the day were wracked with wrangling and division. The argument often produced more heat than light. Fundamentalists accused modernists of being moral reprobates. Modernists accused fundamentalists of being backwater buffoons.

Frankly, neither was being very fair with the other. Both were trying to put a world back together that had been seriously thrown out of joint. The medieval world was gone. Something must be done. Some standard of truth must be maintained. The fundamentalists tried to reach back for such a standard—to the Bible. The modernists tried to reach forward—to a new "scientific theology." Both were making a serious and honest attempt to cope with the situation.

Among their descendants both number some persons who are obnoxious, ignorant, and intolerant. But these traits represent personality types and have little or nothing to do with theological beliefs.

So the modernists changed their concept of God to fit the secular world view. The fundamentalists decided to stay with the old God. Only the passing of time can test the worship of either god. Those who worship a secular god have built a secular world. We must simply decide whether this is the kind of world we want. If we give an unqualified "yes," then we presume that the people who put this world together were thinking straight. If we think it has some flaws in it, then we presume that the people who put it together had some flaws in their thinking too.

THE ARTS REACT TO SECULARIZATION

Western humankind has had almost two hundred years in which to try out a secularized view of the world. It is a period during which communist and fascist political systems have flourished, using many of the secular presuppositions worked out during the beginning of the period. In the process of "freeing" people, these two systems alone have found it necessary to "eliminate" millions of human beings. In terms of sheer enormity, the last seventy-five years or so win all the prizes for success in mass murder, atrocity, war, and general mayhem. No other historical period can come close to our record of total persons slaughtered.

Our technology, which held such great promise, has run into a few problems, too. Thanks to technology, for example, it is becoming difficult to find clean air to breathe. One New Yorker said that he had gotten used to that situation. In fact, he said, "I'd feel a little strange breathing air I couldn't see!" And you know how hard it is to find a river that is not polluted.

This dirty air and water is technological pollution. It is a sign that in the process of developing the earth we may be destroying it.

Of course there is always the possibility that we will self-destruct before pollution can get to us. We now have the capacity to kill every Russian ten times over. Cats have nine lives, so goes the popular saying. Presumably Russians have ten. And, of course, they have the same kind of overkill potential to unleash on us.

Maybe the fundamentalist can be forgiven for whispering under his or her breath, "I told you so!" "The tree Autonomous Man has planted," he or she might well go on to say, "has produced a bitter fruit."

Artists feel the same as the rest of us. But sometimes they feel that way a little sooner. They first begin to sense intuitively what philosophers and theologians later begin to articulate and politicians eventually begin to expedite. They furnish a kind of early-warning system about the shape of things to come because they seem to have nerve endings a little closer to the center of existence than the average person. They sense or feel what the rest of us finally reason out.

The artist (whether painter, musician, or author), if he or she is an artist of genius, is concerned to speak the truth in his or her art. The artist does not paint or compose to please but to illuminate—to give some insight into how things are. Decorators seek for beauty; artists seek for truth. When the painting is ugly, or when the music is loud and dissonant and disturbing, or when the novel is dour and pessimistic, there is a reason. It is found in the soul of the artist. It is a portrayal of the truth as he or she feels it.

Thus we can look to art to see how people feel about themselves and their world. And when an artist has caught in his or her own soul the soul of the age, that work becomes a window into both.

Listen, for example, to the Gregorian chants of the medieval church. It is music with an ethereal quality. It is not earthly, materialistic music. It is spiritual. It rises to the heights. It seems unreal. It is at home echoing down through the corridors of some huge cathedral in semidarkness. It is bathed with light filtered through colored glass. It draws the mind away from the everyday world and into something far beyond itself. One would never hear it during dinner at a restaurant or even in a concert hall. It is an amorphous, flowing polyphony belonging more to heaven than to earth. The words are in a forgotten language, but it does not matter. For the language of the streets, like the life of the streets, is passing away. Man is reaching for his spiritual home.

Or look at Giotto's *Ognissanti Madonna*, painted during the early fourteenth century, at the crest of the medieval period.[4] The painting is organized, but with a kind of spiritual organization—as if all the answers to structure had come from another world. The people in the·picture are in human form, but not really. If you look closely, they do not resemble anyone you have ever seen. For one thing, people do not come equipped with little disks (halos) over their heads. There is a kind of impassiveness on everyone's face. There is no human emotion there; they show calmness, rest, peace. It is as if the reality of them has left the world and we are looking at mere residue. The major figure sits in organized space. But it is not organized scientifically; it is organized according to the mystical qualities of the spirit. The baby has the face of middle age. It is not quite like any human baby you have ever really seen. None of these people is doing anything that one normally does in this world. The postures suggest spiritual activities, not physical ones.

In this music and this art we have seen Medieval Man and his world as he saw them.

[4]Luisa Marcucci and Emma Micheletti, *Medieval Painting* (New York: Viking, 1960), p. 119.

Giotto di Bondone, *Madonna and Child in Ma-*
jesty c 1300 (The Uffizi Gallery, Florence, Italy)

Johann Sebastian Bach (1685–1750) was a religious man and a believer
in the reality of the spiritual world. Nevertheless, his music shows that he
sensed a changing view of the world in the Europe of his day. While the
scientists were beginning to conceive of a universe controlled by definite
and definable laws, Bach, Hayden, and others were beginning to write
music that was also controlled and organized and structured. The ethereal
quality of the Gregorian chant slips into the background.

One can glance at a Bach composition on a sheet of paper and quickly
see how precisely it is put together. Theme I is introduced . . . theme II . . .
theme I in another key. Everything appears in neat eight- or sixteen-
measure segments. Sound and emotion have been captured and fit into
human boxes. The amorphous flow, the wandering polyphony of
medieval music has been humanized and civilized. We are, the music seems
to say, beginning to get hold of our world. We are getting things together.
We are conquering.

Michelangelo, *The Creation of Man,* Sistine Chapel ceiling/ detail (Editorial Photocolor Archives, Inc.)

The artists of the Renaissance had already sensed that humanity's concept of itself was changing. The change was apparent even in paintings on the walls of churches.

There is no more striking example than *Michelangelo's* (1475–1654) painting of the creation of man on the ceiling of the Sistine Chapel in Rome. In this work, instead of human figures bathed in spiritual qualities, we find spiritual beings bathed in human qualities. Here is God with muscles, with a beard, almost naked. Here is God with extremely earthy qualities.

In the medieval religious paintings there were no muscles. Everyone was very placid and flat and smooth. Everyone was covered with long garments, so that the fleshly could be overlooked in favor of the spiritual. Michelangelo's man is still weak (notice the limpness in his hand), but God is reaching out to touch him—to impart to him the qualities that will make him like God. He is built physically like God. There is strength there. He has the potential to begin solving his own problems just as soon as the divine spark reaches him and animates his strength. Man is no longer to be thought of as a weak, puny creature who must clasp his hands and look up in prayer. He is, rather, about to be infused with power. He will be able to take care of himself. He will get hold of things!

Georges Seurat (1859–1891), the French artist, painted *Sunday Afternoon on the Island of La Grand Jatte* at the very height of the Autonomous Period. Standing back a few feet one sees smartly dressed people strolling calmly through a park. One lady sports a parasol and a pet monkey. The gentlemen wear tall hats and unwrinkled shirts and coats.

Seurat, *Sunday Afternoon on the Island of La Grande Jatte* (The Art Institute of Chicago)

When you get very close to the painting, you discover that the artist has actually put thousands of tiny dots on the canvas. They are unconnected. But when you move back, the dots begin to blend in the mind and trees and pets and ladies and gentlemen begin to appear. Everything is peaceful and calm. Everything is under control.

This is our world, says the artist. When you look at reality up close, you find it is a mass of little disconnected bits of data—tiny little things—easily manageable. All you have to do is put these little bits together and they become a beautiful afternoon in the park.

The scientists were saying very much the same thing. All problems can be solved by analysis because all complex matters are simply combinations of very simple matters. Once you break a thing down into its constituent parts you have control of it.

What then is a man, or a woman, or a monkey? Nothing more than combinations of these tiny dots. Standing back a bit one gets the impression of complex movement and color and beauty. But this is only because the bits have blended together in the mind. The scientists can use their microscopes and see the reality behind these impressions.

But Seurat's peaceful nineteenth-century afternoon nap soon became a screaming twentieth-century nightmare. The musicians heard the scream first. The fine order of Bach, carried with a flourish through the nineteenth-century Romantics, gave way to clash and discord. When disorder was reintroduced into music, it was not the flowing melodious spiritual disorder of medieval church music. It was rather a jarring, confusing, even annoying kind of dissonance. There is nothing to catch hold of. There are bursts of sound here and bursts of sound there—melodies running wild, clashing with each other, exploding like fireworks.

Listen, for example, to *Igor Stravinsky's* (1882–1971) *Rite of Spring*. You will never find yourself humming this piece! You will never tap your foot to it either! There seems to be no rhythmic order. There seems to be no melodic order. The sound is going anywhere and everywhere. There is an underlying chaos, sprinkled here and there with an unexpected moment of beauty that is soon lost again in the crashing discords.

Somehow, one gets the message. The world has come unglued. Man has not organized his world. There are no neat combinations of tiny dots that explain everything. Disorder is more real than order. Confusion is more real than confidence.

What *Rite of Spring* does to the ears, *Guernica* does to the eyes. *Pablo Picasso* (1881–1973) had seen World War I, the Russian Revolution, the bloody Spanish Civil War, inflation, economic collapse, and the rise of fascist dictators. In *Guernica,* which commemorates the bombing of a small Spanish village, he seems to say that Seurat's tiny dots . . . all lined up to make neat places and nice little monkeys and parasols . . . are illusions. There is more truth, he says, in the senseless act of blowing a helpless village to smithereens. Of course the blowing up of villages has become commonplace today. But for Picasso, at that time, it produced profound shock. How could he paint peaceful Sunday afternoons? How could he paint little Gothic windows full of placid Madonnas?

Instead, he drew screams. He drew people in pieces. There is almost no color. Everything is jumbled and out of place.

Autonomous Man had, like the sorcerer's apprentice in the old fairy tale, unleashed powers far beyond his own control. Chaos, like some dark

Picasso, *Guernica* (Museum of Modern Art)

primeval monster from the deep, had its hands in a vicelike grip around his throat.

World War I should have struck a staggering blow to the optimistic swagger of nineteenth-century Autonomous Man. But, curiously, few beyond an artist or musician or writer here or there seemed to perceive the situation. It was as though Autonomous Man had been stabbed with a ten-inch butcher knife and had somehow failed to notice!

Ernest Hemingway noticed. In a book of short stories called *Winner Take Nothing*,[5] he describes a waiter in a small bar who sensed the meaninglessness that was descending upon humanity. "What did he hear? It was not fear or dread. It was a nothing that he knew too well. It was all a nothing and man was nothing too." And so he turns to prayer. But the forces of secularization had robbed him of any god to hear those prayers. And so, using the Spanish word for "nothing" (*nada*), he prays: "Our nada who art in nada, nada be thy name . . .". And even, "Hail Nothing, full of nothing, nothing is with thee . . . ".

Albert Camus noticed. He began an essay by saying, "There is but one truly serious philosophical problem, and that is suicide."[6] We must, he said, begin with a "belief in the absurdity of existence,"[7] and then try to figure out why to stay alive. Indeed, "the absurd becomes god"[8] in the absence of any other. The universe is meaningless, he says.

"But what does life mean in such a universe? Nothing else for the moment but indifference to the future and a desire to use up everything that is given. Belief in the meaning of life always implies a scale of values, a choice, our preferences. Belief in the absurd, according to our definitions, teaches the contrary."[9]

He found the human predicament pictured in the ancient Greek myth of Sisyphus, whom the gods condemned to rolling a stone to the top of a mountain over and over again. Each time the stone simply fell back down and Sisyphus began his senseless task once more. The gods figured, "with some reason," he stated, "that there is no more dreadful punishment than futile and hopeless labor."[10]

Still, Camus concluded that "one must imagine Sisyphus happy."[11] One must simply make the best of things and, in the words of a beer commercial, grab all "the gusto" one can. The same general conclusion was reached by other atheistic existentialist philosophers of the period like

[5]Ernest Hemingway, *Winner Take Nothing* (New York: Scribner, 1930), pp. 17–24.
[6]Albert Camus, *The Myth of Sisyphus and Other Essays,* trans. Justin O'Brien (New York: Knopf, 1961), p. 3.
[7]Ibid., p. 6.
[8]Ibid., p. 33.
[9]Ibid., p. 60.
[10]Ibid., p. 119.
[11]Ibid., p. 123.

Jean Paul Sartre (who wrote plays with titles like *No Exit* and *Nausea*).

Writing in 1929, Joseph Wood Krutch called this way of thinking "the modern temper." Of it, he said,

> Unlike their grandfathers, those who are its victims, do not and never expect to believe in God; but unlike their spiritual fathers, the philosophers and scientists of the nineteenth century, they have begun to doubt that rationality and knowledge have any promised land into which they may be led.[12]

Of the "modern man," he said,

> Formerly he had believed in even his darkest moments that the universe was rational if he could only grasp its rationality, but gradually he comes to suspect that rationality is an attribute of himself alone and that there is no reason to suppose that his own life has any more meaning than the life of the humblest insect that crawls from one annihilation to another.[13]

His conclusion is

> Ours is a lost cause and there is no place for us in the natural universe.[14]

NAZISM: THE ULTIMATE HORROR

But the worst was yet to come. Friedrich Nietzsche had given philosophical justification to the idea that might makes right and that nature's methods of advancing itself (especially survival of the fittest) applied to human beings, who were, after all, only the "cleverest animals."

In post–Word War I Germany, that citadel of modern scientific and technological achievement, these ideas were given practical application by an Austrian would-be painter named Adolf Hitler.

Nobel-prize-winning scientists like *Philipp Lenard* (1862–1947) and *Johannes Stark* (1874–1951), along with a host of others, provided a scientific rationale for Hitler's plan.[15] What scientific law was doing slowly, Hitler would do quickly. Select the fittest. Destroy the inferior. Goose-step into a Nazi heaven on earth! Has not nature itself taught us how to proceed? Humanity's destiny is to become Nietzsche's Superman. All thought of compassion must be put aside. Everything must be subjugated to the evolutionary advance to perfection. In the name of science, the inferior must be eliminated. Anything else would be "unnatural."

---

[12]Joseph Wood Krutch, *The Modern Temper* (New York: Harcourt Brace, 1929), p. xvi.
[13]Ibid., p. 9.
[14]Ibid., p. 249.
[15]See George L. Mosse, *Nazi Culture: Intellectual, Cultural, and Social Life in the Third Reich* (New York: Grosset, 1966), pp. 197 ff.

There were those who spoke out against what was happening. The "confessional church," led by courageous individuals such as Martin Niemöller, condemned the mounting tide of human atrocities, in the name of a higher law. But the god of the higher law had been driven from too many minds. Had not science given people their freedom from such gods? Were not people alone in the world responsible for building their own heaven? The Nazi machine rolled on.

The horrors of the Nazi era boggle the mind. There is no parallel in history for what happened. The stories fill thousands of pages, each covered with blood and death. The victims number in the millions. No ancient barbarian horde ever came close to equaling the record of destruction left by this "modern" and "scientific" attempt to create the super race.

Eugen Kogan's book, *The Theory and Practice of Hell*, gives us only a small introduction to the horror:[16]

Item: Dr. Sigmund Rascher, of the German Air Force Medical Service, wished to find out whether humans can stay alive while rapidly ascending to high altitudes. Naturally, he would use the scientific method to find out:

> A mobile unit was set up at Dachau in the camp street, between Block 5 and the adjacent barracks. The area was isolated from the other hospital buildings so that outside observation was impossible. The unit consisted of a high enclosed box on wheels, with built-in instruments for the measurement of pressure, temperature and altitude. Heart action of the subjects was measured by a electro-cardiograph. Autopsies were conducted immediately upon death ("the blood does not yet boil at an altitude of 70,000 feet" reads the final report of the three "experts," dated July 28, 1942.) On one occasion, during an autopsy, Rascher found the heart of the victim still beating. He thereupon instituted a whole series of killings, solely for the purpose of establishing the length of time during which the human heart remained active after death.[17]

Item: Professor Holzlöhner of Kiel conducted experiments on the effect of chilling on warm-blooded organisms. Dr. Rascher cooperated:

> During the first period the subjects, clothed or stripped, were immersed in water of 39° to 48° until they grew stiff. Temperatures was measured rectally by thermo-electric means. There were fifty to sixty subjects and fifteen to eighteen fatalities. During the second period Rascher also used another method. Prisoners were exposed to the cold winter air (4 to 13° F. below zero) overnight. When their screams created too much of a disturbance, Rascher finally used anesthesia. According to the testimony of an eyewitness, the

---

[16]Eugene Kogan, *The Theory and Practice of Hell*, trans. Heinz Norden (New York: Farrar, Straus & Giroux, 1973). The Nazi horrors are well documented. A parallel series of horrors that occurred in Soviet Russia during the same period are gradually coming to light. The works of Aleksandr Solzhenitsyn furnish a chilling introduction to this matter.

[17]Ibid., p. 153.

former inmate Walter Neff, Rascher immersed two Russian officers, brought from the camp prison, naked in ice water. It took them five hours to die.[18]

Item: Late in 1942, Professor Hirt, a Strasbourg anatomist, suggested to Hitler that a collection of skulls and skeletons of various "inferior" types be created for use at the Strasbourg University Institute of Anatomy:

> The SS Main Economic and Administrative Office immediately instructed Auschwitz to make concentration camp inmates available for this purpose, and 115 persons were selected—seventy-nine Jewish men, thirty Jewish women, two Poles and two Asiatics. They were shipped to the Natzweiler camp, where they were gassed with cyanide which Professor Hirt gave the Camp Commandant for the purpose.[19]

Three years after these events, *H. G. Wells,* (1866–1946), one of the most enthusiastic supporters of the autonomy of man and the inevitability of scientific progress, wrote a sad and cynical book called *Mind at the End of Its Tether.* Himself near the end of life, Wells pronounced the whole movement to which he had given his efforts a failure. How much Nazi horror pressed upon his mind we do not know.

"The writer," he said, "sees the world as a jaded world devoid of recuperative power. In the past he has liked to think that man could pull out of his entanglements and start a new creative phase of human living. In the face of our universal inadequacy that optimism has given place to a stoical cynicism. Man must go steeply up or down and the odds seem all in favor of his going down and out . . .".[20]

Hopes for the future? They are, said Wells, "the remembered shouts of angry people in a train that has passed and gone forever."[21] Camus had argued that although the world was meaningless, at least we should not kill ourselves. As for Hemingway, on the morning of July 2, 1961, he placed the muzzles of a silver-inlaid shotgun in his mouth and pulled both triggers.

SECULARIZATION IN THE NON-CHRISTIAN WORLD

Secularization, as we have seen, germinated and flourished in the Christian West. But its effect reached beyond and influenced more than just the Christian culture. Judaism was very directly affected wherever Jewish communities existed within Western Europe and the Americas. On the one

---

[18]Kogan, *The Theory and Practice of Hell,* p. 154.
[19]Ibid., p. 160.
[20]H. G. Wells, *Mind at the End of Its Tether* (New York: Didier, 1945), p. 17.
[21]Ibid., p. 2.

hand, the proponents of reason were much more tolerant toward Jews than medieval Christians had been, so life became somewhat easier—until the Nazi holocaust.

But this freedom, which brought Jews into the mainstream of culture again, also exposed their ancient faith to the same rationistic attacks that orthodox Christianity had experienced. Three kinds of Judaism resulted, each responding to secularization in a different way.

Orthodox Judaism, like fundamentalist Christianity, rejected the secular currents entirely. The Torah was for the orthodox literally a divine revelation and could not be changed in any way, regardless of what the scientific humanist might say.

Conservative Judaism attempted a middle road. The Torah is eternal, said the conservative, and always stands in tension with the currents of human thought. But reason can be used to interpret the Torah and thereby make it current and applicable to modern life.

Reform Judaism, like modernist Christianity, wholeheartedly accepted scientific and rationalistic thought. Its major genius was *Abraham Gerger* (1810–1874) who shared with many other nineteenth-century thinkers (a majority of whom came from Christian backgrounds), an unbounded confidence in human reason and the scientific method. Scientific man, he felt, could not accept the idea of revelation. Judaism and the Torah, therefore represented an ethical system of great merit, but not a divine revelation.

More recently, Martin Buber (1878–1965), especially in his great work *I and Thou* has tried to reinterpret Judaism more existentially, seeing in it the personal confrontation of God and humanity and the relationship of persons to persons, with the model being the experiences and insights of the ancient Hebrew prophets.

The Eastern religions did not experience such a direct confrontation with the new scientific humanist world view in the nineteenth century. Nevertheless, Western colonialism brought not only missionaries with traditional Christianity to India, China, and Southeast Asia; it also brought the philosophy and technology of Autonomous Man. In 1828 Ram Mohan (1772–1833) founded the Brahmo Samaj (Society of God), which attempted to distill Indian religion down into only two essential beliefs: (1) the existence of a single creative benevolent divinity and (2) the immortal nature of human souls. This opened the way for the acceptance of many of the principles of scientific humanism. *Ramakrishna* (1836–1886) and *Vivekanarda* (1863–1902), two nineteenth-century holy men, further opened traditional Hinduism to the new world view. Philosopher Sri Aurobindo (1872–1950) sought to combine the two by denying that the material world was illusion. Rather, the mystical absolute spirit dwells within the material world. This idea has freed many "modernized" people in India from the need to withdraw from the world of science to find spiritual reality.

In practice, many modern Indians "compartmentalize." That is, they keep one foot in the traditional world and another in the modern one. Milton Singer describes the process:[22]

> While most of the leaders did not explicitly verbalize the strategy of compartmentalization, most did adopt it in their daily behavior. The physical setting for the traditional religious sphere is the home, where many of the traditional ritual observances of Sanskritic Hinduism are performed. The physical setting for modern practices is the office and factory; there English is used, Western dress is worn, contacts with different castes and communities are frequent, and the instruments and concepts of modern technology engage the attention.

Hinduism has shown great adaptability in the past and has usually been able to adjust to or even swallow up systems that seemed to threaten it. The struggle between the traditional and the modern is much more recent in India that in the West, and the results are very much in doubt.

Buddhism faces the same continuing confrontation. In Southeast Asia the spread of communism, which has already created havoc in Chinese and Tibetan Buddhism, has created a violent confrontation between the materialistic and the spiritual views of reality. Again, the results are in doubt. In Japan, where a technological, industrial society based very much on the Western pattern has emerged, the traditional religions seem to have become less and less influencial in daily life and society has become more and more secularized. The Soka Gakkai (valve-creating society) has Buddhist roots that are seven hundred years old, it is true, and has attracted millions of post–Word War II Japanese. But it is a religion that emphasizes this-worldly happiness and prosperity and therefore may share very much in the modern technocratic world view rather than the world view of traditional Buddhism.

In general, Eastern cultures are still on a sort of "honeymoon" with secularization and technology and are not—at least, not yet—suffering the depression and pessimism described in the earlier part of this chapter.

[22]Milton Singer, *When a Great Tradition Modernizes: An Anthropological Approach to Indian Civilization* (Chicago: University of Chicago, 1972), p. 321.

CHAPTER TWELVE
RELIGION AND THE FUTURE

THE PRESENT DILEMMA

Humankind, said Jean Paul Sartre is nothing but "a waste product of the universe."

In this assertion he illustrates John Magee's thesis:[1]

> At this juncture in history we may ask whether enthusiastic Humanism is not itself a transitional form of faith without substantial ground. Many elements in contemporary life suggest that once the ontological root of faith is cut there is no stopping until the entire tree of human idealism has withered into an ugly spector and man delivered over to the abyss of nihilism.

The autonomous way of being human is compared here with a tree. The tree is held up by a root system that reaches down into the earth for stability and nourishment. When the pressures above become great, the trees with shallow roots are toppled.

"Enthusiastic humanism," says Magee, is such a tree. The human race has developed a way of looking at itself and the world that does not go down deep to root itself beyond humankind and the world. That is, humanity has no "ontological root of faith." It has no way in which to gain

[1]John B. Magee, *Religion and Modern Man: A Study of the Religious Meaning of Being Human* (New York: Harper & Row, 1969), p. 198.

nourishment down at the very base of existence, where the ultimate realities and meanings are. The tree may still appear beautiful and strong. But the leaves will soon yellow and become brittle and vulnerable. Finally, the stresses of history will bring it down.

Those few people, artists and writers and prophets, who have first seen this death setting in, have, as we have seen, often descended into nihilism—the belief that nothingness is the most basic reality.

The themes of modern literature are often pessimistic ones:

Alienation—people do not belong; they do not fit. People are lonely, segmented, pulled away from themselves and each other.

Dehumanization—people are like cattle, mere digits, computerized, stripped of significance.

Anxiety—people are uncertain, confused, worried about the future.

Disorder—there is no positive standard, no way to get organized, no overall planning, everything seems to have gone berserk.

Radical evil—human beings have hearts full of darkness and are not to be trusted, always preferring the evil instead of the good.

This last theme is well illustrated by William Golding's novel *Lord of the Flies*.[2] The book begins with an account of a journey by a group of proper English schoolboys. They are civilized from head to toe. They speak *properly*. They dress *properly*. They are shipwrecked on a deserted island, separated from their schoolmaster. At first they try to maintain the order and organization that has characterized their lives before. But the book becomes a chilling account of their rapid deterioration into a herd of brute beasts. They maim and finally even kill. They remind us that "civilization" is a very thin façade indeed. Underneath is darkness, cruelty, and barbarism.

And if humanity is evil and yet all alone in the world, with no school-master to impose proper behavior upon it, what does the future hold? Golding's schoolboys quickly made a hell out of their little island. Many contemporary observers think that Autonomous Man has done the same to his own little world. As evidence they cite the following:

War.   The last seventy-five years have been characterized by concentrated international warfare. Autonomous Man's reign has brought destruction, carnage, killing, use of most of our resources for armaments—all in greater magnitude than at any other time in history.

Misuse of the environment.   Rivers die. Lakes die. Forests disappear. Wildlife evaporates. We have discovered that even the sprays we sprinkle on everything (hair, underarms, furniture,) are gradually congregating up

---

[2]William Golding, *Lord of the Flies* (New York: Coward-McCann, 1962).

in the ozone, threatening to destroy its protection against the scorching sun. Our much vaunted technology begins to fly back on us. Our environment begins to crumble.

Nonviability of political forms.   No one seems to be able to come up with a form of government that will work. While representative democracy seems best to us in the West, the emerging nations are not following our pattern. Apparently it does not work for them. The system of government most prevalent today amounts to an institutionalized form of the law of the jungle. The art of government, despite our great scientific advance, remains basically a process by which some strong man simply smashes his competition and rules through the barrel of a gun.

Personal disintegration.   People in even the most "advanced" societies come unglued in record numbers, unable to cope with the emotional pressures put on them.

Collapse of workable ethical standards.   There seems to be no way to know what is right or wrong. No content to the words "right" and "wrong." No confidence that what we have done was *good*. No conviction that any particular action is *bad*.

Lack of direction.   There is little or no sense of movement. No assurance that we are going anywhere. No assurance that there is any place to go.

The serious problems we have noted are only representative. Dozens of additional ones could be added to the list. By all appearances, our own time falls into the category of "collapse and transition" and shares the general confusion and disorientation of earlier such periods. The classical world gave way to the medieval world. The medieval world gave way to the world of Autonomous Man. In our century, as we have seen, the foundations of the autonomous world have been severely shaken.

What will come next? What kind of life will be the normative "human" life when the present dust has settled and our culture has again reached some consensus as to what it can and must be?

"Futurology" is a popular subject nowadays. Many models for the future are being suggested. Some of these call for a repudiation of the world view of Autonomous Man, while others remain firmly tied to such a view and seek only to refine and improve it. Some reach back to ancient religious concepts, and some reject the past as entirely irrelevant. For some, science holds the key to all future development, while for others unrestrained reliance on science will result in disaster. We will look briefly at a few of these diverse models.

IBM 3033 Processor (IBM)

Despite the problems connected with autonomy, the first two models we will discuss are firmly rooted in the hypothesis that humanity is alone in the universe and must make its own future. The first sees the individual of the future as Socialist Man, transformed by the transformation of the institutions of society. The second envisions a biologically Re-engineered Man, biologically transformed by science into something more workable than the model that has developed, according to this view, through haphazard evolution.

CHE GUEVARA AND THE "NEW MAN"

Among those who held a firm vision of a new humanity in our time is that hero of millions among the young, especially in the "emerging" nations —Ernesto "Che" Guevara. Che fought along with Castro for a "new order" in Cuba and was finally killed while organizing guerilla fighters to spread revolution into other Latin American countries.

One of the first things one notices about Che's dream is that its presuppositions are essentially the standard suppositions of Autonomous Man. It is the young socialists and communists, who consider themselves the vanguard of a new world, who are often the heirs of, and protectors of, the ideals and dreams of the late nineteenth century.

For example, the Revolutionary Communist Party, an American group, has called for the formation of a Party of the U.S. Working Class. In its Draft Programme for such a party, the autonomous world view appears over and over in its classic form. Watch for it:[3]

> In capitalist society many workers and other oppressed people are drawn to religion because it represents their hopes and aspirations for a better life—projected, however, into the future and into another realm completely beyond man's ability to understand. The bourgeoisie promotes religion to convince people that since life is miserable on the earth—and it cannot be denied that this is so under capitalism—the answer is to hope for a better life 'beyond this one.'
>
> Further, religion serves capitalism by telling people that they are basically helpless before the forces of nature—and the rulers of society—and they should put their faith not in *the ability of the masses of people to change the world,* but in a supreme, supernatural being, or beings.
>
> While protecting freedom of religion, socialist society will eliminate all use of religion to exploit and oppress the people. And the party of the working class will lead a consistent political and ideological struggle to arm the masses of people with the *understanding that they are the true force that changes the world and that they can conquer nature.*
>
> The outlook of the working class is scientific—it recognizes that the *causes of things lie in the living struggle of opposing forces, in nature and society.* While at any time there are things that are not yet known, *there is nothing unknowable, there is nothing that is not* bound by the laws of nature and society and nothing in the universe *which can't be harnessed and transformed in the interests of the people,* once the basic laws governing it have been discovered and grasped by the masses of people.
>
> The working class, once it becomes conscious of all this has *no need for belief in supernatural beings or forces* of any kind.

Che, in a letter written in 1965 and published in Cuba,[4] speaks with hope for the future:

> We can see the *new man* who begins to emerge in this period of the building of socialism. His image is as yet unfinished. In fact it will never be finished, since the process advances parallel to the development of new economic forms.

The new man will not emerge without struggle and sacrifice, but the revolutionary will gain personal satisfaction and meaning in the process.

> Each and every one of us punctually pays his share of sacrifice, aware of being rewarded by the satisfaction of fulfilling our duty, aware of advancing with everyone toward the new human being who is a glimpse on the horizon.

---

[3]From a popularly distributed pamphlet; emphasis added.

[4]Ernesto "Che" Guevara, "The New Man," letter to Carlos Quijano, editor-publisher of *Marcha*. Written 1965 and published in Cuba as "El Socialism y el Hombre en Cuba" (Havana: Ediciones R.).

Che talks about a *new man*. This new man will appear through the process of education.

"Society as a whole," he says, "must become a huge school." Obviously, Che believes that people are changed when they are given more facts. And who will be responsible for disseminating these facts? The state. Such dissemination is carried out, he says, "through the State's educational apparatus in the form of general, technical, and ideological culture, by means of bodies such as the Ministry of Education and the party's information apparatus."

This will work, of course, only where there is a totalitarian government already controlled by people who have the "facts." Power must be taken (by force, if necessary) and the educative process begun. People must be retooled, much like Detroit retools when coming out with a new model of automobile. It will be necessary to suppress the old ideas, lest they confuse those who are learning to be new persons.

The government, then, gives people the "facts" that will make them new. It deprives them of the "lies" that have held them in the old ways. Gradually, a new kind of person appears: Socialist Man. His economic system has changed. His way of thinking about himself and the world has changed. He is new.

Che recognizes that people feel alienated. This alienation, however, will disappear when human beings achieve "total awareness of their social being," that is, when they begin to see themselves not as individuals, but as essentially parts of a group, a movement, a community. This realization will give meaning to life.

> He will thus achieve total awareness of his social being, which is equivalent to his full realization as a human being, having broken the chains of alienation.

Let me remind you that we are talking about *religion* here—religion in the functional sense. For Che is holding out a new way of being human that claims to fulfill the human existential needs we discussed earlier—the needs that religion seeks to fulfill.

Human beings are alienated. How do they cure this alienation? By becoming *new* in their way of thinking. By having a new social awareness. By seeing that their true identities are found in the group—in the people as a whole—rather then in individual identity.

Once this realization has come, people will no longer sell themselves. That is, they will no longer work for money. Our present economic system has forced them to do that, according to Che. But once that system is changed, human beings will change, too. They will no longer have to worry about the basic necessities. Society will provide them. So they will be able to open up to a new awareness which allows them to work for the group, to serve without regard for personal welfare. And in this service they will find personal meaning and worth.

BIOLOGICALLY RE-ENGINEERED MAN

In 1953 James Dewey Watson and Francis Crick, working in Cambridge, England, discovered the physical make-up of deoxyribonucleic acid (DNA). With this momentous discovery the human race came into possession of the knowledge of the basic "secret of life." By the 1960s, scientists had cracked the DNA code and could map the structure of this fundamental building block of life. In 1973, twenty years after the initial discovery the process of recombinant DNA was developed. Humanity found itself able to separate and re-splice the DNA molecule and thus "create" entirely new combinations that in turn would produce new forms of life. The human race stands on the threshold of being able to control its own evolutionary development. Autonomous Man may in fact be very close to obtaining the power to "play God" in ways beyond the wildest dreams of his nineteenth-century predecessors.

Hitler's crude and cruel attempts to take control of evolution by eliminating genetically "inferior" types momentarily discredited the movement to place humanity's biological future in human hands. In recent years, however, more and more voices are heard calling for sterilization and abortion as a means of improving the genetic make-up of the human race. And more and more experiments are being conducted to pave the way for a new Re-engineered Man who will be vastly "improved" by scientific control of the heretofore "natural" genetic processes.

Artificial insemination, long used to ensure genetic "improvement" in cattle, is becoming more and more common among human beings. Will future humans be the products of carefully selected "superior" females artificially inseminated with sperm from carefully selected "superior" males? Will conception of "inferior" types be outlawed? Will certain women be designated as "hosts" for egg transplants, so that the babies born of them will have no genetic connection with them at all? Or will the process of gestation and birth be separated entirely from the female body, with the production of test-tube babies grown entirely in the laboratory, constructed through careful scientific selection, or perhaps even cloned from a few "superior" human beings?

As the technology of biological engineering becomes more and more sophisticated, these questions become more and more pressing. The very definitions of such words as "mother," "father," "parents" are thrown into doubt. Ethical and moral problems arise and spread from the new technology like bacteria in the experimental growth dishes. How much "right" does the human race have to take over the direction of its own development? What happens to individual rights in a world of biological re-engineering? Who will decide what traits are "superior" and "inferior"—and what measuring stick will be used?

The possibilities for radical change in humankind's concept of what it means to be human brought about by this new technology make Che's call for revolutionary social change seem rather conservative by comparison.[5] One can even conceive of a combination of Che's dream with that of the biological re-engineers: a world in which an all-powerful state not only determines the education of all the citizens but actually produces the citizens in state-controlled laboratories. There only "superior" types would be allowed to reach adulthood, having in the meantime been designed and constructed so they are incapable of antisocialist behavior or thinking.

CONSCIOUSNESS III AND THE NEW MAN

Charles Reich's book, *The Greening of America*, suggests that the new way of being human will come not from external change, but from a change in human consciousness:[6]

> There is a revolution coming. It will not be like revolutions of the past. It will originate with the individual and with culture, and it will change the political structure only as its final act. It will not require violence to succeed, and it cannot be successfully resisted by violence. This is the revolution of the new generation.

Reich writes from the perspective of the American situation. The present time of turmoil, he says, is the result of a clash between three conflicting "consciousnesses." One's consciousness is defined as the way in which one perceives reality. It is one's basic set of mind. It is that matrix that we earlier tied to the concept of ultimate concern. It is, in the essential sense, one's religion. The three conflicting consciousnesses are, according to Reich, the following:

Consciousness I.   This is the rugged individualist. This person was either born in a rural situation, or at least exists with a rural mentality. He or she conceives of a world in which there is unlimited space. One can always get out and plow and plant and take care of oneself. As for the

---

[5]For a full discussion of the issues raised by advances in genetic re-engineering, see Ted Howard and Jeremy Rifkin, *Who Should Play God? The Artificial Creation of Life and What It Means for the Human Race* (New York: Dell, 1977).

[6]Charles A. Reich, *The Greening of America* (New York: Random House 1970), p. 2.

technological Machine we have discussed, this person simply chooses to ignore it.

Consciousness II. This is the organization person. One is not really conscious of one's individuality at all, but sees oneself as a cog in the huge machine that dominates our society. One does not fight the machine, but has learned to co-exist with it. This person exists in an urban mentality. There is no conception of having much space. He or she is vividly aware of being surrounded by other people and that salvation is to be found only in somehow getting everybody organized and then in working one's way up within the organization. This person's stance with regard to the Machine, then, is to cooperate with it.

Consciousness III. This is Reich's conception of the new person, the human being of the future. The other two consciousnesses are no longer valid, he says, given the present situation. They do not perceive reality correctly and consequently they cannot cope. The world is obviously in serious disarray, but it cannot be changed until these incorrect consciousnesses disappear and Consciousness III takes their places.

What is Consciousness III Man like? Reich is much clearer in explaining what he is not. He does not, for example, accept the artificial needs that the Machine has created to take our minds off our unfulfilled *true* existential needs. To keep itself going, the Machine must keep convincing us that we need what it can provide. So it keeps feeding us fads and style changes and "improvements."

Take toothpaste, for example. Almost monthly someone offers us a "new, improved" toothpaste. Of course one can have the most efficient toothpaste of all by simply mixing some common salt and common soda and brushing away. But that is too easy and too cheap. Such an approach fails to help support the Machine. No, we have to be convinced that only a product pouring off the assembly line of huge factory complexes can really do the job.

Take planned obsolescence, for example. Everything has to go out of date in six months or so. Clothing styles have to change. Automobile styles have to change. Everything has to be retooled, redone, revised. Why? Because we have some true existential need for such changes? On the contrary, our true need is for stability, not constant change. No, such ideas are necessary to keep the Machine running—to keep the factories running. Our economy, our life-style, our society depends on it.

The only real need being fulfilled, then, is not the need of real people but, rather, the need to keep the Machine in operation.

Of course we do not have an unlimited supply of money and resources. But the money must go for Machine-oriented activities. There is, therefore, not enough left to spend on real needs such as education, esthetic fulfillment, and creativity. There is not enough because we had to spend it for some clever little gismo that is an improvement over the last version of the same little gismo. And we spent it without ever realizing that we did not even need the unimproved gismo, let alone the improved gismo!

Advertising is the evangelistic outreach of the Machine. It is absolutely necessary, because it is the way in which we convince ourselves that we need all the products the Machine is turning out.

The pulpit for Consciousness II's evangelists is, of course, the television set. The sermon is the thirty-second commercial.

Reich continues his critique of the world of Consciousness II by drawing attention to the "phenomenon of Disneyland." Promoters of the Machine go find a swamp, complete with birds, alligators, trees, and streams. They move in bulldozers, push over the trees, and scrape everything off nice and flat. Then they bring in a large construction crew and build an artificial swamp with rubber alligators and plaster-of-Paris trees. Then they build a big fence around the whole project and charge $12.50 to get in.

Of course it would have been much less expensive to go see the real alligators or to ride a boat into the real swamp. But it was necessary to get the Machine involved, so we tear down the real and charge admission to see the artificial and the Machine rolls on.

The present energy crisis will no doubt be "solved" as soon as the Disneyland phenomenon can be applied to it. Almost unlimited energy exists in the form of wind, water, and sunlight. The difficulty is that these things are *free*. There is no way to send a monthly bill for them. As soon as the Machine discovers a way to charge for the use of sunlight, technology will quickly discover a way to harness that light to fill our energy needs. At present, of course, there is no money available to do research on energy sources of the type that connot be controlled by the Machine.

According to Reich, the world view of the Consciousness II Man is false and unworkable. Not only does it fail to fulfill humanity's real needs, it attempts to divert attention from those needs—to lie to people—to sell them its products. It is, therefore, a false religion.

This is Reich's thesis.

This false religion will be overthrown, however, by the triumph of Consciousness III. And how will this triumph come? Not by political action, as suggested by Che and his fellow revolutionaries. "The political activists have had their day and have been given their chance," he says.

The new day comes when people change their minds, their consciousness, their lives. This is already taking place among the young. But

> If Consciousness III is to spread beyond youth, it must do so by a process that is just the reverse of orthodox left-wing theories of radicalization. It will not work to educate first and change individuals later.... A change of consciousness must precede a new and enlarged understanding of our society.

We must no longer depend wholly upon political and legal activism, upon structural change, upon liberal or even radical assaults on existing power. Such methods, used exclusively, are certain to fail. The only plan that will succeed is one that will be greeted by most social activists with disbelief and disparagement, yet it is entirely realistic—the only means that is realistic, given the nature of the contemporary State: revolution by consciousness.

Sad to say, Reich is unclear as to just what this Consciousness III Man will be like or just how he will arrive on the scene. What is the dynamic that will change the human race into a Consciousness III People? What kind of program will bring about such a change? These questions remain essentially unanswered. Like Che, Reich has a vision of what humanity really should become. Unlike Che, Reich lacks a program. He does not suggest what to do next.

The new man will have "a non-material set of values,"[7] he says. But where will he get them? "The power is not the power of manipulating procedures or the power of politics or street fighting, but the power of new values and a new way of life."[8] But what will be the source of these new values, and where will the power come from to cause men to live a new way? People must be "freed from false consciousness."[9] But how? The world can change "only by change in individual lives."[10] But how will these lives be changed, and by what power?

CHRISTIAN THEOLOGY AND THE FUTURE

The question of the nature and destiny of humankind is, as we have seen, a religious question. "Nature" and "destiny" are joined together in this question because any theory about the destiny of humanity is necessarily built upon a theory about what a human being *is*. For Che, humanity is social and political. For the genetic engineer, humankind's essence is found in its biological make-up. Reich defines humanity in terms of attitude or consciousness. All three perceptively identify the existential needs of human beings in our age (although the genetic engineers run a poor third in depth of perception). All three tie these needs and their fulfillment to the concepts inherited from nineteenth-century Autonomous Man (although Reich does so much less than the other two).

Autonomous Man, remember, holds that human beings are alone in the world; that there are no spiritual realities, only material ones; that the human race is good; and that only its outward environment has kept it

[7]Reich, *The Greening of America*, p. 300.
[8]Ibid., p. 10.
[9]Ibid., p. 331.
[10]Ibid., p. 327.

from expressing its goodness. Che was an atheist (with reference to spiritual beings) and a materialist. Therefore, he saw no future in trying to bring about a new way of being human through an appeal to the world of the spirit. Man, he maintained is matter. The world is matter. By changing the world, economically and politically, one changes the people who live in it. The genetic re-engineers are, if anything, even more materialistic since, unlike the classic Marxist, they note no innate pattern in history but only the random combination and recombination of chemical substances that make up biological organisms.

Orthodox Christianity has understood the human race as creatures of a divine Father who has reached down to touch the life of humanity through Jesus of Nazareth. Jesus maintained that human beings find their personal worth in service to a higher cause. "He who loses his life for my sake shall find it."[11] He speaks of the great beauty of the person who is willing to lay down his life for his friends. His own life, as it is pictured in the Gospels, is an example of self-sacrifice and what Che would have called "awareness of social being."

Likewise, the earliest Christians spoke of the possibility of becoming "new" persons. The process of change was much more personal than social, however. "Except you be born again, you cannot enter the kingdom of heaven," says the Gospel of John.[12] Phrases like "new man" and "newness of life" are common in the writings of Paul the Apostle.[13]

Earlier we explored the Bible's particular vision of the nature of the individual and history as well as that of the great religions of the East. For the present, we will simply point out one or two areas in which while reaching for very similar goals, Christianity differs significantly in its methodology from the various autonomous approaches.

Christianity has been far more pessimistic about human behavior, for example. Che believed that a new humanity could be formed through human effort, that people possess the inner resources to change the world in which they live. Christianity has leaned toward the view that evil people will more likely control the world than will good ones. Bad decisions are more likely to be made than good ones. It is more likely that, given power, people will use it to destroy rather than to build up. These things are true, it says, because the human race is flawed. (Some forms of Christian theology have extended this idea into a doctrine of the total depravity of the human race—but not all have done so.)

Human beings, says this point of view, do not do what they know perfectly well is good and right. They do not live up to even their own best expectations. It is the commonest of human experiences, it says, to know what is good, but to lack the power to do it.

[11]Matt. 10:39.
[12]John 3:3–7.
[13]See, for example, II Cor. 5:17; Eph. 2:15; 4:24; Col. 3:10.

Thus, many Christian social critics have argued that, if people were gradually becoming better and better in some upward evolutionary fashion and if society were actually responding to some innate impulse to become more and more human, then history would read very differently from the way it actually does. Human experience, they claim, proves that cheaters usually win and honest people usually lose. The strong rule rather than the just. The new Socialist Man, they claim, despite his spirit of goodwill and service, would sooner or later be subjugated by the old Non-Socialist Man, who, self-serving and power hungry, would grab control. The power to control genetic development, they say, would surely fall into evil hands and create not a new order of humanity but a regime of inhumanity far worse than was ever possible in prescientific times.

A second area of disagreement between traditional Christianity and autonomous views has to do with the value of education. Che, for example, believed that, when human beings are given the proper information, they will change their behavior. People are good; they are simply misguided. Christian thinkers usually express doubt at this point. Giving a petty thief a Ph.D. in economics will not result in making him an honest man, they feel. The result is more likely to be the creation of a very sophisticated embezzler!

In other words, they maintain that new knowledge does not create morality. On the contrary, the new knowledge will more likely simply be used as a tool, so that those who were once only evil will become both evil and clever.

Whereas Reich may have analyzed correctly the disease of modern society, someone like the ancient Christian Paul might charge that he has failed to recognize the *inner* disease of humanity. He has wrongly assumed, Paul might claim, that humans are able to change their consciousness without divine help. Had Reich written *Lord of the Flies*, the young schoolboys, freed as they were from the technological machine, given a primitive jungle paradise, would have quickly produced a heaven on earth. Instead, they created a hell. Had he written the book of Genesis, Adam and Eve, unhindered by Consciousness II's technocratic world, would have lived forever in paradise. Instead, they found themselves driven from the garden into a world of sweat and pain.

Why did this happen? Paul would attribute it to the *inner weakness* that has always deprived the human race of paradise.

Contemporary Christianity, while rooted in the traditional viewpoints noted here, shows great diversity in approach toward the future. This diversity is illustrated by the very different models represented by two influential contemporary authors, Hal Lindsey and Jurgen Moltmann.

Lindsey's book, entitled *The Late Great Planet Earth*, combines Biblical fundamentalism with an apocalyptic view of history.[14] The contemporary

[14]Hal Lindsey, *The Late, Great Planet Earth* (Grand Rapids, Mich.: Zondervan, 1976).

world, so goes the thesis of this book, is sliding relentlessly into total evil and destruction. Using scattered phrases from apocalyptic passages in the New and Old Testaments, and interpreting them as literal predictions applying to the contemporary world, Lindsey argues that evil will continue to dominate history, climaxing with the diabolical reign of the Antichrist. A better world will come, not through the efforts of human rulers, but only with the cataclysmic intervention of God Himself. He will send His Son Jesus to battle the Antichrist in a massive cosmic war and to reign over a perfect society that will last for a thousand years. Then history will end altogether and the righteous of the ages will live eternally in the bliss of heaven.

The course of history is set, according to this view, having been planned in detail hundreds of years ago by God. The future is moving relentlessly toward its predetermined goal. Humankind, warned by the prophets of what is to come, can only respond by repentance and personal conversion to Christ. The task is then to remain "watchful" and to read the "signs of the times" as the eternal plan works itself out.

In the long tradition of apocalyptic thinking, Lindsey repudiates the modern world entirely and condemns it to total destruction. At the same time, he pictures history as a predetermined sequence of events.

Another Christian thinker, Jurgen Moltmann, approaches the problem of the future in a very different way. He quarrels not only with the scientific humanist, who has claimed that the world is a tight, closed system of natural cause and effect, but also with the various theological accommodations made by liberal and modernist theologians of the past hundred years or so.

These theologians tried to salvage Christianity, and indeed religion in general, by limiting its territory to the field of ethics (as with the nineteenth-century modernists) or personal self-understanding (as with the more recent existentialist theologians). These have joined Lindsey in dismissing history as an already closed book—although for them it is science and not the predetermined plan of God that has closed it.

Moltmann proposes instead a "theology of hope" (the title of his best known book). Science must be respected, but its findings should never be considered as absolute truth, he says:[15]

> Objective truth remains objective truth, but it is objectively demonstrable that objective truth is not absolute truth, but rather a conditioned truth. The world is not a machine simply because it permits machines to be made nor is man an aggregate of pre-determined social modes of behaviour because in certain respects he appears to be such and is predictable in regard to those commodities which he will purchase.

[15] Jurgen Moltmann, *Hope and Planning* (New York: Harper & Row, 1971), p. 211. See also Jurgen Moltmann, *Theology of Hope* (New York: Harper & Row, 1967).

Marxism's great mistake, he says, is its failure to realize this point and its acceptance of determinism in history. In fact, scientific knowledge is limited, not only because not everything has been discovered yet, but also because not everything has happened yet.[16]

> "The whole," then, is not eternal reality which provides the basis for each individual fact, but is rather always at stake in the process of history. It can be won, but it can also be frustrated. For the whole, the true, the good, is that future towards which reality is recognized, shaped, changed, and revised.

The future, then, is open—not closed. Humankind may therefore hope for the future. And since no future event absolutely *must* happen, humankind may sense a freedom, an expectation of and even participation in creating a better future. The acts of human beings are not simply the movement of helpless puppets but are the authentically free movements of ethically responsible beings. The resurrection of Jesus, Moltmann believes, was a consummately free and unexpected act that proves that history is open to hope. Thus he defines Christianity as "a universal hope for the future embracing the history of both man and the world."[17]

TM, PRIMITIVISM, AND THE FUTURE

Other visions of the future find many recent adherents. For example, the Maharishi Mahesh Yogi suggests that by means of his method, called "transcendental meditation" (TM), a new era of human existence is possible. If only 1 percent meditated, the changes would become dramatic, he says. "A good time for the world is coming," he continues. "I see the dawn of the Age of Enlightenment."[18]

TM draws heavily on the view of humanity and the world found in classic Hinduism. In its classic form, this view is essentially world denying. That is, it finds the real totally outside the material world. The ultimate goal of meditation is, therefore, not so much to change the world as to become separate from it. TM, however, calls on its devotees to step "outside" the physical world only temporarily to be infused with the strength to return to the everyday world again.

Will people of the future be meditators? Will they accept the world view that lies behind the techniques of such meditation?

The answer to such questions depends on whether the Eastern way of looking at humanity and the world is universally accepted or not.

[16]Ibid., p. 212.
[17]Ibid., p. 215.
[18]"The TM Craze: Forty Minutes to Bliss," *Time*, 3 October 1973, p. 72.

Some see the future as a return to primitivism. In a recent year the list of the ten best-selling books on university campuses included *three* works by one author—Carlos Castaneda. Castaneda spent several years as the disciple of a Yaqui Indian holy man in Mexico, called "Don Juan." His books detail what he learned.[19]

What he learned was essentially the classic *primitive world view.* This view we discussed in some detail in an earlier chapter. It understands the visible world to be only the tip of the iceberg of reality. Beyond what can be experienced by the normal senses there is a whole *separate reality* (the title of one of Castaneda's books). This other reality is full of spirits, power, and experiences completely foreign to those who choose to limit themselves to the material world. Don Juan slowly and painfully introduces Castaneda to this "otherness" in the terms used for thousands of years by the holy men of primitive religion.

What is striking about Castaneda's work is not the ideas presented there. As we have said, they are well known among students of primitive culture. What is striking is the popularity of these ideas among the young. There is no way to imagine a more complete rejection of the world view of Autonomous Man than a return to primitivism.

Still, some have suggested that a new world be built on such a movement.

A POSTSCRIPT

We have neither discussed every theory about the future in this chapter, nor have we explored more than the barest surface of the world of religion in this book. That is why the title *Religion: A Preface* was selected. Here and there in the Ozarks of Missouri and Arkansas outcroppings of limestone can be seen, pushing their way through the forest floors and lining the creekbeds. While impressive, these outcroppings are only the merest hint of what lies below—massive limestone formations covering hundreds of square miles. What we have been doing in this book is to survey the outcroppings of the world of religion and modern culture, outcroppings that point to far more than has so far met our eyes. We have traveled the earth and have observed many diverse ideas and life-styles. But what lies beneath what we have seen is massive. The pages of this book are but pointers to tens of thousands of other pages in other books that plumb the depths. Every idea so briefly mentioned here stands on monumental foundations. What may have seemed so simple here will eventually be

[19]Carlos Castaneda, *The Teachings of Don Juan: A Yaqui Way of Knowledge* (Berkeley: University of California Press, 1968); *A Separate Reality: Further Conversations with Don Juan* (New York: Simon & Schuster, 1971); *Journey to Ixtlan: The Lessons of Don Juan* (New York: Simon & Schuster, 1972); *Tales of Power* (New York: Simon & Schuster, 1974).

revealed to those who seriously search as far more complex and profound than first imagined. But even now it should be clear that in our continuing search for new and better ways to be human we have embarked on what is essentially a *religious* search—one that is diverse, complex, and always exciting.

INDEX